INFORMATION PROCESSING
IN CHILDREN

CONTRIBUTORS

GUY CELLÉRIER

S. FARNHAM-DIGGORY

JACQUELINE J. GOODNOW

JOHN WILLIAM HAGEN

JOHN R. HAYES

BÄRBEL INHELDER

DAVID KLAHR

ALLEN NEWELL

ROBERT H. POLLACK

H. A. SIMON

J. G. WALLACE

Information Processing in Children

*The Seventh of an Annual Series of Symposia
in the Area of Cognition under the
Sponsorship of Carnegie-Mellon University*

EDITED BY

SYLVIA FARNHAM-DIGGORY

Carnegie-Mellon University

ACADEMIC PRESS   *New York and London*   *1972*

ACADEMIC PRESS, INC.
111 Fifth Avenue, New York, New York 10003

United Kingdom Edition published by
ACADEMIC PRESS, INC. (LONDON) LTD.
24/28 Oval Road, London NW1

LIBRARY OF CONGRESS CATALOG CARD NUMBER: 73-187241

PRINTED IN THE UNITED STATES OF AMERICA

IN MEMORY
OF
WALTER VANDYKE BINGHAM
AND
MILLICENT TODD BINGHAM

It is . . . impossible to infer from the nature which a thing possesses after having passed through all stages of its development, what the condition of the thing has been in the moment when this process commenced. . . . If you make this mistake, and attempt to prove the nature of a thing in potential existence by its properties when actually existing, you will fall into great confusions.

MOSES MAIMONIDES
Guide for the Perplexed, ca. 1185 A.D.

CONTENTS

Part I   OVERVIEW

Chapter 1.   On the Development of the Processor

H. A. Simon

Part IV COMPUTER SIMULATION

Part V FINAL COMMENT

LIST OF CONTRIBUTORS

Numbers in parentheses indicate the pages on which the authors' contributions begin.

GUY CELLÉRIER (115), University of Geneva, Geneva, Switzerland

S. FARNHAM-DIGGORY (43), Department of Psychology, Carnegie-Mellon University, Pittsburgh, Pennsylvania

JACQUELINE J. GOODNOW (83), Department of Psychology, The George Washington University, Washington, D.C.

JOHN WILLIAM HAGEN (65), Department of Psychology, University of Michigan, Ann Arbor, Michigan

JOHN R. HAYES (175), Carnegie-Mellon University, Pittsburgh, Pennsylvania

BÄRBEL INHELDER (103), University of Geneva, Geneva, Switzerland

DAVID KLAHR (143, 183), Carnegie-Mellon University, Pittsburgh, Pennsylvania

ALLEN NEWELL (125), Department of Psychology, Carnegie-Mellon University, Pittsburgh, Pennsylvania.

ROBERT H. POLLACK (25), Department of Psychology, University of Georgia, Athens, Georgia

H. A. SIMON (3), Carnegie-Mellon University, Pittsburgh, Pennsylvania

J. G. WALLACE (143, 183), School of Education, University of Warwick, Coventry, Warwickshire, England

PREFACE

The Carnegie-Mellon annual cognition symposia began in 1965 with a distinguished set of papers on problem-solving in adults (Kleinmuntz, 1966). Last year, the conference focused on problem-solving in primates (Jarrard, 1971). This year it would seem inevitable for children to enter upon the scene, and assume their rightful role as carriers of the continuous functions that we see in rudimentary form in primates, and fully flowered in human adults.

This view of children characterizes the *developmental psychology* of the 1960's and 1970's, in contrast to the *child psychology* of the 1940's and 1950's. Developmental psychologists no longer study children's memories or children's perceptions (for example) as ends in themselves (Carmichael, 1954). We study the growth of memory systems, or the growth of perceptual systems, in our species. The unification of the larger body of adult psychological science, with the special technologies necessary to the study of growth functions, is now producing an explosion of research which is surely among the most exciting of our century (Mussen, 1970).

The coming together of information-processing psychology and developmental psychology in this volume is especially important. From the developmentalist's standpoint, the information-processing approach offers a methodology for precisely specifying the changes in organismic states and systems that are the heart of developmental science. For the information-processing theorist, developmental research provides needed data on the history of adult forms of thought. As one information-processing conferee remarked, following the conference, "If you people are right, then adults are just big kids, using systems and strategies that they've been practicing and modifying for a long time."

The papers in the volume were solicited and organized with these two poles in mind: (1) a display of some of the developmental data that will be necessary to a compleat theory of the human information processor; and (2) a display of current information-processing technologies, useful in the simulation of developmental functions. Parts II and IV of this volume represent these poles.

Part III, including papers by Goodnow, Inhelder, Cellérier, and Newell, represents the important intermediary stage of information or intuitive theorizing, so necessary to the development of psychologically valid computer models.

Part I, Simon's overview, alerts the reader to key aspects of forthcoming papers, and provides us with an expert model of how-to-think about developmental processes in information-processing terms.

Part V, Hayes' discussion, leaves us with a sobering conclusion: the data we gather must be some function of the child's model of the experimental situation. Until we understand that model fully, we may never understand our data at all. The wedding of information-processing psychology and developmental psychology may begin and end right there.

ACKNOWLEDGMENTS

Gratitude is expressed to H. A. Simon, Russell Revlis, and Richard Young for their help with editorial problems. Thanks are also due Allen and Rosalynn Pinkus for special assistance during the final stages of manuscript preparation. And finally, we are all deeply grateful to Betty Boal, who expertly guided the entire symposium process.

The costs of the 1971 Symposium were borne in part by the Walter VanDyke Bingham Memorial Lecture Fund and in part by Carnegie-Mellon University. Editorial preparation of the book was supported by Public Health Service Research Grant MH-07722 from the National Institute of Mental Health.

PART I

OVERVIEW

Herbert Simon is Carnegie-Mellon's R. K. Mellon Professor of Computer Science and Psychology. With Allen Newell and other colleagues, Dr. Simon has been engaged for more than a decade in research in information processing psychology. A summary of his views may be found in *Sciences of the Artificial* (Simon, 1969), and a more extensive discussion in *Human Problem Solving* (Newell & Simon, 1971).

CHAPTER 1

ON THE DEVELOPMENT OF THE PROCESSOR*

H. A. Simon

Carnegie-Mellon University

The papers in this volume deal with information processing in children. One way to give them a common framework—beyond their concern with the young—is to relate them to the schemes we usually use to organize our knowledge of human information processing in general. Against such a background description of the human information processor, the specifically developmental aspects of the work reported here will come into greater relief.

The human information processor is always struggling with the limits of his own processing and storing capabilities in the face of a wealth of information to be processed and stored. Scientists in general, and psychologists in particular, have earned no relief from the processing limits that are common to all men. They cope with these limits by organizing information, detecting the patterns

*This study was supported by Public Health Service Research Grant MH-07722, from the National Institute of Mental Health.

and redundancies contained in it, and recoding it in terms of those powerful systems of generalizations called theories.

In the past several decades, we have progressed a good distance toward describing man as an information processor, and have reached some agreement as to the important components of the description. I will not undertake here to elaborate on them, but rather remind you of what you know about them (Simon, 1969; Newell & Simon, 1971).

1. At the sensory end—the eyes and the ears—the detail of physiological mechanism determines, to a great extent, the ways in which information is processed. The sensory organs and their central connections form a complex interface between man and his environment.

2. As we move through perception to cognition, we find that central processes are less affected by detailed features of the system's construction, and seem to be shaped mainly by its broad architectural outlines and a few key parameters.

3. In describing this architecture, particularly as it affects development and learning processes, we need to give special prominence to these features:

a. The short-term memory, limited in capacity to holding a few chunks;

b. The mechanisms of attention that determine what small fraction of the sensorily available information will be selected for central processing;

c. The long-term memory, potentially unlimited in capacity: probably organized in terms of quite general systems of associations and directed associations; slow to store new information;

d. Hemispheric specialization in long-term memory for storage of information relating to different modalities—visual and auditory, for example;

e. The control of behavior, including the internal behavior of thinking, by stored, learnable and modifiable, strategies or programs.

The largest part of our knowledge of these subsystems and their relations comes from experiments on adults, particularly college sophomores. Therefore, a useful way of looking at the material that was presented at this symposium is to ask to what extent the data on children's information processing fit the theory we have constructed for adult information processing. What new insights do these data give us into that theory, and what extensions do they suggest? What new mechanisms or concepts, if any, do we have to add to it in order to accommodate the data on children?

In this approach of fitting new data into established frameworks, there is a danger that something will be stretched or crushed in the process. Some safeguard against distortion is provided by the fact that this overview precedes the papers about which it comments. If I have not done right by the evidence, you will soon discover my mistakes as you read on in the volume.

Of course, I exaggerate when I suggest that the studies reported in this volume constitute an independent check on our theories of human information processing. Most of the research discussed here is a part of that same concern with man as symbol manipulator that inhabits much of psychology today. The investigators cannot claim that they framed their questions or gathered their data in innocence of information processing theories. On the contrary, during the long period when most of cognitive psychology lay frozen under the glaciers of behaviorism—a glaciation that somehow never touched Swiss valleys—the area of child development, flourishing in these sheltered Alpine valleys, kept alive the concern for complex central processes.

Let me now take up, one by one, the components of the human processing system that I have listed previously, and suggest what the papers in this volume have to say about them.

The Sensory System

The paper by Robert Pollack, which initiates Part II, places appropriate emphasis on the sensory end of the sensory-perceptual-cognitive continuum. As his main text, he takes a series of ingenious and persuasive experiments on some of the standard visual illusions. There has been an increasing tendency in recent years to see how successfully these illusions can be explained by reference to known or hypothesized central mechanisms, and without reference to any very specific physiological properties of the sensory organs. I have indulged in this kind of exercise on a couple of occasions myself (Simon, 1967; Simon & Barenfeld, 1969).

Pollack shows that this approach is only a part of the story. Taking as "simple" a stimulus as the Mueller-Lyer figure, he demonstrates that the magnitude of the illusion varies with the hue and saturation of the stimuli. Perhaps the most striking single result he reports is that if we rank colors according to the magnitude of the illusion they produce, the ranking is reversed in going from colors of low saturation to colors of high saturation.

Pollack then extends his methods and findings to developmental questions. For example, the change in magnitude of illusion with age depends significantly upon whether the figures employ lightness contrast or hue contrast. Hence, Pollack concludes that "ontogenetic trends in the magnitude of the illusion cannot be attributed entirely to cognitive processes; the notion that receptor aging plays a dominant role remains tenable."

None of the other papers presented at the symposium attributed development specifically to physiological changes in the sensory mechanisms. Pollack's results therefore serve as a useful warning to all of us that the eye and ear have very specific properties which affect the information they gather and transmit, and that changes in these properties may have important consequences for the working of the central system. Having stated this *caveat,* I will join my fellow symposiasts in largely neglecting the sensory end of the system and focusing my remarks on more central aspects.

Short-Term Memory

While there is still disagreement on numerous details, there is also a great deal of consensus today on the broad organization of the human memory systems. Incoming visual information is stored briefly (up to about 1 sec), after recognition, in visual immediate memory (VIM). Auditory information (including visual information that has been recoded into auditory mode) and perhaps also unrecoded verbal information is held in a short-term memory (STM) whose capacity is limited to the celebrated seven chunks (possibly fewer), and whose contents can be retained indefinitely, but probably only if they are rehearsed periodically. Information held in STM for a sufficient period of time can be transferred to the more permanent store we usually call long-term memory (LTM). How long a time is "sufficient" is not precisely known: It is unlikely to be less than 2 sec or more than 10, but the exact time requirements are irrelevant to the present discussion.

Now if we are to use a piece of research to test or enlarge our knowledge about this structure of memories, we must understand which memories are exercised by the task presented to the subjects. Attributing the results of experiments to particular features of the memory system becomes especially important in research on development, because we wish to know much more than simply that a child's "memory" changes with age. We need to discover in which memory structure the change occurs, what features or parameters of the structure are altered, and by how much. By varying the task, we can exercise different parts of the structure to varying degrees, hence produce differential effects.

I am not always in agreement with the authors of the papers in their own characterizations of their memory experiments. For example, John Hagen describes what he calls a "short-term memory task" the first part of which involves retaining information about a set of four to six relatively simple stimuli; but the second part involves retrieving information after 14 such sets of stimuli have been presented. It is consistent with what we know about adult STM to suppose that the retention for the first part of the task is indeed occurring in STM. On the other hand, the retention for the second part of the task must almost certainly be attributed to LTM, except perhaps for information about the final set of stimuli. Since the stimulus items were exposed about 5 or 6 sec each, according to Hagen, there was adequate time for the amount of storage in LTM that actually occurred.

The reader will wish to check for himself whether he can accept my interpretation of the memory structures involved in this experiment. He will find, at least, that the interpretation helps other pieces to fall into place—I refer to Hagen's findings on primacy effects (almost certainly involving LTM) and recency effects (equally certainly involving STM). However, whether I am right on this particular issue or not, my methodological point is general: If we are to extract the meanings of such memory experiments—and particularly their implications for development—we must undertake and test detailed interpretations of this kind. I will have more to say about the substantive implications of Hagen's experiments later.

Let me return to data that cast light on the development of STM capacity. Sylvia Farnham-Diggory's experiments bear most directly upon this. At the risk of oversimplifying, we can outline her ingenious approach as follows: She takes as starting point the well-established age norms for digit span in immediate recall: four digits at age five, increasing at a rate of about one digit with each year and a half of chronological age. Then, for each of her tasks, she estimates the number of chunks that would have to be held simultaneously in STM in order to perform the task successfully. From these estimates, she predicts whether children at a given age should be able to perform the task. To flesh out this skeleton of her procedure, I refer the reader to her chapter (Part II).

To carry out this approach, one must have a model, not only of the total capacity of STM, but also of the processing that goes on in that memory. Both of the types of tasks that Farnham-Diggory uses are more complex than immediate recall of a string of stimuli of a single type. In one kind of experiment, what must be recalled is a heterogeneous string (a mixed sequence of digits and localized taps); in another kind of experiment, the correct response is a joint function of several (usually three) stimulus components that are presented in a spatial or temporal sequence. To estimate the STM demands of these tasks, it is necessary to postulate how far the components of the stimulus are encoded in STM, and how the components of the response are retrieved and produced.

For example, in the first type of experiment—recall of a heterogeneous string—it is assumed that there is a chunk in STM for each element of the string, but an additional chunk for each switch from one type of element to the other. Thus, the string:

1—tap right—7—4—tap left—tap middle

is assumed to be encoded:

1—switch—tap right—switch—7—4—switch—tap left—tap middle

With the first encoding, STM would contain six chunks, but with the second, it contains nine. The motivation for the expanded encoding is Broadbent's (1958) finding that this kind of heterogeneity reduced the recall span of adults. However, if they are encoded in this way, *neither* of these tasks should be within the STM memory span of 5-year-old children; yet Farnham-Diggory's subjects succeeded with sequences of this length more than half the time. As she shows, they did it by encoding the strings in ways different from either of those shown previously. To one of these encodings, she applies the name "clustering," to the other "pairing." By an extension of our notation, these can be represented, respectively, by:

$$1-7-4-\text{switch}-\text{tap right}-\text{tap left}-\text{tap middle}$$
$$1 \text{ \& tap right}-7 \text{ \& tap left}-4 \text{ \& tap middle}$$

Using the most obvious way of counting chunks, each of these encodings reduces the STM load from nine chunks to seven or six—still above the level that the child of five should be able to handle. That is, the 5-year-old cannot recall a string of six digits, but *can* often recall two pairs of strings of three stimuli each or a string of three pairs of combined digits and taps. When we spell out the process in this detail, we are drawn toward the conclusion that there are separate STM's for information in different modalities, and that these STM's can be made to supplement each other provided a complex switching pattern does not also have to be stored simultaneously in one of the STM's. This interpretation is reminiscent of earlier findings [discussed by Miller (1956) in his "magic number seven" paper] that the amount of information transmitted by a stimulus can be larger for multidimensional than for one-dimensional stimuli, but I would not want to push the analogy too hard.

The second kind of experiment described by Farnham-Diggory, which requires an integrated response to a sequence of stimuli, also calls for a detailed processing model for its interpretation. Given logographs representing "jump," "over," and "block," a 5-year-old has no difficulty retaining the three stimuli and providing their translations into spoken words, but may be unable to act out the sentence: "Jump over block." Farnham-Diggory argues that to perform the task, the subject "must have held in mind simultaneously the three symbolic concepts, and some ideas about real-world matching events, such as jumping and blocks. Unless the child can mentally survey these five or six information chunks simultaneously, he will not detect the correct relationships among them."

However, this count of STM load cannot be quite correct because we can apply the same reasoning to prove that the child, if someone *said* to him, "Jump over block," could not make the indicated response. For, to perform this task the subject also "must have held in mind simultaneously the three symbolic concepts. . . " etc. Farnham-Diggory reports, however, that the facts are otherwise—the same child who cannot act out the sequence of logographs *can* respond correctly to the oral command. Thus, as in the previous case, a closer look at the processing implied by the model gives us deeper insight into the implications of the experiment for the structure of STM.

In order not to leave this particular story without a denouement, let me hazard my own analysis. The child who cannot perform the logograph task, can nevertheless, respond to the meaning of each of the components of the stimulus. Farnham-Diggory observes that he may jump at "jump," point upward at "over," and point at the block at "block." The child has associated a meaning with each logograph—the meaning taking the form of an act of some sort. His interpretive program is:

> 1. Find next (including first) logograph, if none, stop;
>   Retrieve its meaning;
>   Execute meaning;

However, the "correct" interpretation of the logograph is quite a different program, which might look like this:

> 1. Find next logograph, if none, go to 2;
>   Retrieve its meaning;
>   Modify revised meaning;
>   Go to 1;
>
> 2. Execute meaning; stop.

That is, the subject must first find the meaning of "jump," which is an act that is capable of modification or specification (the specifications answering such questions as "who," "where," "what," "when," "how"). Then, he must interpret "over" and use the meaning to modify JUMP to JUMP (OVER). Finally, he must interpret "block," and modify JUMP (OVER) to JUMP [OVER (BLOCK)]. Only then may he execute the meaning as revised.

I do not hold any brief for the particular way in which I have encoded these programs, but any way of encoding them will show that the program the child needs before he can execute "jump over block" when he is shown the logographs is quite different from the program he needs to interpret the three separate meanings, "jump," "over," and "block."

On the other hand, the program that he needs to execute the logograph command has a form identical with the one he needs to execute the oral command. Only the process, "Retrieve its meaning," has changed. In the case of the oral command, this signifies retrieving the motor command or the modification for the revised motor command corresponding to each successive spoken word. In the case of the logograph sequence, it means retrieving the command or its modification corresponding to each logograph. The latter process may be direct (as in the oral case), or mediated by translation from logograph to word command. In the former case, the meaning (which is quite different from that of the acted-out isolated logograph) must be learned in association with each logograph. In the latter case, the association between each logograph and the word it stands for must be learned. In both cases, the child must learn *not* to act on the individual logographs, but to postpone action until the sequence has been decoded, and the action program assembled.

Described in this way, the new learning required for performance of the logograph task sounds formidable even if the child already has a good competence in executing verbal commands. However, the difficulty does not appear to have anything in particular to do with STM capacity. Furthermore, this analysis suggests that the new skill (program) required to execute the logograph sequences is identical with the program required for reading meaningfully the printed word.

This conjecture appears to be confirmed by the data, which indicate that ability to perform on the logographs is a necessary and sufficient condition for ability to read. If the child can do one, he can do the other.

However, in elaborating on this example, I am getting ahead of my story. I am suggesting that what is involved in this developmental sequence is not simply an increase in the capacity of STM, but the acquisition of new programs. I shall take up that topic again later.

Farnham-Diggory describes another task that is difficult for 5-year-olds: finding a figure that matches the meaning of a written "sentence" (really a logograph sequence again). This task would seem to require almost exactly the same program as the previous one, and for the reasons I have already outlined, I am therefore again skeptical that the difficulties have to do with STM limits. As with the previous task, the child is able to do the matching if the figure is described to him orally. The one difference between the two tasks is that the first one allows the child—in error—to act out each logograph immediately; the second allows only a single response. If he is really following the first (and incorrect) interpretive program I sketched previously, we would predict the recency effect that actually appears—only the last "execute meaning" command can be carried out.

Let me add one final word of caution about the interpretation of the difficulties children encounter in these tasks. If we attempt a Piagetian, sensory-motor *versus* verbal explanation, we are confronted with the empirical fact that the children *can* perform the corresponding tasks in response to oral stimuli. This datum seems to me to create serious problems for the usual explanation.

As I interpret them, the experiments discussed in the symposium do not settle what is perhaps the basic developmental issue about STM: whether the growing capacity of the child to handle even more complex tasks, results entirely, mostly, partly, or not at all from an increase in the maximum number of chunks he can hold in STM. To be sure, the standard digit-span experiment shows that the number of digits or letters he can repeat increases regularly with age. However, that experiment does not prove that the number of *chunks* increases, since it offers no independent evidence of what constitutes a chunk. An alternative explanation (which would fit better what we know about perceptual chunking by adults) would be that, with the accumulation of experience, pairs or even longer strings of symbols become familiarized and stored in memory as chunks. Thus individual digits and letters are no longer separate chunks for the older child or adult.

On the other hand, there are phenomena that are easier to explain on the hypothesis of a growing number of chunks than on the hypothesis of a growing average size of chunk. I refer especially to some impressive experiments by Pascual-Leone (1970), which for reasons of space, are not described here. On the basis of the evidence I have seen—in this symposium and elsewhere—I feel obliged to bring in the Scotch verdict of "Not proven!" and to retain on the agenda of research this question of whether there is actually a growth in the physiological capacity of STM with age, or instead, an ability to call on a growing repertoire of familiar chunks so that a fixed number of chunks designates a steadily growing amount of information.

However, my purpose in discussing the experiments of Hagen and Farnham-Diggory in some detail was not to quarrel with any particular interpretations. Rather, it was to illustrate a technique of analysis that involves, first, postulating the basic characteristics of the information processing system (IPS) that is supposed to be performing the task, and second, considering the kinds of programs the IPS would need to have available in order to perform successfully. A principal advantage offered by the technique is that it enables us to make predictions and comparisons across tasks, hence to increase greatly the refutability of our hypotheses.

Long-Term Memory

Consistent with recent emphasis in cognitive psychology, the papers at this symposium mention long-term memory (LTM) explicitly less often than they do STM. Nevertheless, they suggest a role for LTM in development that is different in one fundamental respect from the role accorded to it classically.

A vulgar view of LTM might picture it as a large bin or filing cabinet in which the child, in the course of his development, accumulates new facts and knowledge. I suppose no one would quarrel with the proposition that this is part of what happens. To acquire a logograph-reading skill, the child must learn the meanings of a suitable vocabulary of logographs. This is a matter of storing away in the filing cabinet properly indexed pairs of associates. However, we have seen that it is equally essential that the child acquire appropriate programs for processing the logographs in accordance with the "reading" instructions.

In almost all references to LTM in this symposium, the speakers talk about the storage of "programs" or "strategies" or "rules, rituals, and tricks of the trade"—that is, of processes rather than information. This, of course, is the touchstone of the information processing point of view in psychology: "Knowing" is largely "knowing how"—that is, skill. It is the viewpoint that led Bartlett, in *Thinking* (1958), to take motor skill as his metaphor for thinking ability.

The Genevans in this symposium, Inhelder and Cellérier, have some interesting points to make about the relation between a structuralist view, which describes the concepts that the child acquires as abstract structures, and an information-processing approach, which describes them as programs—or, in the terminology of Inhelder and Cellérier, as schemata (see Part III).

I am reminded by the structure-schema distinction of the analogous distinction that linguists make between language competence and performance. In the view of some, language competence formulated, say, as a transformational grammar, provides an abstract description of what the native speaker "knows," but does not describe the form in which that knowledge is held in memory or used to process language. I hasten to add that I am not at all sure that Inhelder and Cellérier would accept this analogy with the structure-schema dichotomy.

In her descriptions of some experiments on length conservation, Inhelder offers an interesting hypothesis about what needs to be stored in LTM before the child can perform such tasks. The tasks involve constructing a line of some sort that matches in length a line presented by the experimenter. The lines, or "roads," are constructed from matchsticks, the experimenter using sticks of a different length than those used by the child. Hence, as in all the classic conservation experiments, the situation confronts the child with conflicting cues: He can count matchsticks, or he can estimate lengths. The difficulty in the task, argues Inhelder, lies in reconciling the judgments of equivalence arrived at by these different routes, and choosing a criterion that is consistent with the requirements of the task. She offers a similar analysis of the standard matching test that involves comparing the sizes of sets and subsets.

Now this interpretation is clearly not intended by Inhelder to supercede the usual Geneva analysis, since she speaks explicitly of "resolution through reciprocal assimilation of two different subsystems that do not necessarily belong to the same developmental level." Thus, underlying the learning phenomena are structures stored in LTM that are acquired at different stages of development. If that is so, then we must suppose that each of these structures is associated with (1) processes of attention and perceptual encoding for acquiring information relating to the structure (e.g., counting operations and length-estimating operations for visual stimuli); and (2) an internal representation for encoding and storing in LTM information characterizing the structure.

The work by Klahr and Wallace (Part IV) can be interpreted as an endeavor to make entirely explicit the information processing associated with these kinds of cognitive structures. These authors agree with the other symposiasts in filling LTM mainly with programs; but they detail not only the programs, but also the encoding of information in LTM—the nature of the internal representation. They postulate that such information is stored in the form of lists and description lists—the latter being better known to contemporary psychologists as "feature lists." A description, or feature, is simply a two-termed relation between an object and one of its properties: e.g., the color (relation) of the apple (object) is red (property or value).

An interesting characteristic of this representation is that it makes the contents of LTM rather homogeneous in organization, independently of the sensory channel through which the information was acquired. Thus, a mental picture is made of the same stuff (list structures of features) as a mental symphony. Of course, it is only the form of organization they share in common; the specific relations encoded depend on sensory mode—the feature "red" must have been acquired through the eyes, and "interval of a fifth" through the ears.

Postulating this common organization for encoding stimulus information illuminates one of the central issues discussed (Part III) by Jacqueline Goodnow in her paper: the issue of intersensory correspondences of stimuli. Suppose that a sequence of sounds is encoded as a list:

$$Tap-pause-tap-tap-tap$$

Suppose, further, that the child has a list of pairs (associations) in LTM:

$$tap \rightarrow circle; pause \rightarrow space; tap_2 \text{ after } tap_1 \rightarrow circle_2 \text{ to the right of } circle_1$$

Then, a relatively simple program will allow him to translate the aural stimulus into a visual one, which he can undertake to draw:

$$circle-space-circle-circle-circle$$

What the homogeneous coding explains is the *possibility* of anyone even finding meaningful the task of intermodal correspondence. It does not explain why the task may be difficult for children. In her paper, Goodnow shows us what assumptions are involved in supposing that the child "should know" what intermodal associations the adult has in mind (why not: tap, pause → large circle; tap → small circle? Why not, indeed?). She demonstrates that the child must acquire, and store in LTM, a whole host of conventions, many of them culture-specific, about the correspondences that are "appropriate."

Intermodal Connections

Before we go overboard on the homogeneity of LTM, and treat all problems of intermodal transfer as problems of learning the appropriate correspondences, we need to remind ourselves of one important fact of brain architecture: The left hemisphere usually plays a special role in storing knowledge of oral language, while the right hemisphere may be preferentially involved in processing certain information about visual form.

None of the symposium authors speaks directly to this hemispheric special-ization, or the role of the "great cerebral commissure" that Roger Sperry (1964) and others have illuminated so brilliantly through split-brain studies. Many of the important skills the young child must acquire in the course of his development (e.g., reading) involve the correlation of information and programs relating to two or more modalities. Acquiring such intermodal capabilities may present quite different learning problems from acquiring capabilities that lie within a single modality.

Nor can we rule out the possibility that one hemisphere learns more readily than the other—perhaps due to the differences in their interconnections with the rest of the system. We observed earlier that the program that is needed to act out the meaning of a logograph is essentially identical with the program that is needed to act out the meaning of an oral command. Why, then, is learning to read a difficult task? We do not know; but we must remember that a program stored in one hemisphere may or may not be available for processing information stored in the other. (Incidentally, we do not know either that learning to read is *in fact* any harder for the child than learning to speak. We only know that the former gives the surrounding adults more trouble than the latter.)

Any further comment on this point would carry me beyond my knowledge of the empirical facts. I only comment at all because we did not have in the symposium anyone to represent the physiology of the central nervous system in the same way that Pollack represented the sensory organs and their central connections.* The discussions of intermodal tasks, like those in the papers of Goodnow and Farnham-Diggory, need to be read with these physiological possibilities kept somewhere on the fringe of one's awareness.

Attention

Mention of "awareness" brings us to the important topic of attention. James, in his celebrated chapter on the subject, finessed the problem of definition by beginning boldly, "Everyone knows what attention is." However, to an information processor today, attention is something a little different from this familiar subjective phenomena described by James.

The human IPS, as we describe it today, has a severe bottleneck. Its central processor can do only one or a few things at a time—or over a few hundred milliseconds, to be exact. Its sensory system can extract vast amounts of information from the environment; only a small part of this information can be squeezed through the needle's eye of the central processor. In these terms, attention is the set of processes that filters information, and determines what small part of it will occupy the central processor at any given time. This set of processes is crucial to the operation of the whole system.

Parenthetically, there is probably a close relation between the bottleneck of attention and the limits of STM. If it requires several hundred milliseconds, say, to load or unload chunks in STM, and if every process must find its inputs and deposit its outputs in STM, within the seven-chunk limit, then these parameters

---

*See Geschwind's paper in Jarrard's (1971) edition of the 1970 Carnegie-Mellon Symposium—ED.

of STM determine the maximum rate at which information can be processed centrally. (For a further discussion of this matter, see Chapter 14 of Newell and Simon, 1971.)

The symposium papers are full of phenomena that bear upon attention and its development. Let me begin with the tasks used by Hagen. Hagen's subjects had two tasks: an immediate, or "central," task of remembering the colors of the backgrounds of particular cards in a set; and a delayed, or "incidental," task of later remembering pictures on these cards associated with the colors. The main finding is that performance on the central task improved with age, while performance on the incidental task did not, or even declined.

Hagen proposes an information-processing explanation of this finding, which I should like to summarize—perhaps in a balder form than he would approve. We postulate a fixed fund of attention (i.e., a fixed maximum central-processing rate). Attention cannot be increased or diminished; it can only be reallocated. We postulate that, with increasing age, children become increasingly capable of controlling the allocation of their attention by the adoption of deliberate (but not necessarily conscious) strategies or programs. (See the convincing experiment by Vurpillot, 1968.) Finally, we postulate [an assumption that will remind us of Guthrie and of EPAM. See Hilgard and Bower (1966), and Feigenbaum & Feldman (1963)] that anything will be learned if and only if it is attended to for a sufficient period of time.

Under these assumptions, with increasing age, the subjects will devote increasing fractions of their attention to the central task, learning the color association, and will learn more about those associations and perform better. The additional attention will come from a diminution of attention to other features of the stimuli—including the features essential to performance of the incidental task. Attention to information entirely irrelevant to the card stimulus will disappear at an earlier age than attention to information that is on the card stimulus, but irrelevant to the central task (the earlier strategies will be a coarse filter, the later ones a fine filter).

Anyone whose LTM contains leftovers from the decades of the 1930's and 1940's will be irresistibly reminded of the latent learning controversy of that time (Hilgard, Marquis & Kimble, 1961). The main facts relating to that controversy can be explained by the same postulates. The hungry rat attends only to food-relevant aspects of the environment, hence learns only these. The less hungry rat learns less rapidly about the location of food, but his less focused attention allows him to acquire compensating information about the location of water, for example. Thus, the attention-fund model has considerable power for unifying and explaining a wide range of learning phenomena.

A second attentional phenomenon mentioned in this symposium is Farnham-Diggory's observation that children unable to perform one of the logograph tasks, even after they had repeated it orally, were able to perform if the visual logograph was then removed. Translation: If the young child has insufficient strategic control over attention, he may waste on an irrelevant stimulus processing capacity that he needs to perform the task. Alternative translation: The young child is too stimulus bound to perform the task—his main strategy of attention is to attend to the external stimulus, and he has a low threshold to interruption of central processes by changes in that stimulus.

In addition to this general, unifying proposition about the invariance of the total amount of attention that can be mobilized per unit of time, a few special comments are necessary on attention to visual stimuli. As a point of departure, I will again take the experiments reported by Goodnow in which the child had to translate a string of sounds into a string of visual symbols, or vice versa.

We know that most of the information we take in visually (apart from the information the eye uses to aim its successive saccades) comes in through the fovea—an area of about $2°$ arc. Perhaps this is approximately what the visual information amounts to, recorded in the VIM—the so-called Sperling memory. As we know, this information is lost unless it is again read and recoded within a second or so for storage or processing somewhere else.

By the time this second extraction of information from the original visual stimulus has taken place, the picture that is retained by the "mind's eye" is something very different from a photograph of the pattern of stimulation on the retina. It is probably better described as a linear sequence of tiny mosaic tiles, each of the latter recording a number of features from a very local area of the original scene. The relational information that pieces the tiles together into the larger mosaic is, essentially, information about the direction the eye had to move (or possibly also, the direction the VIM had to be scanned) to get from one tile to the next. That is to say, the internal representation of visual information must be something like the directions for finding pirate treasure:

> Proceed forty yards north to a large ash tree. Turn left and go 210 feet west by $10°$ north down a hill to a granite boulder. . .

and so on. The EPAM theory of perception and memorizing incorporates one scheme of precisely this kind. (Feigenbaum & Feldman, 1963). It has been elaborated by Simon & Barenfeld (1969) to account for some phenomena of chess perception. In the latter version, the eye is supposed to fixate upon some piece on the board, and to acquire information about immediately surrounding pieces. Then a saccade takes the eye to another piece that is related by an attack, defence, or other meaningful chess relation to the one previously fixated. Still another version of such a theory of visual imagery has been developed independently by Noton and Stark (1971).

Independently of the details of these schemes, they all have an important principle in common. Perceptual encoding of visual stimuli translates space into time—a set of simultaneously presented spatial relations becomes a string of symbols encoded in some sequential order. By this means, some of the gross differences of organization between visual and aural stimuli, respectively, are obliterated while the processor is representing them internally.

Even if true, this description of the process of encoding does not mean that establishing a correspondence between a visual string and an aural one, as is required in Goodnow's tasks, becomes effortless. Nothing has been said previously about the *order* of the visual scanning and encoding. Both the successive saccades and the successive extractions of information from the VIM may skip and hop about in all sorts of ways. In fact, fluent reading undoubtedly *requires* them to hop about (but in relatively systematic, not random, ways). We know also that the order in which aural stimuli are recorded is not necessarily identical with the order in which they are presented. Nevertheless, there appear to be considerably more degrees of freedom in the strategies of recording visual, as compared with aural, stimuli. We may include this as another candidate on the list of hypotheses as to why reading is a more difficult skill to acquire than understanding oral language (if it is).

Strategies and Programs

I have already anticipated most of what needs to be said on the topic of strategies. A large part of all the changes that take place in a child's intellective processes during his development appears to be describable as change in the strategies or programs he carries around with him. As we have seen, our symposiasts have provided evidence that some of the change in program refers to the strategies that control the allocation of attention and the extraction of information from visual stimuli. To the present, however, these strategies have been described only in very gross and anecdotal fashion. It is only the past few years that we have taken their existence seriously and literally, and they prove to be very elusive in the fact of the gross experimental manipulations we know how to carry out. Now that we have identified the quarry we are hunting, our tracking methods will undoubtedly improve.

Klahr and Wallace tackle a difficult, but more manageable part of the job of explaining strategies. Taking a standard Piagetian task involving sets and subsets, they construct a detailed description of a processing program (technically, a *production system*) that is capable of simulating the behavior of a child in this task. I say "more manageable" because, initially at least, they can avoid fine-grain questions of the management of attention and short-term memory at the microlevel and focus on the program that organizes performance of the overall task. Thus, the component productions in their system are processes that might take several hundred milliseconds each for their execution. Processes that detail the management of attention will probably have to go down to the level of tens of milliseconds—perhaps an order of magnitude finer resolution.

We may observe, therefore, that the Klahr-Wallace model does not in its present form give a detailed account of the load that is placed on STM; but we may at the same time endorse their strategy of tackling problems one at a time. They have given us the first convincing and concrete description of what a program might look like for performing one of the standard tasks used in research on child development.

If the kind of program that has been constructed for the class inclusion task has to be extended downward to the micro processes of attention and STM, it also has to be extended outward, both to new tasks and to alternative programs for successive stages of development. Klahr and Wallace are explicit in marking the latter extension as the next step in their research strategy. That is what the theory of development is all about—the successive stages that performance programs go through in the course of aging, and the learning processes that take them from one stage to the next. Describing performance programs is the first step toward describing the ways in which those programs change through time, and the mechanisms that produce the changes.

The strategy that Klahr and Wallace propose will undoubtedly occupy many other researchers for many years. None of us will lack things to do.

The Nature of Explanation

Since my comments have moved again from substance to method, I will now look at the symposium papers squarely from the latter viewpoint. The papers are all concerned with explaining one facet or another of children's behavior, or the changes in that behavior in the course of development. To say they are all concerned with "explaining" does not, in itself, say very much, for "explaining" has meant many things in the last century of psychology's history.

For some, explaining has meant demonstrating the physiological mechanism that underlies and produces some kind of behavior. For others, explaining has meant demonstrating a functional relation between variations in a stimulus and corresponding variations in a response. For still others, it has meant showing that a particular variation in a stimulus has *some* effect—as many other things as possible being held constant—on the nature or amount of the response. The first of these three kinds of explanation has been characteristic of physiological psychology, the second of psychophysics, and the third of the behaviorism of significance tests.

The information processing point of view that inhabits the papers of this volume carries with it—implicitly or explicitly—yet another view of explanation. In information processing terms, an explanation of behavior is a description of an organization of simple information processes that (a) is consistent with what we know of the physiology of the nervous system, (b) is consistent with what we know of behavior in tasks other than the one under consideration, (c) is sufficient to produce the behavior that is under consideration, and (d) is relatively definite and concrete.

This general concept of explanation still leaves a great deal of room for variation. At its "lowest," most detailed boundary, it merges with physiological explanation; at its "leftmost," most specific and formal boundary, it merges with computer simulation and artificial intelligence. At its "upper" boundaries with observable behavior, it merges with common sense and description of process in ordinary language.

The visual illusions have always encouraged theorizing of an information processing kind—even before there was anything that could be called "information processing psychology." The history of the moon illusion is a case in point. The Mueller-Lyer illusion is another example discussed by Pollack.

As illustrated by Pollack's paper, the explanations of the illusions have tended closer to the physiological the more sensory organs have been implicated in them. The central explanations, less firmly rooted in physiology, have tended to the informal and commonsensical. Recent years have seen the practitioners of simulation undertake to formalize and detail the process descriptions in computer programs generally stopping short of physiology. However different the specifics of form or content, at a more general level, explanation has meant the same thing—process description—to all. Virtually all psychologists who have dealt with the illusions have behaved like information processing psychologists.

My own biases—which I have not been hiding—lead me to the computer program as the chosen instrument for process description and explanation. A computer program, proposed as an explanation of behavior, can have many faults. First, and most important, it can simply be wrong—can postulate mechanisms different from the ones that actually produce the behavior. However, it has the compensating advantage of being highly susceptible to refutation. The predictions it makes are so strong and specific, it leaves so few ambiguities to hide the facts behind, that it is continually open to testing, modification, and improvement.

In my comments here, I have tried to illustrate, from time to time, another and less systematic use of the language of programs for advancing theory. I have tried to show that our understanding—and in the absence of understanding, our guesses—as to what might be going on in an experiment can be sharpened and deepened by trying to write hypothetical programs describing the processes. This strategy is best illustrated by the discussion of the logograph experiments.

There is a third use of computer programs for explanation that is not illustrated elsewhere in this book. Since it is an important one, and since psychologists have not yet taken much advantage of it, I should like to conclude my introduction with a couple of examples that bear rather directly on the topic of child development. I refer to the construction of artificial intelligence programs that do not aspire to match human behavior or processes in detail, but only to match some aspects of human capability. Though the authors of such programs often disclaim any intent to psychologize, their work is not without value for psychology.

Explanation by Synthesis

The task of discovering process explanations for behavior is work of induction, not deduction. There is no known way to go directly and inexorably from the "facts" to a theory (much less *the* theory) that explains those facts. Theorizing is discovery—but, of course, not unmotivated discovery.

What are the motivators for the synthesis of theory? Where do theories come from? Though theories cannot be deduced from facts, they are often suggested by facts. Thus, doing experiments may help us find theories. If we are lucky enough to carry out an experiment that disappoints our expectations and predictions, the specific discrepancy between actual and predicted fact may help pinpoint where, if not how, the theory needs to be changed. (Of course, if we are unlucky enough to have our theory confirmed by experiment, then the facts will hint at nothing new, and we will have to try again.)

A second motivator of theory is epistemology, in the form of the "Denkexperiment" or in any of its other forms. Kant's synthetic *a priori* is a classical example of the attempt to derive what is from what must necessarily be, and Cellérier points out the affinity of Piaget's epistemology to Kant's. While most of us, including Piaget, would reject many of Kant's conclusions, and even the particular grounds of necessity he espoused, many of us would want to reformulate his venture rather than abandon it. The "language nativism" of Chomsky (1966) and some of his followers is one modern version of epistemological psychology. The cognitive structures of Piaget and his fellow Genevans provide a second. I have had a go at a third version—one that has Brunswikian forerunners in psychology—in my book (Simon, 1969) on the sciences of the artificial. In this book, I argued that any adaptive system must take on, as well as it can, the shape of its environment; hence a careful examination of the environment may tell us a great deal about the adaptive system. I am not sure that this view is identical in thrust with the other two versions of epistemology I have mentioned, but it appears at least compatible with the Genevan views.

A third motivator of theory, closely related to epistemology, is the attempt to use a set of available mechanisms (e.g., computer instructions) to synthesize a process capable of humanoid behaviors. The claim of this approach—artificial intelligence—to relevance for psychology, rests on the proposition that there may be several ways to skin a cat, but probably not dozens of ways. Hence, if *one* way (not admitting magical processes) is found, it may be similar to the way in which cats are actually skinned. If we put further constraints on the solution (e.g., not only must it eschew magic, but it may not use high-speed arithmetic, or other processes that are known not to be available to men), then the probability that it bears resemblance to the human process increases.

In developmental psychology, we would love to have a good theory on how children learn language, initially, oral language, and later, how they learn to read. Perhaps we can get a leg up on the problem by discovering how a computer can learn language. Let me describe briefly a recent venture of this kind.

There is reason to suppose that before a child acquires oral language he acquires an ability to represent internally simple situations that are presented to his senses: his mother and father conversing, for example; or his cat lapping milk. Let us call these internal representations of sensed objects or situations "semantic representation."

The child generally learns oral language in the presence of objects and situations that he can already represent semantically. Can we find some simple mechanisms that will do that trick—without magic, and without using unimaginably rapid processes? Can we write a computer program that, after training with paired semantic representations and natural language sentences that describe them, will acquire the ability to output appropriate sentences when it is later confronted with semantic representations of new (but similar) situations? Laurent Siklóssy (in Siklóssy and Simon (1972)) has written a computer program that does just this. What import does it have for psychology? We will know only if we examine it in detail and use it to suggest experiments to test its predictions.

To take a final example, when a child is confronted with a task slightly different from any he has performed before, and shows that he can cope with it, we conclude that he must have some process for generating a program for handling it in the face of the task itself. How does he do it? From everyday observation, we know that we can often help him by providing him with worked-out examples of the task. How does he extract information from these examples?

Can we write a computer program that will learn to perform a task (not unrelated to other tasks it can perform) by being shown worked-out examples? Donald Williams (1972) has written such a program. Does it give any hints as to how the child does it? We will know that only when we have examined Williams' program in detail and tried out the experiments it suggests.

There already exists in the literature of artificial intelligence—in computer programs that have been written and debugged—a gold mine (let us say, more conservatively, some veins that may bear gold) of hypotheses on how an information processor—and possibly a human information processor—performs certain tasks. Perhaps in some instances the cat has already been skinned, and skinned in a humanoid (if not humane) way. As psychologists, we must look to computer simulation as an important new source of inspiration for psychological theory.

Conclusion

In this introductory chapter, I have tried to provide a common framework for the papers in this volume. Such a common framework is possible because the authors appear to share the view that to explain human behavior and the development of behavior strategies is to construct theories of the information processes that underlie that behavior.

The framework I have used is assembled from components that are now familiar, and widely accepted as appropriate categories for describing the human information processing system: the sensory system, STM, LTM, the two hemispheres of the central nervous system, attentional mechanisms, and stored programs. About each of these I have asked the following questions. What do the symposium papers tell us about how the child resembles, or differs from the adult on this dimension? To what extent do the differences appear qualitative in nature, and to what extent, on the contrary, do they appear to be explainable in terms of learning—the storage of new knowledge and new programs in long-term memory?

On the whole, the papers impress me more with the continuity than with the discontinuity of development. Perhaps matters would appear differently if we had looked more closely at the very young child—the child under five—however the work that was reviewed relates to children from that age upward.

The developmental changes in short-term memory limits remain controversial. I have tried to indicate how they *might* be explained by the storage of new chunks in LTM, rather than by an actual growth in the physiological capacity of the memory. On neither side of the question is the evidence conclusive.

We also have Pollack's evidence of physiological changes in the sensory system. Beyond this, the emphasis in all of the papers has been upon presumably learnable skills, where the required learning is primarily the storage of new strategies or programs in long-term memory. While it is clear that the sequence of developmental changes must take place in an orderly way—some skills are prerequisite to others—little evidence was presented that would tie development to a physiological clock.

I hope the authors, in reading this summary, will not object too strongly to being laid promiscuously in a common bed, and that they will not find the bed too Procrustean in shape. There are many variant versions of information processing psychology, and broad opportunity for each of us to follow his bent and hunches, substantive and methodological. The papers themselves provide the best evidence of the richness of our opportunities.

PART II

BASIC MECHANISMS

Dr. Robert Pollack received his undergraduate degree from the City College of New York, and his Ph.D. from Clark University. For several years he was Chief of the Division of Cognitive Development at the Institute for Juvenile Research in Chicago, and he is currently Chairman of the graduate program in experimental psychology at the University of Georgia.

For over ten years, Dr. Pollack has devoted his research to the detailed analysis of the precise mechanisms of perceptual development. Although he has attempted to maintain a relatively neutral position with reference to developmental theory, his research findings have led him into some controversial positions (Pollack, 1969). These findings are further elucidated in the following progress report.

CHAPTER 2

PERCEPTUAL DEVELOPMENT: A PROGRESS REPORT

Robert H. Pollack

University of Georgia

This narration of work carried out both at the Institute for Juvenile Research and the University of Georgia begins where my last summary statement left off (Pollack, 1969). Because of the change in location of the laboratory, recent restriction of research funds, and the presence of a number of theoretical loose ends, the research carried out was concerned mainly with basic sensory and perceptual problems. Although some progress was made at the cognition interface, it has been tentative and in the nature of a "tooling up" operation for the next big step. One thing is certain; our understanding of the operation of

25

many basic stimulus variables in relation to ontogenetic change is much clearer now than it was in 1969. It is also clearer than ever that a precise specification of experimental viewing conditions and procedures is necessary before either theory construction or demolition can take place effectively.

The theoretical framework within which the research to be summarized was carried out has not changed materially since my last summary (Pollack, 1969). In brief, two sorts of ontogenetic change are postulated. Type-I phenomena change as a function of the physiological aging of receptor processes within the organism and are not related to higher complex functions. This is especially so for figures presented tachistoscopically under fixation conditions subtending no more than 4° of visual angle. The course of the change in Type-I phenomena is not developmental. Development is seen as involving either differentiation with increasing hierarchic organization (progression), or dedifferentiation with a breakdown of hierarchic organization (regression).

In contrast, Type-II phenomena change as a result of development, and in turn fall into two classes. The members of the simpler class (e.g., size and distance judgment and intersensory effects) undergo a single progressive change, most likely to occur in middle childhood, which represents a shift from an egocentric mode of viewing to an object central mode. The determinants of the shift have not yet been found, but since it takes place in almost all individuals from retardates to geniuses it does not appear to be related to higher-level cognitive processes. The more complex class of Type-II phenomena increases more continuously with increasing age, exhibiting a closer relationship to mental age than to chronological age. The outstanding characteristic of these phenomena is that they tend to involve the integration of successive bits of information over time, thereby involving mechanisms well beyond the capacities of the visual system alone. Both Type-I and Type-II phenomena appear to reverse age trends in later life. While the apparent regression of Type-II phenomena can be accounted for in developmental terms involving the senile breakdown of higher-order functions, the mechanisms behind the Type-I reversal are as yet not clear.

The studies to be described fall into three groups, dealing with the stimulus determinants of Type-I phenomena, the classification of phenomena, and the relationship between cognitive activities and Type-II phenomena. The first group is the largest, containing studies dealing with stimulus persistence; the effects of hue, saturation, and lightness contrast on such diverse phenomena as visual acuity and the Mueller-Lyer illusion; the relationship of optical pigmentation to illusion magnitude; and the effects of filtered light on such magnitudes. The second group consists of two studies on the Ponzo illusion, which cast considerable doubt on its present classification as a Type-II illusion. Finally, the third group includes a number of small experiments showing a linkage between temporal integration tasks and a Type-II illusion.

Stimulus Determinants of Type-I Phenomena

One of the basic assumptions made in the preceding theoretical position is that receptor sensitivity to intensity contrast declines as a function of age. It has been demonstrated that the threshold for contour detection as a function of absolute contrast rises through childhood (Pollack, 1963). Another consequence of declining sensitivity with increasing age could be a lessening of stimulus persistence, conceived as a kind of minimal afterimage activity. This notion was used earlier to predict the drop in backward figural masking through middle childhood (Pollack, 1965b). A more direct measure of the effects of a decrease in stimulus persistence with age could be a reduction in the interstimulus interval necessary for detection of a dark interval between two equally intense foveal flashes, as the initial stimulus persists (and thus interferes) less and less. The dark interval threshold (DIT) was measured on 240 children aged 6 to 17 years (Pollack, Ptashne, & Carter, 1968, Pollack, 1969). A significant ($p < .001$) linear decrease in threshold as a function of age was found. Correlation between DIT and chronological age (CA) was higher than that between DIT and mental age (MA). Partialling out MA yielded a coefficient of $-.43$ ($p < .001$) with CA, indicating that aging rather than intelligence is related to the drop (see Fig. 2.1).

Attention was next turned to the disagreement between ontogenetic trends relating to intensity contrast and hue contrast. Hue detection thresholds were shown earlier not to change between ages 7 and 12, although there were significant differences between hues with respect to detectability (Pollack, 1965a) (see Fig. 2.2). An orange sample was easier to detect than either a green or a purple-blue (Fig. 2.3). Some pilot work by Skoff (Pollack, 1969) using adult subjects, showed that acuity based on minimal bar separation was finer for red than for blue bars on a neutral background of equal lightness. Yellow bars were tried as well, but were impossible to use because of their tremendous irradiation.

Later, Skoff and Pollack (1969) confirmed this finding with children ranging in age from 7 to 14 (Figs. 2.4-2.5), but they found neither age differences nor an age-by-hue interaction once subjects had been trained to focus clearly. Initially, children younger than 11 had shown relatively poorer acuity with blue bars, most probably because they were not compensating for normal foveal myopia for blue objects and were thus tolerating blue rather than accommodating. The finding of hue differences in the absence of age differences led to additional experimentation, employing the overestimated or open component of the Mueller-Lyer figure.

The first question asked was whether or not the results obtained for hue detection and for acuity would generalize to the magnitude of a Type-I illusion. An experiment (Pollack, 1970a) was carried out on 50 adults (25 males and 25 females) using four colored figures—red, yellow, green, and blue—on neutral gray backgrounds of equal lightness. Once again there were marked hue differences. Red and blue produced the largest illusions, while those produced by yellow and

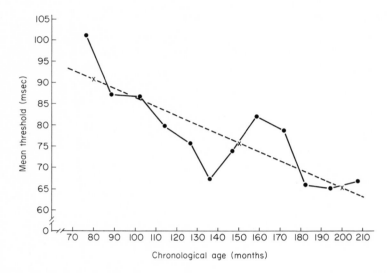

Fig. 2.1. Dark interval threshold as a function of chronological age. The solid line indicates observed data; the broken line indicates the line of best fit ($Y' = -.2134X' + 107.83$).

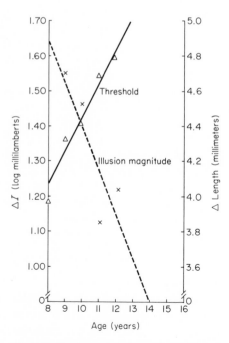

Fig. 2.2. Contour detection threshold and illusion magnitude as a function of chronological age (Pollack, 1963).

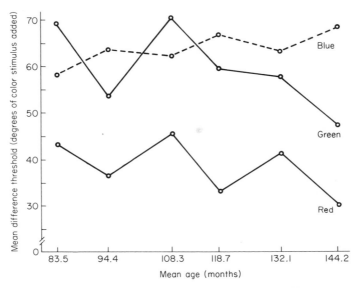

Fig. 2.3. Hue detection threshold as a function of chronological age (Pollack, 1965a).

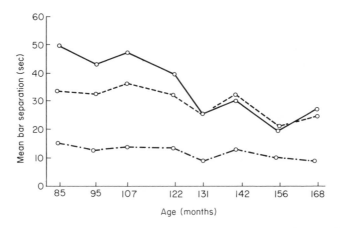

Fig. 2.4. Experiment I—Visual acuity as a function of hue and chronological age. Solid line = blue; dashed line = red; dot-dash line = black and white; N = 96 (Skoff & Pollack, 1969).

green were significantly smaller. As before, subjects reported occasional blurring of the yellow figure and also the green (Fig. 2.6). In order to permit the use of all four colors at equal lightness levels, relatively unsaturated samples were used.

A second experiment (Ebert & Pollack, 1971) was performed comparing the original data for the red, yellow and blue figures with those obtained with highly saturated samples. Green was dropped because it was impossible to obtain green

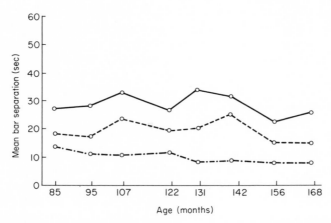

Fig. 2.5. Experiment II–Visual acuity as a function of hue and chronological age with pre-trial focusing. Solid line = blue; dashed line = red; dot-dash line = black and white; N = 96 (Skoff & Pollack, 1969).

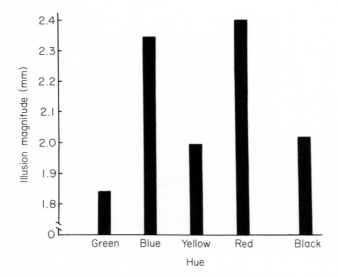

Fig. 2.6. Illusion magnitude as a function of hue.

Munsell papers of sufficient saturation. An additional 50 subjects were run. No main effect for either saturation or hue was found, but there was a significant interaction. Curiously, increasing saturation for the red figure significantly *reduced* the magnitude of its illusion. The main finding, however, was that the original order of magnitude of the low saturation figures (red > blue > yellow) was reversed when saturation was markedly increased. Obviously, a mechanism different from that obtaining for lightness contrast (Wickelgren, 1965) must be operating, since increasing the contrast of the inducing lines increased illusion magnitude in Wickelgren's study. A follow-up experiment is presently underway in which figures representing three levels of lightness contrast are being used. Preliminary data indicate that the greater the contrast, the greater the illusion for short durations (500 msec). There is a significant linear decrease in illusion magnitude as the figure is changed from black (Munsell, 1.5) to midgray (5/) to light gray (2./) on a white (9.5/) background. The pattern, however, may be different for longer exposures (1500 msec). A contrast (midgray and light gray) and duration (.5 and 1.5 sec) analyses of variance yielded a main effect of duration and a huge contrast by duration interaction. The longer duration produced a reversal of the contrast pattern in that lower contrast produced a greater illusion magnitude.

The obvious next step to be taken was the comparison of the ontogenetic course of a Type-I illusion whose figure is produced by lightness contrast only, with the same illusion when its figure is produced by hue contrast alone. The expectations based on previous data (Pollack 1963, 1964, 1965a; Skoff & Pollack, 1969) were crystal clear: The lightness contrast figure would show the usual diminution in magnitude with increasing age while the hue contrast figures would not. The experiment (Pollack, 1970a) was carried out using red, yellow, green and blue midhue figures of equal chroma on neutral gray backgrounds of equivalent lightness, as well as a white figure on a black ground. The subjects included 120 children aged 9 to 14, 60 male and 60 female, and 20 university students aged 18 to 25, 10 male, 10 female. A preliminary analysis of variance of the hue contrast figures alone across age yielded only a main effect of hue ($p < .001$). Red produced a significantly greater illusion than blue and yellow, which did not differ from each other, while green produced a significantly smaller magnitude than all the others. Since there was no age by hue interaction, the data for the hues was averaged. A further analysis of variance of contrast type by age was carried out, yielding a main effect for contrast type (lightness > hue) and a type-by-age interaction (Fig. 2.7). One-way analyses across age revealed only a significant linear decline for lightness contrast as age increased. Thus, the theoretical view that ontogenetic trends in Type-I phenomena can be accounted for entirely by cognitive processes (Piaget, 1969) cannot be sustained. At the same time, the notion that receptor aging plays a dominant role remains tenable.

Following the initial findings (Silvar & Pollack, 1967; Pollack & Silvar, 1967) that gross differences in the lightness of fundus pigmentation are reflected in susceptibility to a Mueller-Lyer figure presented in blue light (lightly pigmented subjects have bigger illusions), a long period was occupied in developing instrumentation by means of which pigmentation lightness could be recorded so

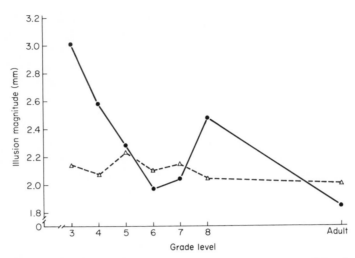

Fig. 2.7. Magnitude of Mueller-Lyer illusion as a function of school grade level; solid line indicates white/black, broken line indicates average color (Pollack, 1970b).

that finer work could be undertaken. Preliminary work employing a trained observer using a hand ophthalmoscope with an all white sample produced unreliable ordering of subjects. In the end, a Bausch and Lomb binocular ophthalmoscope was purchased. One of the eyepieces was modified so that it could be mated to the sensor of a multivolt lightmeter. The other eyepiece was used for sighting, to locate an area just outside the foveal depression from which meter readings would be taken.

The first experiment undertaken with these apparatus, yielded data from subjects who also experienced highly saturated, colored Mueller-Lyer figures (Ebert & Pollack, 1971). Correlations between illusion magnitude and lightness of pigmentation tended to be small, but that obtained for the yellow figure was significant $(r = .29, N = 50)$. This result coincides with some of De Valois' (1970) work on the sensitivities of various opponent color cells in the lateral geniculate nucleus. He found that the yellow excitatory-blue inhibitory cells are the most sensitive to intensity changes of the four hue-sensitive cell types. Our data indicate, therefore, that the action of pigmentation lightness must be mainly on overall sensitivity to contrast intensity, and not on color detection. An experiment is now under way to compare illusion magnitudes of light gray, midgray and black Mueller-Lyer figures on white grounds and to correlate these data with pigmentation lightness. Preliminary findings indicate that the relationship will be most manifest with minimal figure ground contrast, as one might expect.

The final pair of studies in this group dealing with Type-I phenomena represents a new departure in the research program. An attempt has been made to manipulate experimentally one of the variables operating in the aging process of the eye. One of my students, Kris Sjöstrom, and I have measured the effect of simulated lens-yellowing on the magnitude of the Delboeuf illusion (Type I) (Fig. 2.8) and the Usnadze effect (Type II) (Fig. 2.9). A fairly narrow-band yellow filter (dominant wave-length 581.2 μm) which transmits 86% of normal light when placed in front of the eyes, created our aged condition. The initial study (Sjöstrom & Pollack, 1971a) was carried out monocularly on two samples of adults aged either 20 or 45 on the average. It was expected that the yellow filter would effect the Delboeuf illusion considerably, because of our view that Type-I phenomena are largely determined by variables affecting light intensity. In contrast, little change in the Usnadze effect was expected, since its occurrence depends upon the integration of the trace of the initially presented unequal circles with the subsequently presented equal ones, a cognitive process which will operate as long as the stimuli are above threshold. The results confirmed our expectations, in that the magnitude of the Delboeuf illusion diminished significantly when viewed through the yellow filter, while the Usnadze effect did not change significantly (Fig. 2.10). There was no overall age effect, which was due, most probably, to a poor selection of age groups. Wapner, Werner, and Comalli (1960) had found a reversal of illusion age trends in the early 1940s which would preclude an age difference in our study. The reasons for these reversals, especially in Type-I phenomena, are still unknown and will not be speculated upon here.

Because no trends were apparent, a second experiment was carried out, employing binocular vision and more youthful subjects (Sjöstrom & Pollack, 1971 b). The subjects were 48 children, 24 males and 24 females, divided into three age-groups—8, 11, and 14. This time, an age-by-illusion-by-condition analysis of variance was carried out, yielding significant main effects for age and illusion and no significant interactions between age and illusion and condition and illusion. The age-by-illusion interaction showed the familiar pattern of diminution in the Delboeuf and enhancement of the Usnadze. Once again the filter significantly reduced the magnitude of the Delboeuf, but left the Usnadze relatively unchanged (see Fig. 2.11). There was no age-by-condition interaction, indicating that the filter acted in additive fashion to diminish the Delboeuf equally at all ages. This additive relationship further bolsters the argument that receptor aging is an essentially nondevelopmental process. Research is continuing with an emphasis on stimulus duration.

Classification of Illusion Phenomena

The second group of only two experiments deals with the classification and the determinants of the Ponzo illusion. The first experiment (Quina & Pollack, 1971a) was designed to test three theoretical accounts for the phenomenon. In

Fig. 2.8. Delboeuf illusion.

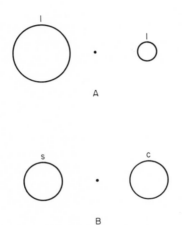

Fig. 2.9. Usnadze effect. The upper circles (A) are presented first followed by an interval and then by the lower circles (B).

general, the Ponzo has been considered as an illusion which increases through childhood (Leibowitz & Judisch, 1967), and therefore apparently belongs in Type II. Further bolstering for such a position comes from the age regression study of Parish, Lundy, and Leibowitz (1968), in which age regressed subjects reduced the magnitude of their illusions significantly. More recent work attempting to relate the Ponzo illusion to a general appreciation of perspective (Leibowitz *et al,* 1969) has shown this relationship to be more apparent than real, in that the basic geometrical illusion obtains in population samples (natives of Guam) that do not respond to real perspective cues. In addition, rotation of the basic geometric figure, which tends to reduce perspective cues, has no effect on the magnitude of the illusion. Work in Leibowitz's laboratory (personal communication, 1970) has shown a reversal of the visual age trends using the basic figure. The picture is confused further by Fisher (1968) and Greene and Lawson (1970) who find no effect of induced depth cues on the magnitude of the illusion either by using the Necker cube or by stereoscopically inducing depth.

Older work, by Köhler and Wallach (1944), attributed the Ponzo illusion to

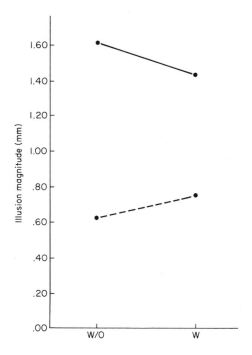

Fig. 2.10. Interaction between Delboeuf (solid line) and Usnadze (broken line) illusions without (w/o) and with (w) filter conditions (Sjöstrom & Pollack, 1971a).

the satiation effects produced by the inducing angle which caused shrinkage of the two vertical lines placed within its arms. The line more distal from the apex was said to shrink more, because of the distance paradox apparent in all figural aftereffect displacements. If Köhler and Wallach were indeed correct, then one would expect a decline in illusion magnitude with age because of the postulated buildup of permanent satiation in the cortex with age, which reduces the immediate distributing effects of experienced patterns. The occurrence of figural aftereffects does, indeed, decline up to age 10 (Pollack, 1969) before the age trend reverses itself.

Another finding by Greene and Lawson (1970) suggested the strategy adopted by Quina and Pollack (1971b). These authors used small squares as their test figures. They discovered that the square distal to the apex shrank with respect to one outside the wedge, while the proximal square was overestimated. Such results are consistent neither with a perspective nor a satiation theory. We placed vertical lines within a horizontal wedge at six distances from the apex. Their apparent lengths were compared with vertical lines well outside of the wedge.

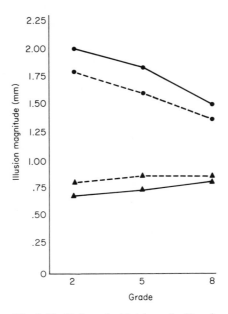

Fig. 2.11. Delboeuf (dots) and Usnadze (triangles) illusion magnitude under conditions of with (broken lines) and without (solid lines) filter, for three grade levels (Sjöstrom & Pollack, 1971b).

The line closest to the apex completed an equilateral triangle and the most distal line was just outside of the wedge (Fig. 2.12). Our usual practice of using small figures (maximum visual angle: 3°15′) presented tachistoscopically (250 msec) under fixation conditions was followed. The results obtained from two trained adult subjects are quite clear. The two lines closest to the apex are overestimated while those most distal are underestimated (Fig. 2.13). The intermediate lines remain relatively unchanged. Theories appealing to perspective cannot account for the underestimations of the distal lines unless they argue that the wedge is subjectively pivoted at its middle so that its open end is subjectively closer to the observer than the fronto-parallel plane of the figure. Satiation theory cannot account for the overestimations near the apex. In our view, we are dealing with separate phenomena. There is assimilation at the apical end of the wedge such that the test line serves to complete a triangle. Pollack (1964) showed previously that fixated triangles have a tendency to be overestimated in size. At the distal end, contrast is operating in that the test line is compared to the relatively large extent of empty space between its ends and the lines of the wedge thus giving the appearance of reduced size. It is also possible that the

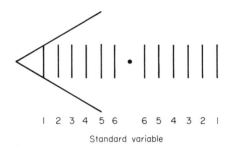

Standard variable

Fig. 2.12   The Ponzo illusion figure (Quina, 1971).

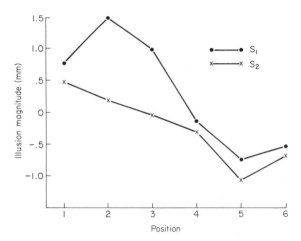

Fig. 2.13. Magnitude of illusion as a function of the position of the test line relative to the apex of the Ponzo wedge; dots = S_1, crosses = S_2.

often found overestimations of acute angles is operating to exaggerate the distance between the ends of the test line and the wedge. If such an explanation holds, then the Ponzo figure represents two illusions which may have quite distinct age courses.

Quina (1971) went on to study ontogenetic effects using test lines at the two positions which produced the most overestimation and the most under-estimation in the previous experiment (see Fig. 2.14). The subjects were four groups of five males and five females each in grades two, four, six and eight. As before, the line closer to the apex was consistently overestimated while the distal line was underestimated. Analysis of variance yielded a significant interaction between age and test line position as well as an age main effect. Trend analyses for the two positions across age revealed a significant linear decrease in illusion magnitude with age for the apical position, whereas the distal

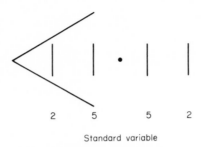

Standard variable

Fig. 2.14. The Ponzo illusion figure.

position showed a quadratic trend increasing from ages seven to nine and dropping thereafter (Fig. 2.15). Correlational analysis of illusion magnitude, MA and CA for each position yields significant results for the apical position (CA × I: $r = -.57$, $p < .001$, $N = 40$; MA × I: $r = -.30$, $p < .01$, $N = 40$). The difference between these correlations is significant ($p < .001$). Partial correlation increases the coefficient with CA to $-.60$ and changes that with MA to a positive value, .38 which is significant. Considering the overall age trend, CA is the more important variable. Since the relationship between the contrast effect and age was curvilinear, etas were calculated. The coefficients obtained were .90 and .70, respectively, for MA and CA with both highly significant ($p < .001$, $N = 40$). The eta for MA was significantly greater than that for CA ($p < .01$), indicating that the attentional shift which makes the appreciation of contrast effect on the distal line possible is related to intellectual functioning, but the pattern of illusion decline thereafter follows Type-I ontogenesis. The overestimation of the angle of the wedge most likely declines with age since it represents a primitive contour interaction. The trend of the main effect of age has both highly significant linear and quadratic components, which illustrate the greater overall magnitude of the contrast illusion beyond age eight. When the two illusions are subtracted algebraically to show the total illusory effect, no significant trend is found. The shape of the curve, however, looks much like that obtained by Comalli who also found a maximum at age nine.

In sum, the Ponzo illusion appears to be two separate phenomena. Lines near the apex show an assimilation effect of overestimation probably due to contour processes which are fairly primitive. This effect tends to decline linearly with increasing age. Distal lines show a contrast effect, which increases up to age nine and declines thereafter. The trend has the earmarks of a Piagetian Type-III (1969) illusion, which typically increases through middle childhood and then declines. The larger component of the total illusion is assimilatory at age seven, indicating perhaps that relatively little attention is focused on the more distal line. From age nine onwards, however, the contrast component is much larger, but still declining. It could mean that once the distal line is focused upon, the contrast effect is a contour effect resulting from the apparent enlargement of the

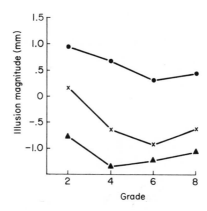

Fig. 2.15. Magnitude of illusion as a function of age for two positions of the test line relative to the apex of the Ponzo wedge. Position 2 (dots) is near the apex, and position 5 (triangles) corresponds with the ends of the wedge. Sum (crosses) indicates the algebraic summation of the means for the two positions.

acute angle of the wedge which itself declines due to the aging process. What is involved thereafter is a widening of the child's effective field of attention, which produces a pseudoincrease in a Type-I illusion made up of two distinct Type-I phenomena which differ as a result of the location of the test lines and their distances from the contours of the wedge.

The final group of studies deal with the relationship of Hearnshaw's concept of temporal integration (1956) to Type-II phenomena.

Cognition and Type-II Phenomena

Hearnshaw considered that the ability to integrate sequential information, and by doing so to anticipate future events, was a distinct component of overall intelligence. Unfortunately, little work has been done to follow up on Hearnshaw's original demonstrations. If, however, a relationship between the magnitude of a Type-II illusion and one of Hearnshaw's anticipation tasks could be found, then a link between perceptual behavior and a component of intellectual functioning could be established. The Hearnshaw-type task consists of three concentric circles divided by 12 equidistant radii (see Fig. 2.16). Black dots are set at intersections of radii and circles. In the simpler problem, one dot is set and fixed at an intersection on the innermost circle. Another dot is placed at an intersection on the middle circle. In successive presentations, the latter is moved about the circle in a standard pattern. After two series of moves, subjects

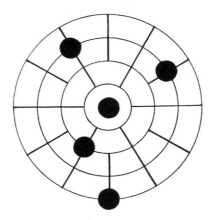

Fig. 2.16. The Hearnshaw task (Hearnshaw, 1956).

are asked to predict the next two moves according to the pattern. In the more difficult task, a third dot is placed at an intersection on the outer circle as well. This dot is moved about the circle in a random pattern. The subject is asked now to pick out the random and the standard patterns and to anticipate the next two moves for the standard pattern.

Mrs. Carter Seeman's work began with an examination of the possible role of afterimages in the successive version of the Mueller-Lyer illusion (Figs. 2.17-2.19) (Pollack, 1964). It was felt that if the exposure time of the inducing lines of the figure were lengthened, the age course would be altered. That is, the youngest subjects would show a relatively larger illusion, which would decrease with age and then increase due to a shift from a situation in which the trace of the inducing lines would have to be integrated with the subsequent appearance of the test line. In the first experiment (Carter, 1970), inspection time was increased from Pollack's (1964) 500 msec to 1000 msec and two interstimulus-intervals (ISI), 500 msec and 2000 msec, were used. The shorter ISI replicated the earlier typical Type-II age pattern, but there was no trend for the longer ISI. Apparently the shorter exposure time was too short for afterimages, and the longer ISI was too long for interaction purposes.

A second experiment was carried out using the same ISI's but longer inspection times, 2 and 5 sec. No age trends were apparent. An examination of the experimental conditions and subjects revealed a larger degree of intersubject variability, which could be related to the fact that, unlike the upper middle class, high achieving, urban population of the 1964 study, the present sample members were mainly lower class, rural children. Also, there was a change from male to female experimenters. The next experiment, therefore, instituted a pretest control condition of judgments of equal line length which could be used as a

Fig. 2.17. Inducing lines for the successive Mueller-Lyer illusion.

Fig. 2.18. Comparison lines for the successive Mueller-Lyer illusion.

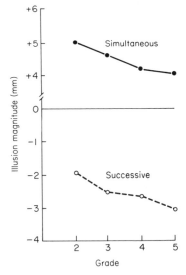

Fig. 2.19. Magnitude of simultaneous and successive illusion as a function of age level (Pollack, 1964).

baseline from which to measure illusion magnitude. In addition, only female subjects, 10 in each of grades two, four, six and eight were used with the female experimenter. Inspection time was 1000 msec ISI's of 500 msec and 2 sec. The 500-msec ISI results were as before, but the 2-sec ISI produced a lower magnitude of illusion with the youngest subjects than before, but a steeper increase with age than the 500-msec ISI. The latter magnitude also correlated significantly with two versions of Hearnshaw's dot matrix task (Hearnshaw, 1956)—.49 and .44 respectively, thus indicating the strong possibility of a common temporal integration mechanism underlying the successive Mueller-Lyer illusion and the Hearnshaw tasks.

Because correct solutions of the task and illusions were obtained at all the age levels studied, plans have been made to search out the origins of these phenomena in preschool children. Obviously, more work will have to be done as well with the temporal parameters of the tasks. This line of research appears to be profitable, however, since it may well lead to the origins of the perceptual-cognitive interface.

In summary, then, the bulk of our work since early 1969 has been concerned with exploration of the psychological microstructure of the mechanisms underlying Type-I phenomena. The results have served in general to confirm our earlier theoretical notions, but they have forced some necessary changes. In the process, our knowledge of perception per se has increased, and the directions for future research have been clarified.

Sylvia Farnham-Diggory received her bachelor's degree from the University of Chicago, and her doctorate from the University of Pennsylvania. For several years she carried out a program of psychiatric research culminating in a monograph on the conceptual development of brain-damaged and psychotic children (Farnham-Diggory, 1966).

Following a year of postdoctoral training at the University of California, Los Angeles, she joined the psychology faculty at Carnegie-Mellon, where she authored *Cognitive Processes in Education* (Farnham-Diggory, 1972) and directed her research toward the cognitive developmental problems of black children (Farnham-Diggory, 1970). The following paper, however, is concerned with some basic theoretical issues.

CHAPTER 3

THE DEVELOPMENT OF EQUIVALENCE SYSTEMS*

S. Farnham-Diggory

Carnegie-Mellon University

Several years ago I began investigating a type of complex, integrated behavior that I called *cognitively synthesized* behavior (Farnham-Diggory, 1967). Here is an example: A child first learns a list of logographs, like those shown in Figure 3.1. These are whole word symbols for such words as *jump, block, over, around, teacher,* and so forth. These logographs do not, obviously, require alphabetic discriminations, so we can bypass the perceptual confusion that may beset young readers. Even 3-year-olds can learn these symbols quite easily. They can

*The research reported here was supported in part by Public Health Service Research Grant MH-07722 from the National Institutes of Mental Health.

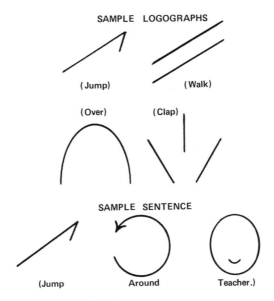

Fig. 3.1. Sample logograph stimuli.

also easily read sentences composed of the symbols, like *jump over block,* or *jump around teacher.* However, a problem may arise when they are asked to demonstrate the meaning of a logograph sentence. For example, a 5-year-old is presented with the sentence, *jump over block.* Conveniently, there is a block on the floor that he knows about. In fact, he may already have practiced jumping over it. After the child reads the sentence, the experimenter says to him, "All right, now let me see you *do* it." The child may look perplexed for a moment, and then his face brightens, he jumps up in the air, makes a sign for *over,* and then points to the block on the floor. He acts out each element of the sentence *jump over block* separately. He fails to integrate or synthesize cognitively the separate chunks of information.

This is a relatively intractable deficiency which can be demonstrated on many different kinds of experimental materials. I have used four basic tasks: the artificial reading task just described, a maplike task, a task using quantitative concepts, and a new task involving the integration of color and form. I will be describing them in more detail. I do not have extensive age norms, but the development of synthesis capacities seems to parallel the general development of operational capacities as defined by Piaget and Inhelder (1969). In fact, it has seemed to me intuitively that synthesized behavior is broadly analogous to compensation. The child who can recognize that a change in one dimension is accompanied by a compensatory change in another dimension is integrating two kinds of information simultaneously. In general, children who fail to conserve on the conservation of liquids task are also nonsynthesizers (Farnham-Diggory & Bermon, 1968), as was demonstrated in an experiment a few years ago. However, some Syracuse colleagues (Hall *et al.,* 1970) pointed out quite rightly that I had not properly controlled for age, and showed that when this was done, the correlation between conservation and synthesis disappeared. Regardless of whether or not he is a conserver, a child below the age of about 7 is unlikely to synthesize the logograph sentences. The Syracuse investigators felt that reading training was important, and it is certainly true that reading ability can be predicted by scores on the logograph synthesis task (Denner, 1970). However, none of us has been able to show that reading training alone will substantially influence synthesis capacities (Farnham-Diggory, 1970).

Rather than approach the problem through the collection of age norms or behavioral correlates, I have pursued a different research strategy. A group of children are selected who show a baseline synthesis level of 30-50%. That is, the age is determined at which children will be correct on a synthesis task no more than half of the time, but no less than one-third of the time. Beginning at this level, one stands a chance of accelerating synthesis behaviors through training procedures. The success of one training procedure compared with another then tells us something about the intersensory structure of the natural developmental process.

However, this has not been satisfying as an explanatory mechanism. It leaves me wandering from brain cell to brain cell, wondering if anything has myelinated lately. So I reanalyzed the behaviors in question, and decided that what my subjects were really doing was matching one type of behavior to another. In order to do that, they had to first construct a mental program that is equivalent, in some sense, to another mental program.

Consider the first example again. The subject reads *jump over block,* and then jumps over the block on the floor. To do this, he must have held in mind simultaneously the three symbolic concepts (whether in the form of words or of logograph images), and some ideas (whether in the form of images or kinesthetic presentiments) about real-world matching events, such as jumping and blocks. Unless the child can mentally survey these five or six information chunks simultaneously, he will not detect the correct relationships among them.

This task requirement is beyond the apprehension capacities of a typical 5-year-old. Apprehension span at that age is a solid four chunks (Starr, 1923). A 5-year-old is therefore not likely to discover the correct response. What does he do instead? Something exceedingly clever. He matches each action event with its symbol, and outputs a series of pairs. He pairs the concept *jump* with the action event of jumping; he pairs the concept *over* with a sign; and he pairs the concept *block* with a concrete object.

It is important to note that the child does not, in the course of this procedure, forget any elements of the original instructions. He jumps, he makes a sign for *over,* and he points to the block. He has efficiently reduced a five- or six-chunk load to a three-chunk load of *pairs*—and three chunks are well within his capacities.

Exactly the same strategy can be seen in another synthesis task, shown in Figure 3.2. The child first learns four string symbols for bridge, river, roa `, and crossroad, respectively. The cues for the symbols—line drawings on white cards—are left in view. The child is then asked to "Make a bridge, going across a river, with a road on each side."

The correct equivalence-matching operation would require that the three words *bridge, across,* and *river*—to take just the first part of the sentence—be matched to three symbols, and that these concepts be held in mind simultaneously long enough to detect the relationships among them. That is, then, a six-chunk operation, almost at the outer limits for an adult. Young children, of course, do not perform it. Very efficiently, they pair each string symbol with its cue card and ignore the verbal instructions entirely.

The pairwise printout of an overloaded system can be seen in a pure form by combining digit span and block tapping span testing procedures. Figure 3.3 schematizes two examples of the way in which this can be done. The blocks are placed before the subject. The letters R, L, and M refer to right, left, and middle, respectively. The letters, of course, do not appear on the blocks. The numbers also do not appear. Instead, they are spoken. Thus, the first trial will be "1," right block tapped, "7, 4," left block, middle block. The entire pattern is first displayed by the experimenter, and the child immediately tries to duplicate it. The stimulus events are paced at about 1 sec. Exact pacing is not especially important. Apprehension span seems impervious to small variations in speed, and to practice (Neisser, 1967; Norman, 1969). Even when a child is given an opportunity to repeat a trial, he will make almost exactly the same errors the second or third time around.

Figure 3.3 illustrates two six-chunk trials: three blocks and three digits are presented in each trial. The figure also illustrates two onset modalities. In Trial 1, the onset modality is auditory—the digit is spoken first. In Trial 2, it is visual—the block is tapped first. The rest of the Trial 2 elements are modal reversals of the Trial 2 elements, as you can see. The figure further illustrates three intermodal switches: In Trial 1, the first switch is between the one and the right block; the second switch is between the right block and the seven; and the third switch is between the four and the left block. Chunks, switches, onset modality, and sex were the four independent variables in the study I am about to report.

The switching variable is of special interest because it signifies an additional load. Broadbent (1958) believes a switch requires something less than a whole chunk, but it certainly requires some portion of available apprehension capacity. Along with block taps and digits, information about order must be stored.

Fig. 3.2. Child performing string-matching task incorrectly (from Farnham-Diggory, 1970).

Trial 1 **1** R **7** **4** L M

Trial 2 M **9** L R **2** **5**

Fig. 3.3. Sample stimuli for digit/block span task.

Therefore, we would expect an increase in switches to have an effect that is similar to an increase in chunks. That means that an 8-chunk/3-switch condition, for example, may be equivalent to a 10-chunk load.

Thirty-six children of kindergarten age participated in this study. I had already obtained some normative data from local children as a check on the continuing validity of Starr's (1923) norms from 2000 children—showing that the 5-year-old apprehension span is four chunks. The span shifts to five chunks between the ages of 6 and 7, and it is much more likely to be 7 years in the disadvantaged populations where I do most of my research.

Apprehension span for block-tapping is the same as the span for digits—if you do not count reversals as errors. When a fairly complex block-tapping pattern has been accurately reproduced, except for a left-right reversal of the entire pattern, it seems to me that the information is all there. It has been transformed, but it has all been remembered. Therefore, I hesitate to call a reversal a span error.

However, I try to train subjects not to make reversals, so the problem comes up infrequently.

Twelve of my experimental children (six boys and six girls) received four-chunk block and digit patterns—two blocks, and two digits per trial. Twelve received six-chunk patterns, and twelve received eight-chunk patterns. Each child did not receive a sample of all three patterns because that would have necessitated continuous removal and replacement of blocks. Only the number of blocks that were to be tapped were placed before the subjects, and the blocks remained in view throughout all trials.

In the four-chunk condition, there were 12 trials, representing one, two and three switches, in two onset modalities each. There were two trials per onset modality. In the six- and eight-chunk conditions, there were 20 trials, representing different numbers of switch patterns, each presented twice in two onset modalities.

We can ask first about number correct. The children were 100% correct on the four-chunk task; 54% correct on the six-chunk task; and 46% correct on the eight-chunk task. In other words, almost half the time 5-year-olds can, through various strategies that I shall explain in a moment, cope correctly with a memory span task that must severely overload their capacities.

There are two ways in which they try to do this. One way is to cluster the digits and the blocks separately. For example, in the first trial shown in Figure 3.2, a clustering subject would report, "1, 7, 4" and then tap RLM. He would not alternate between digits and blocks, as the experimenter had demonstrated. Clustering is a stable characteristic of some children. Fifteen of my 36 experimental subjects showed consistent tendencies to cluster, the number of clustering trials ranging from two to 15 per child in this group.

There were some differences in initial clustering modality. Four boys and three girls always clustered digits first; that is, they always reported their digit cluster first. Four boys clustered blocks first, but no girl did this. Three girls and one boy clustered blocks first sometimes, and digits first sometimes. As Figure 3.4 shows, boys are somewhat more likely than girls to cluster blocks, and girls are somewhat more likely to cluster digits.

Onset modality had no effect on this, or on anything else, somewhat surprisingly.

Figure 3.5 shows that girls make more errors on both blocks and digits than do boys. That should not surprise us, since this sort of sex difference in quantitative and spatial skills is well documented. However, I know of no previous research that reveals a possible mechanism so clearly: Girls apparently have a basic problem registering the stimuli. Naturally, this will handicap their subsequent use of numerical and spatial information on the more complex tasks that appear on aptitude and achievement tests.

Figure 3.5 also suggest that there are generally more block errors than digit

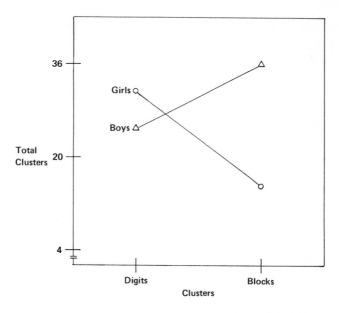

Fig. 3.4. Clustering responses of boys and girls on the digit/block span task.

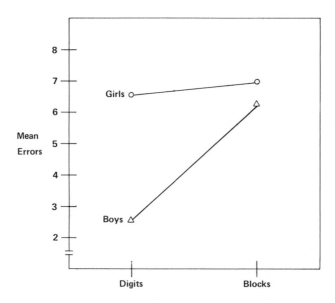

Fig. 3.5. Mean errors of boys and girls on the digit/block span task.

errors. The error rate for digits is 4.7; the rate for blocks is 6.6. I suspect the digits are somewhat more salient than blocks, because each digit sounds different, while all the blocks look alike. If you are going to forget something under these conditions, it is probably easier to forget a block.

Our main interest here is how the children manage to preserve the block-digit information that is ordinarily beyond their capacity to remember. Their favorite strategy for doing so is through pairing: They pair a block with a digit, and output them both as a pair-series. For example, in Trial 1 of Figure 3.3, the output would be 1R, 7L, and 4M. They touched each block, labeling it by its paired number. This pairing response is automatic and usually intractable. A pairing child will be unable to respond correctly in any other way. If you force him to stop pairing (which is extremely hard to do), he will lose the information.

In Figure 3.6, we can see what happens to errors, clusters, and pairs as a function of chunks. In the four-chunk condition, the error rate is 0, and the pair rate is 56—that is, 56% of the time, the children were pairing digits and blocks. The error rate increases sharply when the task is extended beyond 5-year-old span capacity, to six chunks, but the pair rate remains above it. By eight chunks, the pair rate drops to 31% and the error rate soars accordingly. By contrast, the cluster rate remains low and relatively constant.

We can see more clearly in Figure 3.7, where number of switches is the independent variable, how errors and pairs mirror each other. An additional variation here involved switching regularity. One set of three-switch trials was an irregular pattern; one set was a regular pattern. You can see that both errors and pairing responded to this variation, by increasing with irregularity. The highly regular seven-switch pattern, which was actually an alternation of blocks and digits, produced a sharp increase in pairs, but a relatively small increase in errors. The clustering function, however, remained low and constant. Whatever else clustering may be, it does not seem to be an especially efficient system for responding to an increase in span load. That is, clustering does not negatively covary with the error function.

The fact that the pairing function does negatively covary with errors is of special interest developmentally because it is a cross-modal function. Some of Milner's (1970) recent data would suggest that digit-block pairing may be an interhemispheric coordination. Milner has evidence that block span functions are damaged by right hemispheric lesions, whereas digit span is damaged by left hemispheric lesions. This suggests that the automatic pairing responses which we see in our 5-year-olds may provide the foundation for rich conceptual interconnections. For one thing, the use of a cross-modal pairing mechanism to reduce information load probably makes many kinds of equivalence discoveries possible. These discoveries, in turn, may be the basis for higher-order recoding discoveries.

Consider the problem of comprehending a complex graph. A separate cluster

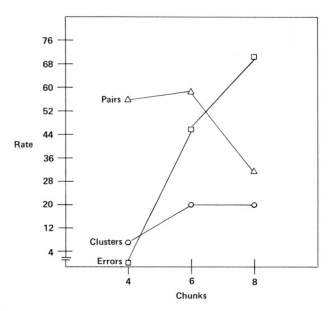

Fig. 3.6. Rate of pairs, clusters and errors, as a function of chunks, on the digit/block span task.

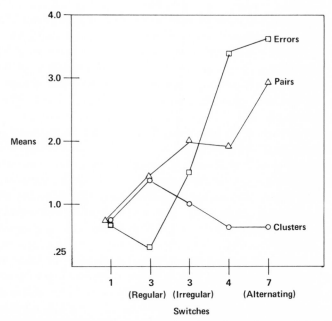

Fig. 3.7. Mean clusters, pairs, and errors, as a function of switches, on the digit/block span task.

of images on the one hand, and of words on the other, would not be of much help. However, when we can pair words with graphic features, and (on a higher level) pair sentences with graphic patterns, then we can begin to understand the display. The underlying mechanism here may be the same simple load-reduction system we have seen in 5-year-olds: Pair it up to make it less.

Of course there are other kinds of load-reducing mechanisms, and we have used some of them to devise ways of helping children to perform equivalence matches, or cognitive syntheses of various kinds. I would like to discuss two methods in particular: rote linking, and marking or attentional control.

By rote linking, I mean the following: A child learns a portion of a task so well that it becomes largely automatic. This rote behavior now need be only partially apprehended. When it is cued in as part of a synthesis task, it will take up only one apprehension chunk. It can then be more readily related to other information.

Essentially, this is part learning, but it is often not recognized as such. For example, the connection of spoken language to its written form may not seem to be putting two parts of a whole together. That is because the writing part is not usually as well practiced as the spoken part. It could be, and in traditional Chinese families, for example, it is. Formal training begins at the age of 2. Montessori also prepared children extensively for writing their own language, and she did this entirely through rote techniques.

By means of rote linking, I have been able to raise the behavior of 5-year-olds on the logograph (block-jumping) task to an 8-year-old level. The children practiced the behavior segments (like jumping over the block) before they learned the logographs. In one condition, they also overlearned the logograph sentences. Since several portions of the task now no longer required active apprehension, the few remaining critical relationships could be accurately scanned and recognized.

A second major load-reduction technique involves the more direct control of attention. This may be handled through pretraining procedures, or through a restructuring of the task environment itself. In the string task, where the child makes a bridge going across a river, more mature solutions can be produced simply by removing the cue cards. The child memorizes the string symbols first, which is easy for him to do. Then he "makes a bridge going across a river, with a road on each side" from verbal instructions. Without the distraction of the cue cards, he can pay closer attention to his own language.

I have seen a similar procedure demonstrated by a gifted art teacher working with slow first graders. If you ask such a child to draw a picture of his house, for example, you get a few discouragingly stereotyped forms, and that is the end of that. However, the teacher in this case, one of our fine arts graduates, Joan Brindle, would not let the children pick up a crayon until they had talked extensively about the details of their houses. They spent 15 or 20 minutes just discussing such questions as, "If you looked through the front window of your house, what would you see? On what side of the roof is your TV antenna? How many steps are in front? Can you count them? Does your front door have a doorknob or a handle? Does it have a window?" When the children were finally permitted to begin to draw what they had talked about, they burst forth with complex, detailed pictures that would do justice to 10-year-olds. They were, in our terms, pairing a series of motor schemata (drawing patterns) with items on a verbal list. This is very different from trying to match motor actions to visual images—which is what we usually do when we try to draw a pictorial representation from memory. Most of the children in Dr. Brindle's class suffered from visual-motor disorders. So she essentially taught them a rerouting procedure. First talk to yourself about a visual memory, and then draw what you *said*. This is an attention control program.

It is also, obviously, a chain of equivalence matches. You find a verbal representation of a visual memory, and then you find a motoric representation of the verbalization. It is important to understand that the order of such procedures is critical, and may differ from task to task. Certainly we must be aware of any simple-minded assumption that verbal mediation, or a verbal step in the chain, is a universal aid. I have found, for example, that verbalization is helpful if the end result is going to be a motor or kinesthetic activity. However, verbalization is, if anything, a hindrance in tasks that have a perceptual or visual restructuring as a final outcome.

For example, Figure 3.8 shows a three-term serial ordering task (Farnham-Diggory, 1970). The blocks, in the order shown in the figure, are placed before the child. The dot cards are scrambled, face up, and the child is then asked to "put the cards with the blocks, the way they are supposed to go." The 30% group for this task is about 4 years old. Five-year-olds polish it off with dispatch,

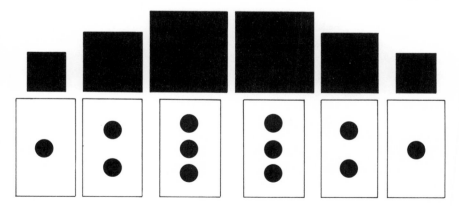

Fig. 3.8. Stimuli for the block-dot matching task (from Farnham-Diggory, 1970).

but the 4-year-olds struggle. They can quite well recognize that one card has more dots than another, and that one block has more area than another. However, they do not easily discover the higher-order equivalence: The fact that a greater-than relation in one dimension is equivalent to a greater-than relation in another dimension.

To help them discover this equivalence, they were drilled verbally on the blocks and the dot-cards, prior to the final synthesis task. Each child had 30 trials on pairs of dot-cards, and on pairs of blocks. The child would say, in the best Bereiter and Engelman (1966) tradition, "This is more than this," pointing (with guidance if necessary) to one block as compared to another, or pointing to one dot-card as compared to another. He practiced the mediating common phrase *more than* 15 times with reference to the blocks, and 15 times with reference to the dots. Then he was tested. One would certainly expect the common phrase to help the child make appropriate connections between the block series and the dot series. It did not; the verbal drill had little or no experimental effect.

Herbert Clark, who was then at Carnegie-Mellon, took issue with my procedure because he felt that I had not used a sufficiently primitive linguistic marker. He thought I should have emphasized the underlying dimension of bigness, rather than the inequality. So I tried the drill system again, only this time the children said, "This is big and this is little," rather than "This is more than this." Again, the verbal pretraining had no effect.

Interestingly, what did have an effect were some sensorimotor pretraining procedures—for example, playing this kind of a game: I would hold up a one-dot card, and the child would learn to stamp one time when he saw it. Or I would hold up the big block, and the child would learn to take a giant step when he saw that. After 30 pretraining trials involving only visual-motor attention control, and no verbalization at all, 4-year-olds were much more successful on the series-matching task.

I have considered this to be confirmation of Piaget's theoretical emphasis on the sensorimotor—as opposed to verbal—foundations of this kind of logic. However, I also wanted to gain more controlled insight into the general problem of the relationship of verbal representations to the kind of perceptual restructuring that has been illustrated by the series problem. The quality of the task that I have been working on recently can be most easily shown by an example.

Figure 3.9 shows a stimulus "sentence" composed of a number, a color, and a form. The child reads the sentence from left to right, saying aloud "one red square." He is then shown a response card (Fig. 3.10) containing eight cells, and is asked to "find what you said." Ideally, he will point to the red square.

This is a 30% task for a 5-year-old. In order to find the correct response, the child must simultaneously hold in mind the three stimulus concepts—one, red,

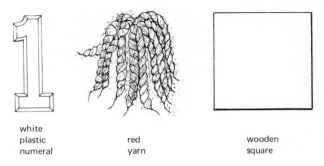

white
plastic   red   wooden
numeral   yarn   square

Fig. 3.9. Sample stimuli for the color-form-number synthesis task.

and square—and test them against at least two attributes of a response choice. He can probably ignore one attribute temporarily, but he must keep at least two of them in mind. Matching the three stimulus attributes to two response attributes requires a five-chunk apprehension span, and so a 5-year-old generally flubs it. He falls back on his characteristic pairing strategy: first he points to a square. Then, if the experimenter continues to look at him expectantly, he will point to something red, such as a red circle, and finally he will point to one of something. Actually, I score only the first response of the series, because waiting for the entire printout becomes a bit tedious.

In order to gain systematic information about the role of verbal marking or attention control on this kind of equivalence matching, I have carried out a series of experiments which have as a final test 18 trials on three term equivalences, like those shown in Figs. 3.9 and 3.10. Only two numbers were used: 1 and 2. Four forms were used: square, circle, triangle, and diamond; and four colors: red, blue, green, and yellow. Eighteen stimulus sentences were randomly selected from all possible combinations of the 10 variables. No two sentences were alike. The response cards, as you see in Fig. 3.10, were eight-celled displays of two numbers, two colors, and two forms, conjunctively represented. The location of the concepts on the response cards was randomly determined, with whatever restrictions necessary to foreclose the confounding of a correct response with a position preference.

The first experiment was concerned with the role of labeling, or marking, as a pretraining procedure. Many 5-year-olds are shaky on labels for even this limited set of colors, forms, and numbers. So it is reasonable to drill first on the labels they will actually be using in the equivalence matching task. The question then arises as to the proper choice of training materials. Would equivalence matching be facilitated by speech training on the stimulus sentences ("What color is this? . . ."), or by auditory training ("Find something red, show me a square. . . ") on the response or pictorial materials? A second question concerned context. Would equivalence matching be facilitated by training on

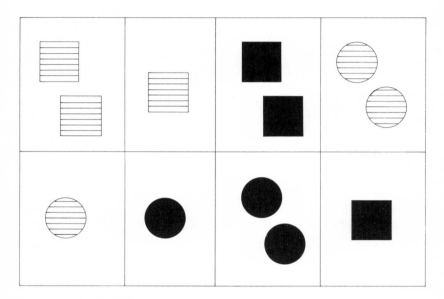

Fig. 3.10. Sample response card for the color-form-number task.

one value at a time, or by training on the three critical terms as a unit? These questions generated a 2 × 2 design, wherein 25% of the subjects were drilled on the stimulus materials, one at a time; 25% on the stimulus materials in three-element "sentences"; 25% on the response materials, one variable at a time—for example, the experimenter would focus the subject's attention only on the color aspect of a red square, or only on the square aspect of the same figure; and, finally, 25% of the subjects were drilled on the conjunctive representation of all three terms at once—one red square, two blue triangles, and the like, using the response panels. There were 96 training trials altogether. Following them, all subjects received the 18 test sentences.

So far as number correct is concerned, the procedure using the conjunctive representations on the response panel was a bit more successful than the others, but by successful I mean only that it moved the subjects from a 30% hit rate to a 50% hit rate. Since none of the label drills actually reduced the apprehension load very much, we should not expect substantial improvement. The more interesting analysis concerns the shift in error functions from training to test.

Errors were recorded at all stages—during the training trials, during the reading of the stimulus "sentences," and during the response panel test sessions. There were, of course, three possible types of errors: color errors, form errors, and number errors. Figure 3.11 shows what happened to these errors.

During the training sessions, color and form errors were more numerous than number errors. This discrepancy increased during the "reading" trials, but it

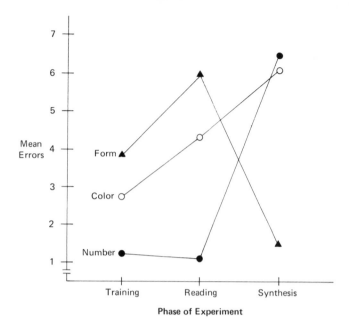

Fig. 3.11. Mean form, color, and number errors during phases of the experiment.

shifted dramatically during the synthesis or equivalence matching trials. This is because the subjects were making their response panel choice on the basis of form—which is the last term in their little sentence. They knew their form *labels* least well as earlier phases of the experiment showed, but apparently used the visual representation of each form as a basis for a response decision, and as their only basis. They ignored number and color, which is why those two error functions shot up.

We can show an equally dramatic reversal of the effect simply by changing the last term in the sentence from a form to a color. That is, we can use sentences like "one square red" instead of "one red square." Under these conditions, the form errors on the 18 equivalence task trials go quite high, and the color errors drop. Figure 3.12 shows the effect in two samples.

You will have noted, of course, a strong recency effect. This may arise from the fact that the children verbalize the stimulus sentence, thus increasing the salience of the last item (Hagen & Kingsley, 1968; Crowder, 1970). However, it is noteworthy that in the block-jumping task, which is also verbalized, recency effects of this sort never appear: the children always begin with the first instruction (*jump*), never with the word *block*. This difference probably arises from the sentence forms, i.e., from the fact that the stimulus sets are not nonsense lists. Further, the subjects are using the information to make a

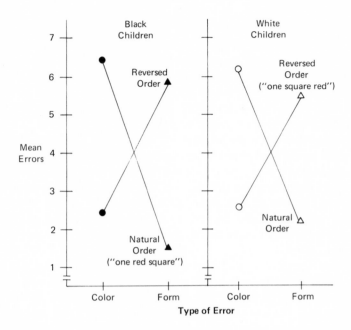

Fig. 3.12. Shifts in the color and form response errors as a function of stimulus word order.

decision. They are not simply outputting buffer contents, as in the block and digit span tests.

The fact that primacy/recency effects will vary with context or list structure, and with the nature of contingent decisions, should make us cautious about generalizing from buffer functions. Similarly, we need to be cautious about the assumption that a child's decision will be a straightforward function of how well he has learned something, as we have seen. Children simply may not use a pretrained system in coping with a particular task. The extent to which they will use it is going to be determined by the processing requirements of the immediate problem.

In this particular case, the span constraints force a pair-serialization of the stimulus and response attributes. That pairing is presumably done visually—a form is visually matched to another form, or a color is matched to another color. Labels have nothing to do with it, and in fact the intrusion of a label simply adds to the load.

If training is to be effective in a task of this sort, it must use a combination of attention control and rote link procedures. The most disturbing aspect of this task is that 5-year-olds already know how to do it—if you simply remove the stimulus materials and tell them what you want. If you say, "Show me a red square," they can easily do so, even using a complex response panel which requires considerable scanning. Similarly, if you say, "Show me two blue triangles, show me a green circle, show me two yellow squares, etc.," a normal 5-year-old can do so. Even in my disadvantaged population, which is plagued with retardation and perceptual-motor dysfunctions of various kinds, it is not unusual to find a child who will be 100% correct on the "show me" task, and less than 10% correct on exactly the same concepts—when he must read the concepts for himself from a stimulus sentence.

The problem then is to devise ways of helping such children link the visual stimulus cues to different visual representations of the same concepts. I am still convinced that a verbal representation is a necessary intermediary step, if I can find a way of persuading the children to use it. I have tried screening the visual cues after they were read. The child closes his eyes, repeats the sentence, "One red square," and then looks directly at the response panel. I hoped he would thereby pay more attention to the information in his own speech. This was not especially successful.

I have also tried cueing the subject more directly, during the test sessions. When a child says "one red square" and points to a blue square, I say, "What color is that?" the child says "Blue," and then I point back to the stimulus materials and say, "And what color did you say?" The child responds "Red," and then I have him read the whole sentence again, and I say to him, very meaningfully, "Now find what you *said*." That, of course, would be counted as a second trial.

Some children profit from this cueing, and some do not. If we separate, at the median, children who can successfully correct their own errors, following cueing, from children who cannot, we get the first-trial function shown in Fig. 3.13. That is, the graph shows how well children who previously had a correction trial were able to apply their new insight to new trials.

The better group is leveling off at a hit rate of about 70%, but the poorer group remains at a 30% level. Presumably, the use of a verbal step can be taught to some children, if the attention control strategy is properly timed. However, there may be intractable differences in rate of intersensory capabilities; some children simply may not be able to make an adequate connection between something seen and something said until their central neural systems are more mature.

To gain more insight into these rates, I am falling back to regroup at an earlier developmental level. My current research involves a new equivalence matching task, for use with very young children. The pictures are projected, from the rear, onto a touch-sensitive screen. It is a simple matching-to-sample setup: The child touches the lower, response picture that is equivalent to the middle, stimulus picture. His touch sends a signal to our on-line computer, which records both latency and errors, and also advances the slide projector. The children never see the same pictures twice.

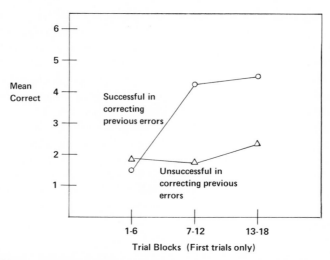

Fig. 3.13. Mean number of synthesis responses correct in children who were, or were not, responsive to a previous correction procedure.

The design actually includes something like a reversal feature, since the children begin with a series of trials that permit identity matches. Among other things, these trials teach the child how to use the machine and what the game is all about. Of more interest theoretically, is the fact that identity matches can probably be made on the basis of visual-visual pairing. Then the equivalence series begins, without warning. A direct visual-visual pairing is no longer possible. How is the match to be made? All of the pictures involved are of materials familiar to the middle class children being used in the study. They have had sensorimotor experiences with similar materials. Is that enough? Do we know a shoe is like a boot because we can put them both on a foot? Or must we have a word to mediate an equivalence match? If a word is necessary, must it be spoken? Or merely comprehended? Is it enough for a child to be able to point to the picture of a shoe, on request, or must he be able to say "shoe," before he is able to perform a pictorial equivalence match?

I wish I could give answers now, but the experiments have barely begun. I plan to collect longitudinal data, beginning some months before a child can solve this problem, and hope to be able to plot the onset of this pictorial equivalence-matching function, and to correlate it with the development of language comprehension and production.

Let me now briefly summarize the major principles that characterize this program of research. First, there are certain intractable physiological limitations upon children's ability to process information. Foremost among these are apprehension span, and intersensory connections. The ability to discover equivalences depends heavily upon both of these constraints. If apprehension span is not exceeded, children discover equivalences easily. If it is exceeded, they may respond by pairing up portions of the equivalence sets, chunk by chunk. What gets paired is partly a function of the task objective, and partly a function of intersensory connectivity.

By working with experimental groups that cannot quite perform certain tasks, and by attempting to devise successful acceleration procedures, we can gain some insight into the course of psychological growth processes that result from continual attempts to cope with excessive information. McLaughlin (1963) has argued, for example, that the classification skills described by Piaget, and studied by Klahr and Wallace (1970a), can be exactly predicted by known increases in a child's memory span. For example, if a young child is shown some brown beads and some white beads, he may correctly tell a questioner that the brown beads are wooden and that the white beads are wooden. But,

> . . . if he is shown a box containing a larger number of brown than white beads, and he is asked whether it holds more brown beads or more wooden beads, he will insist that there are more brown beads. This would be predicted of a [young child] who cannot think of three concepts simultaneously; for, if he has already classified the white wooden beads as "wooden" and the brown wooden beads as "brown" or even "brown wooden," he has not the capacity to restructure his concepts to form a third concept "wooden of any colour" [McLaughlin, 1963, p. 65].

I do not mean to imply that span limitation explains the classification strategies that a child may adopt. Such limitations are merely one of several factors that may make it necessary for him to adopt a strategy that differs from the one he may adopt when his span has grown. The adult conceptual structures inside our heads are not merely physiologically maximized. They are also the result of coping strategies forged during a long period of physiological limitation. Unless we study these strategies while they are evolving, we will never fully understand their final state.

REPLY TO SIMON

Dr. Simon's discussion of my logograph task, and of my position on STM as a fundamental factor in the correct performance of this task, resembles Braine's (1963) theory of syntactical learning as the gathering of contextual associations. Problems with theories of this type have been summarized by Bever et al. (1965). Essentially, (1) It is difficult to specify the conditions of contextual learning. Children, for example, are not frequently provided with good performance models that they become capable of generating (at least as frequency is defined in the laboratory). (2) It is difficult to show that sufficient time exists for "stamping in" contextual associations. Simon himself has noted that the logograph task sounds formidable when described in these terms.

Generally, of course, it is true that contextual associations play a role in both language learning and in logograph sentence learning. Several experimenters (for example, Hall *et al.,* 1970) have shown that some of the less familiar logograph sentences such as "walk over block" are more difficult for children to integrate than more familiar ones such as "walk around teacher." A number of language experiments—for example, those of Miller and Selfridge (1950)—have shown that contextual associations figure importantly in sentence processing.

However, contextual associations do not seem to be as fundamental as memory span. In language learning, the one-chunk span of the 18-month-old may be the basic factor in his production of holophrases. Perhaps the tiny span is also responsible for his deficiencies in contextual learning. In any event, the only possible output of a one-chunk span is a one-word sentence. As span increases, the two-word pivot grammar appears. Presumably contextual associations of pivots like "hi," for example, with the names of people help the child perform some important recodings that free up chunks. However, these recodings do not continue indefinitely. If a two-year-old collapses "hi" and "daddy" into a one-chunk "hidaddy," he still will have only one chunk left for such fancy new sentences as "hidaddy car."

Similarly, in the logograph experiments, contextual associations seem less critical to the production of integrated behavior than is memory span. The span permits mutual associations to be discovered. If one of those words falls out of memory before those associations have time to generate and hook up, then the integration cannot be discovered. The 5-year-old child may cope with this deficiency by employing an intermodal pairing strategy, similar to the one shown in the digit-block experiment. He produces a three-chunk chain of word-action *pairs.* However, the program seems to me to be the same as that used by a 7-year-old.

> *S*: (reading) "jump over block"
> *E*: Now, let me see you *do* it.
>   1. Find "it," if none, stop;
>   Find action that matches "it";
>   2. Go to 1.

For the 5-year-old, "it" is one logograph at a time. For the 7-year-old, "it" is three logographs at a time. The program is the same, but the 7-year-old's increased span makes it possible for him to match a *set* of "its" to an action.

Of course, familiarity may quicken the associative network, but the result of drilling children under the age of four or five may simply be to increase their facility in the use of the pairing strategy. At the age of five, practice begins to facilitate a new type of recoding, which I have called rote-linking. This is still not the full contextual discovery of the 7-year-old, although it looks like it, behaviorally. Beyond the age of seven, children immediately, without any practice whatsoever, perform the logograph task correctly. The increase in STM capacity seems to make possible a flowering of new processing strategies, linguistic and otherwise.

A final note about modality problems. The auditory representation of "jump over block" is easier for children to integrate behaviorally. The visual representation (reading the logographs) is more difficult. As has been detailed elsewhere, (Farnham-Diggory, 1970) the visual onset system must eventually hook up to the auditory system, if comprehension is to occur. The meaning is in the familiar language, not in the unfamiliar logographs. Thus, the reading child must connect the visually-apprehended logograph to the spoken word—a two-step process. The auditory onset (hear and then do) is only a one-step process. At this symposium, Marion Blank pointed out that the same phenomenon can be observed with reference to the auditory-speech chain. It is more difficult for young children to hear an instruction, repeat it aloud, and then do it, than it is for them to hear it and do it, without the speech requirement. Luria (1959, 1961) has shown that the ability to handle an increasing number of steps is a fundamental symptom of development.

An important and difficult experimental question therefore involves distinctions between the STM "width," and STM "depth" or step capacity, as well as inter-modal capacities. That is, where is the major hangup? The number of chunks that can be held in mind simultaneously (width)? The number of sequential steps required for the execution of a behavior (depth)? Or in neurological connections? For example, do children have difficulty learning to read because of the number of visual units (letters or syllables or words) that must be simultaneously apprehended? Or because of the number of steps in the visual-auditory-speech chain? Or because of insufficiently myelinated neuronal tracts connecting visual, auditory, and speech brain areas?

A critical aspect of this is the distinction between the serializing capacities of the motor, auditory and speech systems, and the nonserializing gestalt functions of the visual system. When we "see" something, comprehension has a simultaneous, all-at-once aspect. When we hear something, comprehension unfolds serially. The fact that the earliest, sensorimotor representations are serial in nature may be one reason why auditory comprehension is easier (especially if critical periods are involved). In any event, it seems clear that translations of gestalt representations into serial representations, and vice-versa, poses special problems developmentally. Lashley's (1951) classical paper still stands as the best definition of the issues.

Despite our momentarily differing views of my two experiments, I agree completely with Simon's analytical approach, and profoundly value our continuing dialogue. One of the most important outcomes of the 1971 symposium has been the fact that we developmentalists managed to capture Herbert Simon's attention. His continuing interest promises to result in a number of important theoretical contributions to our field, within the near future.

John Hagen received his bachelor's degree from the University of Minnesota, and his doctorate from Stanford University. He is now Chairman of the developmental psychology program at the University of Michigan.

Unlike many of us, Dr. Hagen seems to have remained focused upon an area of research closely related to his doctoral thesis. With his students, he has generated an extensive series of studies probing selective attention and short-term recall in normals and retardates, and is now the first person one thinks of with reference to the general topic of children's memory. A summary of this work follows.

CHAPTER 4

*STRATEGIES FOR REMEMBERING**

John William Hagen

University of Michigan

There has been considerable interest in the study of memory among developmental psychologists during the past few years, but prior to that time research in the area on children was minimal (Goulet, 1968). Since its beginning, experimental psychology has dealt with memory. The information-processing approach was a real breakthrough both in terms of conceptualizing the issues and generating new empirical evidence concerning the processes involved. Some new concepts and constructs are needed to understand better the developmental aspects of memory, and the research and thinking presented in this paper are addressed to this need.

The research by my colleagues and myself has investigated attention and

*Thanks to Jean Gascon for his reading and comments on the manuscript.

65

mediation in memory. These two factors have been studied by many in attempting to understand developmental changes in perception, learning, and cognition, but relatively few investigators have addressed themselves to memory per se. The findings have led us to conclude that with development, the child becomes an increasingly active participant in the memory process.

Selective Attention and Memory

A brief summary of the research on selective attention should illustrate how my views have evolved. The initial study was by Maccoby and myself (1965). Broadbent's model (1958) of filtering mechanisms was used to derive the predictions. These mechanisms allow certain cues to be attended to selectively while others are ignored. Information to be encoded is held in a memory store before it is passed through the filters for further processing. Ignored information does not pass through the filters and simply fades from memory. Two developmental hypotheses were made. First, improvement in memory as a function of age occurs at least in part because the ability to attend to certain cues while at the same time to ignore others improves. Second, under information overload conditions, incidental information is ignored in order to maintain performance on the central task, and this ability increases with age.

A short-term memory task was used which contained two memory measures, central and incidental. An array of picture cards was presented for a brief exposure (approximately 5 sec). The child was told his task was to remember the locations of certain pictures. In this initial study, each card contained a picture of some object such as a toy train or an animal surrounded by a bright, distinctive color background. After the array of cards was shown (array length varied from four to six), it was placed face down, and a cue card was shown which was the same color as the background of one of the presentation cards. The child's task was to locate the card in the series which had the matching color background. Thus, the picture was not used to obtain this central memory measure. After the 14 trials of picture arrays were presented and the responses were recorded, incidental recall was measured. The incidental task was to match each picture with the appropriate color with which it previously had appeared. The number of correct matches constituted the incidental task measure.

A distractor task was added to ensure information overload. Half the children at each age level performed the task under the distraction condition—a tape recording of piano notes. Whenever a very low note occurred, the child was required to tap the table with a small hammer. Four grade-levels were tested: first, third, fifth, and seventh.

The results were as follows. Central memory task performance increased as a function of age level, while incidental performance did not and actually declined at the oldest level. Thus the proportion of central recall relative to total recall increased developmentally, confirming the first hypothesis. The information overload condition did result in a decrement in performance on central memory, and about as much for the oldest as for the younger children. Incidental performance was affected only at the oldest age level, where it was reduced. Thus only at the oldest age level was support obtained for the second hypothesis.

The next study (Hagen, 1967) was designed to eliminate certain problems in the first. The stimuli used here have been used in most of the subsequent studies. Each stimulus card contained two pictures, an animal and a household object. Thus the figure-background relation of the first stimuli was avoided (see Fig. 4.1). We knew that if the pictures themselves were used as the central recall measure, there would be little or no incidental learning of the background colors. For the new stimuli, central and incidental pictures could be counter-balanced. Half the subjects were instructed to recall locations of animals and half household objects for the central task. The incidental measure was pairing each animal with the household object with which it had originally occurred. The grades tested were again first, third, fifth, and seventh. In addition, a series of trials was included in which only the central pictures appeared on the cards to determine the effect of the presence of the second stimulus.

It was again found that central memory improved with age, whereas incidental performance did not. The distraction condition resulted in lower central performance about equally across age levels. Incidental performance declined at the oldest age level only in the distraction condition. The central-picture-only condition resulted in higher central memory scores at all age levels. An additional result appeared in this study. The correlations between the two response measures were positive at the younger grades, but negative at the oldest. Thus, among the younger children, those who did well on central memory also did well on incidental memory. At the oldest level, however, those who did well on central seemed to ignore the incidental information. This finding supports the hypothesis that the ability to maintain task performance by excluding incidental information improves with age.

In four subsequent studies, we attempted to explore the effects of certain stimulus properties and characteristics of the experimental design. Hagen and Sabo (1967) modified the paradigm so that testing for central performance followed testing for incidental recall for half the subjects, thereby checking to discover if the differences found were related to the order of testing. The original results were replicated, showing that order was not a confounding factor.

A study by Hagen and Frisch (1968) varied the presentation of the incidental stimuli in three different ways. One condition replicated the earlier method of presentation in which the incidental picture was always paired with the same central picture. In the other two conditions, the pairings were not constant. In

Fig. 4.1. Stimulus materials for the central-incidental memory task.

one, pairing was random, and in the other the *same* incidental picture appeared with each of the central pictures on a given trial. The exact same number of instances of each picture appeared in each condition; only the pairings differed. A recognition rather than the recall measure was used for incidental since the pairing task was not appropriate for the latter two conditions. It was expected that central performance would be affected for the younger children when constant pairing of incidental pictures did not occur. However, no differences were found in central task performance as a function of pairing conditions. The central-incidental-task-by-age interaction found in the previous studies was replicated. Thus it seems that younger children do not attend to the incidental pictures simply because they are paired with the central pictures. The mere presence of the incidental pictures distracts from the central task at hand.

Another study attempted to produce differences in memory performance by manipulating stimulus arrangement factors (Druker & Hagen, 1969). It was expected that changes in the visual discriminability of the stimuli would differentially affect selective task performance as a function of age. Discriminability between the relevant (central) and irrelevant (incidental) pictures was varied in two ways. The contiguous picture pairing arrangement which has been used previously was compared with an arrangement in which the pictures of a pair were separated spatially from each other. The second condition involved nonalternating versus alternating spatial arrangements. In the nonalternating condition, the central picture always appeared above the incidental picture. In the alternating arrangement, it was randomly determined whether the central or incidental picture appeared in the upper position. The expectation was that when incidental stimuli could be more easily differentiated from central stimuli via certain spatial arrangements, younger children would be more able to ignore them. The results did not confirm this expectation, although it was again found that central recall scores increased with age while incidental decreased relative to the total amount of recall. This study also employed a posttest questionnaire. From these data, two response tendencies were found to be related to age: specific verbal labeling of the central stimuli and focused visual scanning (see Figs. 4.2 and 4.3). Thus, the developmental changes in memory task performance were not found to be related to stimulus discriminability, but were related to certain encoding strategies as revealed by the questionnaire results.

A dissertation recently completed by Sally Baker (1970) employed the central-incidental memory task to explore the effects of frequency of presentation of the incidental stimuli as Siegel (1968) had done in a discrimination learning task. He found, contrary to expectations, that 8-year-old subjects performed the same as 14-year-olds; but his task seemed to confound task difficulty with number of presentations. Baker compared performance of an 8-trial condition with a 16-trial condition. Third, fifth, and seventh grade subjects were tested. For the two younger age groups, incidental recall was higher for the 16-trial condition than the 8-trial condition; but incidental recall was about the same for the oldest age group for both conditions. Central task performance was not affected, but improved with increasing age. It appears that, again, children at the oldest age level (12-14 years) were least affected by the presence of the incidental stimuli.

It became clear to us that the study of specific stimulus properties would not lead to the understanding of improvement in memory performance in children we were seeking. The research of Belmont and Butterfield (1969) and Flavell (1970) as well as another ongoing research project of our own (Hagen & Kingsley, 1968; Kingsley & Hagen, 1969), had shown that, with development, strategies are used increasingly in short-term memory performance. The results suggested that the study of encoding strategies in short-term memory performance should be fruitful. What evidence do we have thus far for the "cognitive strategy" hypothesis?

Recall that in the first two studies described, a distractor task had been employed. It had a detrimental effect on central task performance. In the second of those studies (Hagen, 1967), it was found that the presence of incidental pictures produced a detrimental effect on central memory performance. The

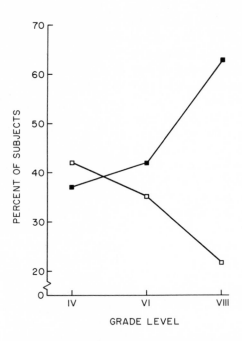

Fig. 4.2. Percentage of subjects reporting use of relevant (■) versus irrelevant (□) labels during implicit rehearsal for three grade levels. (From Druker & Hagen, 1969).

same comparison condition was included in another study with adult subjects (Hagen, Meacham, & Mesibov, 1970). No decremental effect due to the presence of the incidental pictures was found for the adults. However, the adults' performance was hindered significantly if they were required to say aloud the names of the pictures as they were presented. Thus three factors have been shown to have deleterious effects on short-term memory: an imposed auditory distractor, the presence of an incidental or irrelevant stimulus, and an imposed labeling of the to-be-remembered stimuli. However, whether the deleterious effects occur depends entirely upon the developmental level, or chronological age, of the subjects. Imposed irrelevant stimuli, such as piano notes or pictures, impede performance for the younger, but not the older individuals. The younger child seems to be dependent upon immediate stimuli in his environment, but perhaps he does not have well-developed strategies for coping with the specific task at hand. The older subject has these strategies and can ignore imposed, irrelevant stimuli, unless they interfere directly with the employment of strategies, as the imposed verbal labels seem to do. More evidence on this argument is presented later.

The correlations between task performance measures lend further support to

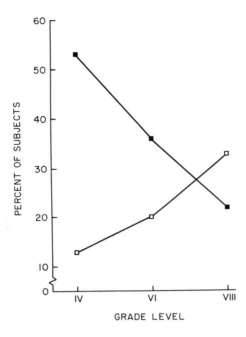

Fig. 4.3. Percentage of subjects reporting amount of visual scanning for three grade-levels. Solid squares indicate subjects who scan both relevant and irrelevant items; open squares indicate subjects who scan relevant items only. (From Druker & Hagen, 1969).

the theory that older subjects employ cognitive strategies in short-term memory performance. It has already been said that central versus incidental memory correlated positively at the younger ages and negatively at the older. This finding has been replicated several times, including in the study described just previously. In this study, the correlations were negative as expected. The correlation was larger in the no-label condition than in the label condition. In the earlier study when a distractor task was used, the correlations disappeared under the distracting condition. Both types of externally imposed stimuli have the same effect: The tendency for high central to be associated with low incidental memory performance is diminished. Perhaps the use of strategies to facilitate selective processing is disrupted.

The correlations of the two memory-task measures with IQ measures are also revealing. It was found in the earlier studies that central task performance correlated increasingly in the positive direction with IQ as age increases. Incidental task performance typically showed no correlation pattern. In the study which tested adults under both label and no-label conditions, it was found that central task performance correlated positively with Scholastic Aptitudes Test (SAT) performance (verbal, .38; mathematical, .51) in the no-label condition, but the correlations were near zero (verbal, −.02; mathematical, −.06) in the label condition. High scorers on the SAT lose their advantage in short-term memory performance in the more experimentally controlled task situation. Thus the most widely used measures of cognitive ability show clear-cut relations to performance in the central-incidental memory task, but these relations are vulnerable to external factors.

Children of varying IQ levels have also been tested. Retarded children were found to be deficient in central-incidental task performance, but the deficiency was greater for institutionalized retardates than for retardates of the same IQ level living at home (Hagen & Huntsman, 1971). In another study (Hagen & West, 1970), a training procedure was used and retarded children improved in selective-attention performance. These studies offer further evidence that intellectual development plays a role, and that appropriate training can facilitate task performance.

It is evident that the memory measures under investigation are related to other measures of cognitive and intellectual development. Further, the evidence is consistent with the hypothesis that during the acquisition phase of the memory task, cognitive strategies are employed which facilitate performance. Improvement in selectivity of task-relevant information seems to be more a function of processes similar to Neisser's (1967) second stage of selective attention, rather than Broadbent's filter mechanisms or Neisser's first, preattentive, stage. In order to gain more definitive evidence for the "cognitive strategy" hypothesis, research on mediation and memory is considered next.

Mediation and Memory

Many investigators consider mediational mechanisms to be important determinants of children's cognitive abilities in addition to, or instead of, attentional factors (e.g., Kendler & Kendler, 1962; Kendler, 1963; Spiker, 1963). It has been demonstrated that the child names or labels objects in his environment, and when he does, his performance in certain tasks improves. The labeling, according to theory, serves as a mediator which facilitates performance in certain tasks at certain ages. Reese (1962) has offered the mediational-deficiency hypothesis, which states there is a stage in the child's development during which verbal responses to stimuli occur but do not serve as mediators. He summarizes a large body of data which supports this hypothesis.

We have conducted a series of studies on the development of memory which explored mediation theory. The initial question asked was: Do verbal labels mediate memory? The task was modified from the memory task described above, except it was constructed so that serial position data could be obtained as Atkinson, Hansen, and Bernbach had done earlier (1964). The picture cards were presented successively rather than simultaneously, and there was only one (central) picture per card. After each card in the series had been presented and then placed face down in a row, the cue card was presented and the child identified by pointing to the card in the series that matched the cue card. Each subject was tested an equal number of times at each of the eight positions.

In the first study (Hagen & Kingsley, 1968), two experiments were performed. The task for recall of serial positions was administered to nursery-school children approximately 5 years old. One group was required to label overtly the names of the animals as the cards were presented. A second group did no overt labeling. No difference in memory performance was found between the groups.

The second experiment replicated the first, except older children at age levels 6, 7, 8, and 10 years were tested. There were three predictions. First, an increase would be found in overall memory performance with increasing age. Second, verbal labeling should facilitate the performance of younger children who do not use them spontaneously, while verbal labeling should not facilitate as much the performance of older children who spontaneously label. Third, it was expected that serial position analyses of data of the older children would approximate those of adults with elevated performance at the primacy positions as well as the recency positions.

The three predictions were in general supported. There was an increase in memory performance as a function of increasing chronological age. Overt verbal naming resulted in increased memory performance for the three younger age levels, but not the oldest. Figure 4.4 illustrates these results, and includes the performance of the preschool groups from the first experiment. It is clear that at both the youngest and oldest age levels, labeling did not facilitate overall memory performance. At the intermediate levels, performance was facilitated by the verbal labeling. The serial position analyses are presented in Fig. 4.5 for all the age levels of the second experiment. Three findings should be noted. Overall performance level increased across age levels. At the primacy positions, or the left-hand portions, there was no facilitation due to labeling. At the oldest age level, the performance of the no label group was clearly higher. Finally, at the recency portions, labeling did facilitate performance at all age levels. Thus labeling facilitated memory, but only for those items presented just before recall was measured. At the oldest age level, the gain at recency was canceled by the loss at primacy; and no overall change in performance was found. It was concluded that verbal labeling of the stimuli in a short-term memory task does, under certain circumstances, facilitate performance. However, it is obvious that more is happening than a simple enhancing effect. We must look further for an explanation.

Phillip Kingsley and myself now took a new look at our results. Flavell, Beach, and Chinsky (1966) observed that older children rehearsed stimulus names during a waiting period between stimulus presentation and actual testing for memory. Perhaps rehearsal, in addition to labeling, facilitates recall. Might

John William Hagen

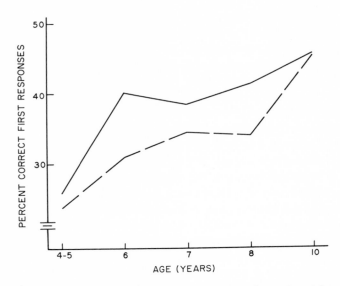

Fig. 4.4. Proportion of correct first responses as a function of experimental group and age level; solid line = group L, broken line = group N. (From Hagen & Kingsley, 1968.)

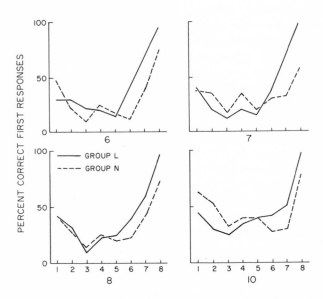

Fig. 4.5. Proportion of correct first responses as a function of serial position and experimental condition for four age-levels; solid line = group L, broken line = group N. (From Hagen & Kingsley, 1968.)

rehearsal facilitate especially primacy performance? It seemed reasonable that the older children from our study repeated to themselves during the presentation period the names of the pictures that had already been exposed. The first ones would be easy, but the task becomes more difficult as the list gets longer. The first ones also are practiced the most. Hence these items are recalled best. Now consider the possible effect of the required labeling. If the child attempts to rehearse, the labeling would make the task more difficult. The imposed overt labeling might well interfere with the covert rehearsing. Two new studies attempted to examine more precisely the roles of verbal labeling and rehearsal.

Induced rehearsal was compared to labeling in the memory task previously described (Kingsley & Hagen, 1969). Children at age 5 were tested, the age at which no overall labeling facilitation or primacy effect had been found previously. The induced rehearsal required the children to repeat out loud the names of the pictures. For example, when the first was presented, the child said, "Fish." The second was then presented, and he said, "Fish, bear." As each picture was presented, its name was added to the series of overtly rehearsed names. The series length was five in this study. The children had no problem rehearsing the first two or three, but confusions sometimes occurred toward the end. Children tested in this induced rehearsal condition recalled more picture locations than those in the simple labeling condition. Moreover, facilitation occurred at the primacy portion of the serial position curve, where children of this age do not typically perform well. The two groups did not differ in recency performance. It was concluded that young children who do not typically rehearse can be induced to do so, and their memory performance is facilitated when they do. Keeney, Cannizzo, and Flavell (1967) also showed that rehearsal can be induced and memory performance improved.

Hagen, Meacham, and Mesibov (1970) adapted the paradigm so that both central versus incidental recall measures and serial position analyses of the central scores could be obtained. The age range in which the selective processing shift had been found to occur in the earlier studies was included, 9 through 14 years. At each age tested, half the subjects were required to say the name of the stimuli as presented and half did not name. It was found that labeling did not affect either central or incidental performance. The interaction between central and incidental performance was found again. Serial-position data for the central task showed that primacy performance was higher for the no labeling condition at all age levels. Recency performance was higher for the labeling condition at all ages, presumably because of auditory memory trace. These results confirm Hagen and Kingsley's interpretation that children at age 10 and older spontaneously employ rehearsal in order to remember. Rehearsal facilitates primacy performance, and labeling interrupts rehearsal, thereby decreasing primacy memory. No overall labeling effect occurred, since the facilitation at recency cancelled the decrement at primacy.

A second study, mentioned earlier, replicated the one just described with college students as subjects. Labeling resulted in a *decrement* in overall central performance this time. The overall central memory performance of the college-age subjects was higher than for any other group tested. Incidental recall was low, but significantly above chance. As expected, the labeling decrement was associated mainly with the primacy positions, and in fact it spread to include all but the two most recently presented items. Thus, it was established that central short-term memory performance continues to improve into adulthood and the improvement is related to the use of rehearsal strategies. These strategies are interrupted by required verbal labeling, and the deleterious effect of interruption increases with increasing age.

These results support our hypothesis that older children and adults engage in active rehearsal strategies, and requiring labeling hinders the use of these strategies. For those subjects who perform best in the memory task, the college students, labeling produced the most deleterious effect.

Conclusions and Implications

Several tentative conclusions are justified by the research reviewed here. First, both selective attention and verbal processes play a role in the development of memory. Second, short-term memory performance improves as a function of development, but the changes cannot be attributed simply to improved memory span or ability to remember. Third, when task demands are made, older children as compared to younger more actively respond and utilize task-appropriate strategies that facilitate task performance.

The research with the selective attention paradigm pointed to the importance of the use of these strategies. A recent study (Sabo & Hagen, 1971) provides more definitive evidence. A delay period was imposed between the presentation of stimuli and test for recall. In one condition, the children were told to "think about the pictures" during the delay; while in the other condition they were required to count aloud, a highly distracting task. It was predicted that preventing rehearsal would not affect performance of younger children, but would decrease performance for the older. The prediction was confirmed. Central memory increased with age, but only in the condition which permitted rehearsal. Thus, it seems that the younger children did not utilize strategies for remembering the central stimuli.

The improvement in selectivity of task-relevant information found in the several studies reviewed previously seems to occur because of processes similar to those described in Neisser's (1967) attention model, Stage two.

In Stage one, called preattentive, information is dealt with in a global, undifferentiated way. It is in Stage two that the individual actively analyzes and makes certain constructions of the available information. Now to take a developmental perspective. The child comes to know that certain materials are supposed to be remembered while others are superfluous. He also acquires a greater repertoire of task appropriate strategies. Incidental information may not be affected directly by these developmental changes, but it may decline when measured due to the interference of encoding and storing of central information. It is this second stage of attentional processes which does not seem to reach full development until ages 11-13. Future research will have to determine if this developmental application of Neisser's two-stage model fits better with reality than models used previously.

The research on the verbal mediation hypothesis leads to the conclusion that the effects of verbal labeling depend on the developmental level of the subjects and the particular memory measures employed. The original view of a mediator which is automatically activated at a certain point in development and serves to facilitate performance is unwarranted. Rather, mediators function in a more complicated fashion. Flavell (1970) describes *mnemonic mediation* as, "a planful, instrumental, cognitive act, akin to problem-solving behavior [p. 208]."

The development of the use of strategies occurs because of two types of developmental changes, according to Flavell (1970). The *specific* changes are those which a particular mediator, such as verbal rehearsal, goes through. Labeling is not done by the young child at all. With development, overt labeling of stimulus objects in the environment becomes the normal response. When learning or remembering becomes important, strings of labels are repeated covertly. Finally, particular strategies and rules specific to the task demands at hand become perfected. The other type of developmental change is called *general*, and it involves planfulness on the part of the child. The child becomes aware that if he does some sort of activity now, he will improve his likelihood of success in the future. The rehearsal strategies will only be implemented when there is a plan in mind indicating it will be useful to do so. The child sees a purpose in his plan.

The model that has been presented fits well with what is known about the course of development in natural settings. The young child learns very early in life that certain performances are rewarded and others are not. He wants to make sure that his rewards are forthcoming and his expectations increase with age. The school environment takes up increasingly significant proportions of the child's time and activity; and it is obvious this environment is important in the development of information processing skills. Studying is an example of an activity which occurs frequently and is much practiced (Flavell, 1970). One goal of studying is to remember information for some specific time in the future. The study of studying behavior is being pursued. We are attempting to identify the use of plans, attention strategies, verbalizations, and mnemonics in this behavior. The identification of individual differences in these activities should be useful for understanding how children go about learning to remember.

The development of memory skills involves the composite of many factors and occurs over a wide age span. An important part of the process involves the active participation of the child. Attention, verbal skills, and mnemonic strategies play key roles in the process. Future research should be aimed at answering the basic, but still unanswered questions. Just *how* is the young child limited in the employment of strategies? Does he not employ certain rehearsal strategies because they make demands beyond his capacities? What are the precise developmental changes that take place in the use of rehearsal strategies? Are there alternative strategies for achieving the same results? Are there differences in the process when the information to be remembered is presented in other than the visual mode? How similar is the account of memory presented here to Piaget's view of memory processes? Is memory really just a subcategory of cognition? These and other questions should provide fertile research areas for the future.

REPLY TO SIMON

The issue of the definition of short-term memory (STM) is raised by Dr. Simon regarding its appropriateness as applied to the tasks described in my chapter. For the task that involves a central and an incidental memory measure, it is pointed out in my chapter that in one study (Hagen & Sabo, 1967) the order of recall was balanced so that for half the subjects the incidental measure was taken after the central measure as in the earlier studies; but for the other half of the subjects, the incidental measure was taken first. There were no differences in the results due to order of measurement. Thus, for this task, it does not really matter functionally whether the recall measures are said to be from STM or long-term memory (LTM).

For the task in which serial position recall was measured, Dr. Simon argues that the primacy data "almost certainly" involve LTM and the recency data involve STM. They certainly do seem to involve two different mechanisms, as I have pointed out in numerous places including my chapter in this volume. However, rather than becoming involved over the STM-LTM controversy, I have preferred to stay with a functional distinction between the (at least) two processes which are involved. No one agrees just how long STM actually is, or whether **time** is the best measure to use to define it. When primacy recall is measured, it might well be that both STM and LTM are involved. It cannot be said at this time whether the rehearsal which affects primacy recall provides a way to store the items in STM or a way to code items into LTM. However, rehearsal does facilitate recall and is used increasingly by older subjects.

The comments by Dr. Simon on the development of attention are well chosen, and his synopsis of the studies reflects my views accurately. However, I wish to clarify my position on one point. In the original model, Maccoby and I postulated that there was a limited channel capacity which did not increase with age. Under overload conditions, older subjects were more efficient at directing more of their attention to the task at hand. While there is of course a limit to the system, I now believe that it is not just because this limit is exceeded that "selective" attention occurs. Rather, external demands interact with the subject's state at the particular time. A particular task set is imposed by some external source, i.e., a parent, a teacher, or an experimenter. This set is received differently by children of different ages. Older children understand better the nature of the demands placed on them and have available appropriate strategies to deal with them. I agree that there is a close relation between attention and STM, and limitations in the system must of course play a role, but only through further research will we be able to describe the precise nature of the interactions.

PART III

BUILDING A MODEL—
PSYCHOLOGICAL CONSIDERATIONS

Jacqueline Goodnow was born in Toowoomba, Australia. She received her bachelor's degree with honors from the University of Sydney, and her Ph.D. from Harvard University. She is currently on the faculty of George Washington University, and is completing a 5-year career grant award from the National Institutes of Health.

Dr. Goodnow's early research dealt with studies of probability learning and concept attainment. In 1960, while in Hong Kong, she began investigating the effects of cultural milieu on some of Piaget's tasks (Goodnow, 1962), and rapidly became one of our foremost American authorities on culture and cognition (Goodnow, 1969b). Her interest in analyzing the details of cultural influences on thought led her into a type of information processing task analysis that is of special interest to us here at Carnegie-Mellon.

CHAPTER 5

RULES AND REPERTOIRES, RITUALS AND TRICKS OF THE TRADE: SOCIAL AND INFORMATIONAL ASPECTS TO COGNITIVE AND REPRESENTATIONAL DEVELOPMENT*

Jacqueline J. Goodnow

The George Washington University

In some recent work, I have been watching the way children copy shapes, draw humans, and interpret graphic patterns. I have also been searching for concepts that would help pull these diverse behaviors together. This chapter describes some of the behavior and some of the concepts. It also extends, to cognitive development in general, a few ideas that appear to have some general promise,

*Support from the National Institute of Child Health and Human Development made possible the research on representation and the preparation of this paper (1-K03-HD 36971, 1-R01-HD03105-04). At a more personal level, I am happy to acknowledge the help of many students and assistants (Phyllis Evans and Rochelle Levine, in particular), and of my colleagues Richard Walk and Elyse Lehman.

useful toward the overall goal of understanding how children of different ages and different backgrounds come to give different performances on cognitive tasks.

The material is in three sections: the first two deal with representational tasks, the third with extensions to a variety of other tasks. Throughout all sections, one of the recurring themes is the argument that to understand performance, we must consider two sets of conditions. One is informational: It concerns questions of load, capacity, compatibility, sequential constraint—the type of condition usually to the fore in information-processing analyses. The other set is social: It concerns the way any given society defines a "good" or "mature" performance, and the opportunities it provides for learning.

A second recurring theme deals with a particular way of looking at the nature of a performance and the nature of learning. On any occasion, the argument runs, performance is a selection from a repertoire of behaviors. Age and experience may expand or constrict the repertoire, although expansion would appear to be the usual case during childhood. Age and experience also alter our sense of the right behavior for the right occasion. We acquire ground-rules that specify, for the task at hand, a range of possible behaviors and, within this range, the most appropriate behavior: most suited to our resources or goals, most likely to be expected, tolerated, or greeted with surprise by another, most likely to move a problem in a needed direction.

This second theme—performance as selection from a repertoire—has a corollary. "Errors" on any task may be approached with the question: What makes it difficult to achieve an effective match between the demands of the occasion and the performance selected? We may find it easier to understand "errors," I suggest, if we ask about the ground-rules involved, the difficulties they present, the extent to which they are customs or conventions, and the conditions under which they are learned.

Before starting on the data, I would like to give a little space to the second theme and its corollary.

Performance as Selection from a Repertoire

The idea of behavior as a selection from a range or repertoire is by no means unique to me or to the area of cognitive development. It is explicit, for example, in the area of sociolinguistics, where several people have suggested that, over and above grammar, we acquire a range of ways to talk, varying with the person we talk to and the nature of the talk. Much of our response to people, it has been suggested, is based on their knowing and using the appropriate form for particular occasions. To take an example which I find especially intriguing, Labov (1969) has suggested that some of the disciplinary difficulties "lower-class" children encounter in "middle class" schools stem from their not knowing or not using the expected small words and "mitigating terms" that make it possible to say no or disagree without provoking an authority figure or escalating an argument. Actually, we can illustrate the matching process in any interaction between speaker and audience or author and reader. I possess a range of behaviors that I may bring to this occasion: I may go over things lightly or in detail, may try to impress you or involve you in some real exchange, may invite you to suspend belief for a while or to be as critical as possible. You also possess a range of behaviors and expectations, and the sense of a "good" talk or a "good" paper will stem from a matching selection on both sides. These aspects of performance, I would like to point out, have been superbly described by Goffman (1956;1969), and by Cole, Gay, Glick, and Sharp (1971).

Sources of Difficulty in Achieving a Match.

A good match will be difficult to achieve if it calls for an unknown rule, or for juggling more rules and conditions than an individual can manage. A good match will also be difficult to achieve when some particular behaviors are given the status of rituals: They may be used indiscriminately, without regard for the particular occasion, or they may be called "right" and "wrong" in a highly restrictive way ("not quite right" being equated with "all-wrong"). In a Brunswickian sense, the match is made difficult in one case by a very high probability that the behavior selected will be the same for every occasion, and, in the other case, by a very low probability that performance will be exactly on target.

A good match will also be difficult for all members of a group to achieve when the rules are implicit, or can be learned only by way of some specific experiences, when they become, in effect, "tricks of the trade."

These social conditions, I feel, are all the more important because they arise so easily and are so seldom discussed. As people, we move very easily towards the assumption that some selections from the repertoire—usually our own—are good things in themselves, forgetting, after a while, to ask what purposes the selection originally served and what are the alternatives. One possible way becomes the right way, and its rightness seems somehow "obvious" or "natural." In addition, we move very easily towards thinking of behavior that does not follow our rules as being without rules, without order. The child's performance is easily seen as random, the outgroup's performance as "lawless." We have progressed, for instance, only with difficulty from talking about the "substandard" speech of some groups to talking about their "nonstandard" speech, gingerly entertaining the notion that this seemingly debased version of our grammar may be lawful in its own right, that only the rules may be different.

These very human tendencies can create difficulties for us when we come to ask about the reasons for children not doing "well" on our tasks: We have known the rules so long that the need for learning and the feasibility of alternative actions are not easy to recognize. Difficulties are also generated for the beginning learner. Many of our rules—whether they deal with social, linguistic, or intellectual "good" behavior—are far from explicit. It is simply understood that some behaviors are more correct than others. As a result, we may not, as teachers, see the need to make the rules explicit or to ask what the cues are that tell a child how to select appropriate behavior.

The next two sections provide the first layer of flesh for this skeleton of ideas. Each of the experiments is an occasion for asking about rules that need to be learned or applied and the sources of difficulty that may arise.

Representational Tasks—Finding Equivalents

We often present children with pictures or graphic patterns and ask them to match these to one another or to some "real" event: an object, a set of actions, or a series of sounds. Both Sylvia Farnham-Diggory (1967, 1970) and I have been working with some complex versions of such tasks, and I wish to start now by discussing one that I have been mulling over. The match is between a series of sounds and a series of dots. The child may hear the sounds first and be asked to write out an equivalent (Goodnow, 1971), or to choose an equivalent from such alternatives (for a 2-2-2 pattern) as (·· ··· ··), (·· ·· ··), or (······) (Birch & Belmont, 1964, 1965). Alternatively, he may be shown the written series first, and asked to tap out its equivalent (Stambak, 1951, 1962).

At first sight, the task seems to call for the coordination of modalities. To account for age differences or individual differences, we might do best to look toward changes in cortical connections. This was, in fact, the approach initially taken by Birch and Belmont (1965). However, if we ask about the correspondences or equivalences that have to be respected in order to be called "correct," the problem begins to appear in a different light. To be correct, an individual has to know that

> a dot can stand for a sound;
> the direction left-to-right stands for the time order, first-to-last;
> a larger space between the dots stands for a longer interval between the sounds.

Any or all of these equivalences may give a child trouble. The problem for us, as observers, is to tell where the trouble is when we find that children in a particular age or social group are not making a "correct" match. In the sample I worked with, it was the third equivalence—space interval for time interval—that marked the difference between kindergarten and first grade. The kindergarten children, when they wrote out their versions of the auditory series, were able to use marks for sounds, to use left-to-right for first-to-last, and to match the number of marks to the number of dots, but they did not use blank spaces on the paper to represent the intervals between groups of sounds. What they often used instead was a motor pause. For a 2-2-2 pattern, many of them would write two dots, pause, then two dots, pause, and another two dots. In effect, there was a rule of correspondence present. One act of waiting was traded for another act of waiting. One can easily imagine children finding this rule more reasonable than the adult practice of representing an act with an empty space, a visual "nothing."

The same task illustrates as well another aspect of what makes a match difficult, namely the number of rules we have to apply at any one time. Blank, Weider, and Bridger (1968) have suggested that children who have difficulty with this task, and with reading, may do so because they cannot cope with so many features at one time: If they pay attention to the number of sounds, they lose track of the pauses, and vice versa. In effect, they know the equivalence rules, but they have not learned how to juggle several at one time. This phenomenon, in relation to poor readers, fits my own observations and earlier observations by Stambak (1951).

So far we have the suggestion that the rules of correspondence or equivalence underlying a match may be difficult for a child because

no one has told him about them;
the adult correspondence may conflict with a different correspondence he has established;
he has to cope with too many correspondences at once.

To this list, I shall add two more points:

The child may not include some needed properties in his translation. Some children, for instance, ignore the presence of intervals; some ignore the number of items; and, among younger children, some ignore both, producing simply a series of dots that covers the whole page.

The child may be putting into the translation more than is needed. He may try to cover properties that an adult considers not critical, or he may give more than the minimal equivalent we expect to see.

The last possibility is especially important, and the easiest way to illustrate this point is by looking at some actual write-outs. Figure 5.1 shows all the write-outs for twenty children in a first-grade class. You can see variations in the size of the dots (the single dot is usually larger), as well as some variations in up-down positions on the page. For some of the children, the larger size of the single dot stood for its sounding "louder" (an "excess" property in this task). For others, the large size stood for its being "all by itself" (an "excess" sign when there is already a separation in space).

In contrast, variations in size are rare in the set of equivalents written out by some older children (these children were asked to write out all of the ways they could think of). Figure 5.2 gives some examples. Each of these three children has

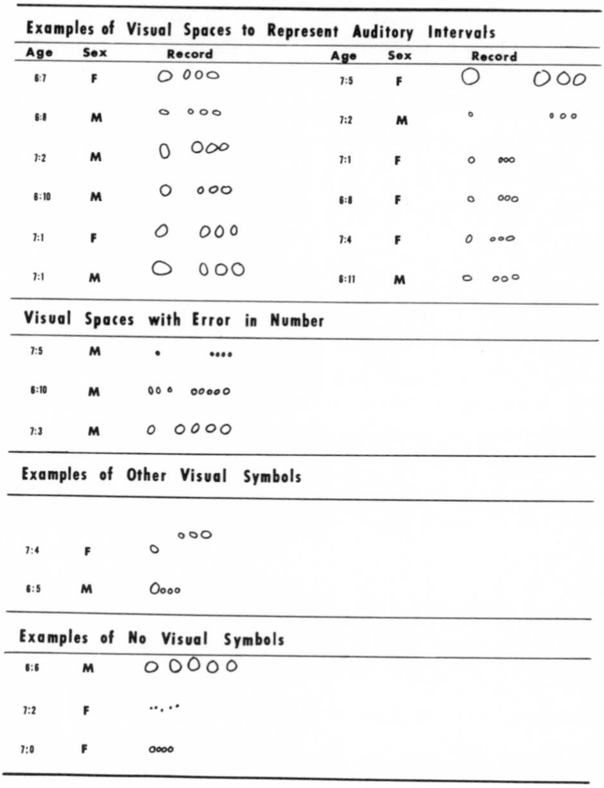

Examples of Visual Spaces to Represent Auditory Intervals

Age	Sex	Record	Age	Sex	Record
8:7	F	O 0OO	7:5	F	O OOO
8:8	M	o °°°	7:2	M	° ° °°
7:2	M	0 OΦΦ	7:1	F	o ∞∞
8:10	M	O o°°	6:8	F	o ∞∞
7:1	F	O OOO	7:4	F	o o∞
7:1	M	O OOO	8:11	M	o oo°

Visual Spaces with Error in Number

7:5	M	• ••••
6:10	M	OO ° °°°°°
7:3	M	o OOOO

Examples of Other Visual Symbols

7:4	F	o OOO o
8:5	M	Oooo

Examples of No Visual Symbols

8:8	M	O OOOO
7:2	F	••, ••
7:0	F	oooo

Fig. 5.1. First grade write-outs of a tapped series. (From Goodnow, 1971.)

acquired a range of ways to write out the same message, but only one of them includes a variation in size. The fourth grader uses an "excess" sign, i.e., another symbol as well as a space to show "you should stop here," but the sign is not a variation in size. The sixth grader gives a stripped-down translation: no "excess" signs, and no "excess" properties. The seventh grader (a child with learning difficulties) is the exception to most of the older children I have seen. She used pauses (row 1) and also variations in size and space (row 2 and 3). On one occasion, in fact (row 3), all three signs were present. The single circle was drawn large *and* very slowly, while the circles in the group of three were drawn at a distance, smaller, and more quickly.

Relatively little is known as yet about how children learn which properties to represent and by what sign. Work on the psychology of art, particularly the work of Arnheim (1954, 1969) and Gombrich (1960), is an excellent source. Arnheim's argument, for example—representation is a search for equivalents

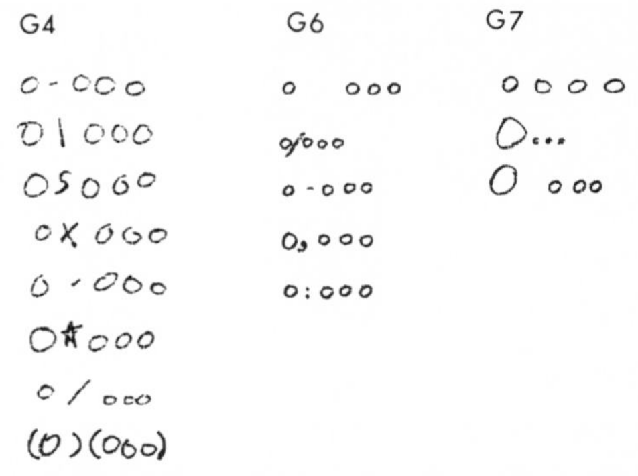

G4	G6	G7
o - oo o	o ooo	o o o o
o	ooo	o/ooo	o...
o5o6o	o - ooo	o ooo
ox ooo	o, ooo	
o · oo o	o: ooo	
ox ooo		
o / oo		
(o)(ooo)		

Fig. 5.2. Write-outs from some older children, asked to give several write-outs (dot always indicates tap). The first series is from a girl in grade 4 (age 9 years, 8 months); the second from a boy in grade 6 (age 11 years, 10 months); the third from a girl in grade 7 (age 12 years, 7 months), with a record of "learning problems".

within the limits of a medium and an intention—is of obvious relevance. So also is Gombrich's argument that the schemata or stabilized representations we use form some kind of range. In addition, the interested reader should note Siegel and McBurney's (1970) studies of cross-modal scaling, and should watch for the work of Jeanne Bamberger, who has recently been asking children to write out their versions of musical pieces. [Dr. Bamberger, a pianist interested in music education (Brofsky & Bamberger, 1969) is based at M.I.T..]

For the present, I would like to draw attention to two general questions raised by these complex equivalence or translation tasks. If we regard the task as requiring a match between properties and signs, then:

(1) What properties or signs are most likely to be used by children at one age, but not at another?

(2) How do we come to select some properties or signs as the "right" ones to use, while others are regarded as inappropriate or as unnecessary "decorations" and "flourishes"? What are the grounds for this selection, and for our ideas about ideal correspondences between properties and signs?

Favored Properties and Signs

In children's representations of series, for example, variations in size appear to be a favored sign, one that often does not have a one-to-one relationship with a particular property. In fact, children are highly likely to use size as a way to represent variations in many properties—loudness, duration, separateness—and the double or triple meanings may occur within the representations of a single child.

At the same time, end points appear to be favored properties. They are especially likely to be matched carefully or given extra signs and markers. These favored properties are a less obvious phenomenon and I would like to spend a little time on them, describing two examples of an age change in the occurrence of end-to-end matching.

One example comes from some recent data collected by Elyse Lehman on the way children reproduce and code a tapped-out series (in this case ·· ···). We were especially interested in the use of number coding and in age changes in number coding. The most striking change, it turned out, was between second and fourth grade, when the modal coding shifted from 12345 to 12123. Now there is some change here in the type of grouping or chunking (even though children in both grades reproduced the series as two groups). However, I feel this is only part of the story. What 12123 does that 12345 does not is to break away from a direct matching of end to end, a matching of largest number to last sound.

Stambak's (1951) task supplies another example. Children are shown a written pattern—a series of dots—and asked to tap out the message on the table, using a tap for each dot. Among the young children we worked with, a striking form of behavior emerged: Taps were often spread from one side of the 3-foot table to the other. Older children reduced the size of the spread until by the end of grade two, 50% were tapping on a single spot. The older children are trading only time for space. The younger children are instead trading space for space, but not, it is important to note, in any directly imitative manner (the dots were centered on a 5 × 8-inch card, with about 2 inches margin on each side). On the contrary, they may be described as transposing, changing the scale of the pattern to fit the space available, and marking off with special clarity the beginning and end of the series.

In more complex series, the favored properties may be of a higher order. For example, Jeanne Bamberger suggests that in representing a musical piece, children often try to represent not only end points, but some forms of phrasing and some progressions towards endpoints. To use her term, the child displays a "configurational logic": His goal is a representation of the way sounds form phenomenal groups.

In sum, spontaneous representations of series offer a rich array of possibilities for asking about the signs most likely to be used, the properties most likely to be represented, and the kinds of match most likely to occur between properties and signs.

I would not like to have it appear, however, that the questions raised are limited to the representations of series. There is a good deal of similarity, I suggest, between the way children use variations in size to represent degrees of loudness and the way they use variations in size to represent degrees of importance in drawing scenes or human figures. In both cases, we need to tease out rather carefully the properties an individual is trying to represent and the range of equivalents he regards as feasible. In both cases, also, this teasing out is not likely to be easy. To take one example, people have been analyzing children's figure drawings for some time, and we still do not know how to tell, on any particular occasion of drawing, whether a child draws hands extra large because they have extra emotional value for him, because he is giving extra thought to the importance of all five fingers, or because he finds them easier to draw large.

Similarly, it will not be easy to tease out the original source of an established match. The source may be phenomenal: Largeness in size may go in some natural way with loudness in sound; closeness in space may have the same "feel" as closeness in time or affect. Alternatively, the matches may be incidental. Variations in size, for example, and status as end points may simply happen to be at the top of their respective hierarchies and, entirely on the basis of probability, come to be matched and then to "feel right." Finally, some correspondences may come to appear natural and obvious to us because they have been selected by our culture as appropriate matches, and we learned them so long ago that they seem now to be the "best" and often the only matches possible.

Grounds for Such Labels as "Right" or "Excess"

Part of what a child is learning appears to be the selection of only those properties and those signs that we regard as appropriate for a particular task. At this point, I would like to argue that custom rather than the demands of information processing underlies many of our selections.

From this position, we may argue that there is no real need to confine all one's taps to one part of the table. There is no logical argument against using variations in size to represent grouping, or against putting variations in phenomenal loudness or phenomenal speed into a representation. (Jeanne Bamberger, in fact, suggests that children's spontaneous notations may include some properties that standard musical notations would do well to include). Rather than any unique or universal truth, there is a consensual agreement that some aspects or early representations are "wrong" or "not necessary" and, among older, well-socialized children, these become infrequent and may even disappear. The phenomenon is especially easy to recognize in children's drawings, where many early properties and early signs drop out in the course of learning that the goal must always be one of "naturalistic" representation.

Over and above the selection of particular properties and particular signs, custom also appears to have a role in the way we assume that one-to-one relationships between properties and signs are always ideal, rather than asking *when* such stripped-down relationships are useful matches. Newell has suggested one set of occasions: If a series is extremely long and the goal is exact recovery of its numerical structure, then "flourishes" may become a burden. The most effective way to proceed would be by the use of "minimal sign," the use of "only the sign which suffices" (a phrase from Matisse, quoted by Brett, 1969, p. 14).

Another set of circumstances probably has to do with the need for others to read off a representation, to translate it back. In such circumstances, an idiosyncratic set of signs would present a difficulty, but the use of several signs for one property would not. All of them could lead to the same response, and be used in combination for a deliberate reason, in much the same way that we indicate the importance of a heading in an article by using several signs at once: a special place, a special size, and a special type.

In effect, we can easily think of situations where departing from a one-to-one relationship may make no particular difference or even be an asset. Our expectation that children will learn and display one-to-one relationships on a task like series-matching probably stems from the hidden assumption that this is a task where "scientific" rather than "expressive" notation is appropriate, i.e., the appropriate notation, even on an easy task, will be one that could fit the need for exact recovery in the face of a demanding situation.

Our difficulties begin when we start to regard one-to-one relationships as always right—ours is a "scientific" culture, Arnheim (1969) would say—and when we come to regard some particular relationships as so obviously right that we fail to recognize either the need for them to be taught or the possibility of alternatives.

Let me give two examples, both dealing with interpretations of position on a page. One of them has been commented on recently by John Holt (1971), pointing out that we often say that some letters come "before" others, "as if it were self-evident that 'before' meant 'on the left side' and 'after' meant 'on the right side' . . . . In fact, there is nothing self-evident or natural or reasonable about it at all. We just do it that way [p. B5]."

We also take for granted that children will easily recognize the equivalence of "up" in the air and "up" on a page, even though, objectively speaking, the correspondence is between "up and down" vertically and "far and near" horizontally. It had not occurred to me that this correspondence was something children had to learn; and the first time I encountered it, I did not take it seriously. The first time was an occasion when I asked Lila Ghent Braine why she always placed her stimuli, in experiments on judgments about orientation, upright rather than down on the desk. Her answer was that one should not assume, especially with young children, that the two "tops" are regarded as equivalent or scanned in the same way. After my experience with the auditory-visual task, and its set of equivalents, I began to take the problem seriously, and Lila Braine and I have begun to do some work on when children get this particular correspondence under control, and what may be the difficulties. The learning on my part, however, has been a useful reminder of the ease with which we assume that the correspondences we are used to are "natural" and "obvious" ones.

Representational Tasks:
Lawfulness in the Equivalents Children Produce

I have been dealing with tasks where an individual either judges two things to be "the same" or produces an equivalent for some object or pattern we give him. Within these tasks, a large part of my emphasis has fallen on the child's approach to various matches between signs and properties, and on the several ways in which a particular match may come about.

At this point, I would like to expand the material on one particular possibility. This is the possibility that some "errors" in matching are an expression of lawful behavior. They are the consequences of rules—rules different from ours, perhaps, or like ours, but applied with excessive zeal and no regard for exceptions. I have a special fondness for this possibility, because I think we often assume its opposite too readily, i.e., we assume that an error represents an inability to discriminate, or an indifference to a property we define as critical.

The material covers two studies, both examples of behavior where the child's equivalent seems at first to be based on the lack of a rule, but turns out to be based on some fairly definite rules.

One example is a very old phenomenon in children's drawings, namely the occurrence of human figures drawn "upside down" or "sideways," relative, that is, to our judgment that the body should run from the "top" to the "bottom" of the page. The oldest interpretation of this behavior is that the child is indifferent to spatial orientation, an interpretation that has often been challenged (cf. Ghent, 1961). When I first encountered this behavior, I thought that the child might be defining "top" in a way different from ours, but the nature of this definition was a mystery. Luckily, Phyllis Evans and I were collecting data on sequences in the way children drew human figures, and an interesting factor began to emerge. As a rule, the first part to be drawn, among 4- and 5-year-olds, is a circular form that stands for either the head or the head-plus-trunk. The usual next step is placing some eyes into the circle, followed by limbs (or facial features). We were intrigued by the way some of the upside down or sideways figures seemed to be determined by wherever the eyes were drawn, and, after a while, we constructed two incomplete figures. In one, two eyes were drawn down toward the base of a circle, the circle being centered on the page. In the other, the eyes were drawn in sideways (Figure 5.3).

We asked a number of 4- and 5-year-olds to finish for us a drawing that "someone else had started." If they attempted to turn the page (and most of the 5-year-olds did), we asked them not to. Among the 4-year-olds, we were able to

Fig. 5.3. Incomplete figures (children asked to finish what "someone else started").

produce a large number of upside down and sideways drawings with this technique. The rule, apparently, is that the rest of the face or body goes on the side furthest from the eyes. In a way, the position of the eyes in the circle defines the "top" of the body. Given this variable and a certain amount of carelessness or lack of motor control in the placement of eye-marks, we can expect then to see upside down or sideways drawings among 4-year-olds.

Few 5-year-olds, we should note, displayed this behavior. As one 5-year-old told us: "You can't draw him; you have to move the page; his feet have to be on the ground." For this child, the equivalence of ground-line and bottom of the page were firmly established. We assured her, and others like her, that it could be done, and the result was a wonderful set of compromises. One figure was drawn upside down, but was described as deliberately so: He was hanging from rings in a gymnasium. Others were drawn with the mouth opposite the eyes, but the body aligned down the page: The figure was described as having his head tilted "way back." Others were drawn so that all inconsistency was eliminated: The eyemarks (we had never described them as such) were converted into rosy cheeks, dimples at the ends of a mouth, and so forth. These children met both the rule that the eyes should be at the far end from the join of head to trunk and the rule that the eyes should be the feature closest to the top of the page.

The second example of a "lawful error" is the confusion, in writing, of letters like "b" and "d." It is tempting to say that the child cannot tell the difference between the two, or has not yet been told often enough that a left-right flip-over in this case means he should say "different." Both these factors are probably part of the story. Certainly, a number of recent training experiments point to the need to consider carefully how far the child knows the criteria for "same" and "different" in this particular game (cf. Caldwell & Hall, 1969; Wohlwill & Weiner, 1964; Koenigsberg, 1971). However, some recent data of ours suggest that there is more to the story.

The data is again sequential data, stemming from an attempt to find the rules that underlie sequences of strokes in copying simple shapes. A number of people have pointed out that children often draw shapes like squares, triangles, or diamonds with very similar stroke sequences, and that these sequences may change with age (cf. Gesell & Ames, 1946; Ilg & Ames, 1964). Rochelle Levine and I were seeking to pull these results together and, in particular, to find a way of describing paths (the latter on the assumption that some apparently different paths might still be following the same rules).

The first point to be made is that rules can be isolated, and a progression of rules can be charted against age. Somewhere between 4 and 5, the nursery-school children we tested began to start most figures from the topmost point and, if possible, also from the leftmost points of a figure. If possible, they would also start with a vertical rather than a horizontal line. If the figure was simple (a cross, for example), they drew the vertical line from top to bottom, and the horizontal line from left to right. In a sense, the traffic on these lines is "one-way": The "one-way traffic rules," however, are ignored from about 5 to 7½ years if the figure can be threaded, i.e., drawn with a single continuous line, as can a square, triangle, or U-shaped figure. After this age, threading drops out and one-way traffic rules begin to take over again, applied this time to more and more complex figures (Goodnow & Levine, 1971).

At this point, I am going to bypass the question one asks most often about rules, namely the question of their origin, and concentrate on the question of their consequences. The major points to be made are as follows.

1. The drawing rules often contribute to left-right reversals. Children often write И for N, for example. Their failure to see a difference between the model and their product may be called a lack of discrimination, but the И is nonetheless not a random production. It stems from two common rules: start at the top left corner, and draw as a thread.

2. Reversals are asymmetrical, i.e. if we compare designs like b and d, then b is more often produced for d than vice versa. We have constructed several pairs of these designs, all consisting of a vertical bar with an additional part (a dot, or a continuing line) placed either to the left or the right of the bar (e.g. .| versus |.). In over two samples of kindergarten children, 30 left-right reversals have occurred with these designs, and 24 are reversals of the "d-type" design. The error is again not a random production. The child responds to two rules: draw the vertical bar first, and draw horizontal features in a left-to-right fashion.

These effects shed a different light on the nature of left-right reversals. They might even be errors one grows into at a certain age rather than out of, rather like the lawful errors that occur in children's speech when they start producing lawful, but culturally incorrect plurals such as "foots" or "doed" (Ervin & Miller, 1963). For our present purposes, such errors serve two ends: They are a demonstration of some specific rules, and a reminder that we may easily think of children's behavior as "unformed" or "lawless" when in fact it is simply following rules different from our own.

The General Course of Cognitive Development

I have been describing a variety of behaviors on representational tasks. As the data accumulated, I found myself pleased with the way some of the underlying order was becoming clearer, but less than pleased on two other counts.

One of these concerned the limits to any list of rules. Sooner or later, one must ask, "What are the general properties of rules?" "What makes one rule different from or compatible with another?" "What are the conditions, across tasks, that make rules difficult to learn or apply?" From these broader questions, I selected one as a starter: "What conditions make it difficult to achieve an effective match between occasion and performance?"

The second area of concern was the generality of the concepts with which I found myself playing. To be really useful, they should be able to break up some old habits and suggest some new ways of looking at behavior on nonrepresentational tasks.

To ease these two concerns, I began asking myself about similar phenomena in other cognitive areas, and this last section is the result of such self-questioning. First, I wish to offer some further examples of the core concepts—performance as a selection from a range of possible behaviors, learning as the development of knowledge about possible, usual, and most appropriate selections for a given situation. Second, I wish to pick out some sources of difficulty that seem especially relevant to other cognitive areas and to our understanding of how age differences and cultural differences come about.

Before starting on these checks for generality, however, let me point to two more major efforts to bring out the general properties of rules and rule-learning. One of these is the work of Piaget and his colleagues, with its special emphasis on an important rule-property, namely the way rules are interrelated, and on a major source of difficulty, namely the young child's difficulty in decentering and in coping simultaneously with two or more properties.

The other major effort is the work of Simon and Newell. Their approach is less well-known in developmental circles than the Geneva approach, and I would like to make some particular comment on it at this time.

Back in 1962, when I first read a brief developmental extension of Simon and Newell's approach, I was impressed by their idea that mathematics, problem-solving, language development, in fact life in general, could be thought of as the solution of a vast number of correspondence problems. We learn correspondences between an object and its representation; between two representations; between means and ends, between words like "clean" that describe a state, and words like "washed" or "cleaned" that describe a process. From this point of view, "most of our skill in dealing with the environment is embodied in elaborate *heuristics* or rules of thumb, which allow us to act on that world predictably" (Simon & Newell, 1962, p. 105).

Also intriguing was their answer to the question: What makes some problems harder than others? In some cases, they suggested, the rule of correspondence is relatively simple. Their example is "the relation between decimal and octal representations of number. There is a simple and direct algorithm that solves all problems of the form: If a is the decimal representation of a number, what is its octal representation?" (Simon & Newell, 1962, p. 149). In other cases, it may not be easy to find "in language B the representation of an object that is described in language A [p. 169]." The "correspondence between the vocabularies may be purely conventional or arbitrary. Then, rote learning is the only means for building up the translation dictionary, and, if the correct translations must also be discovered, immense amounts of trial-and-error search may be required [p. 150]."

Both approaches—Piaget's, and Simon and Newell's—are excellent sources for material on how we may describe differences between one rule and another. The differences may apply to rules as they exist in some outside world (e.g., differences in the extent to which correspondences between two sets of events can be covered by a single statement, in the extent to which a rule "always works"). Or the differences may apply to individuals, specifying the types of rule they have acquired, the breadth and style of their "operations" or "translation dictionaries."

My own effort, as the reader will easily see, is both more restricted and more biased toward the role of culture.

Performance as Selection from a Repertoire

One of the general properties of rules, I have suggested, is the way they specify a range of possible behaviors, along with the proper behavior for a particular occasion. Age and experience may either enlarge or narrow the range, in much the same way that they may narrow or enlarge the cast of social roles we play. Age and experience may also change the occasions on which we give particular performances, or make us more aware of the behavior that will be expected, tolerated, and warmly approved in a given type of situation.

Examples of such ranges of behavior are not difficult to find in cognitive behavior. We learn, if we are lucky, to fit the degree of effort and the degree of commitment to what the task requires, to select an appropriate goal. We also learn, if we are lucky, that problems can be solved in a variety of ways: inductively or deductively, with speed or at leisure, by asking someone, by looking up the answer, or by working it out ourselves. In all cases, "reasonable" or "skilled" behavior may be regarded as the selection of a goal and a method appropriate to the task and the resources at hand.

The sharpest examples of this phenomenon come from tasks that involve judgments about "same," "similar," and "different." A series such as "abcdabc....," for instance, may be completed in a variety of ways. The majority of answers, however, will fall within a narrow range, as Bartlett (1958) and Simon and Kotovsky (1963) have pointed out (most answers will be abcdabcd, unless subjects have some notion that originality rather than speed is expected).

Similarly, we may give a variety of answers—and be called "correct"—when faced with a bunch of colored yarns, including "pure" greens, blue-greens, and yellow-greens, and told only: "Show me the ones that go together." A great deal of learning goes into our expectation that an acceptable answer will need to cover more than two pieces of yarn, but less than all the yarns, with a fair amount of leeway about the exact number. We would feel shaken and betrayed, but probably all move towards a narrower category, Arnheim (1969) argues, if we felt our lives depended on finding exactly the width of category that an experimenter had in mind.

Implicit in this kind of match is the expectation that everyone knows, and is prepared to go along with, the requirements signaled by the task or by the other person. When a teacher or experimenter says "this is a test," or, even more ambiguously, "I have some games for you to play," the expectation is that the subject will respond by putting out a fair amount of effort. The subject should also know that the expected answers are "scientific" ones. To take another of Arnheim's (1969) examples (from a chapter entitled "With our Feet on the Ground"), "scientific" answers are expected when someone asks, as part of the Wechsler scale, "How are wood and alcohol alike?" The answer, "They both knock you out" may be regarded as witty in some settings, Arnheim points out, but it will rate you zero points in a testing situation. "Good" "scientific" answers, of course—e.g., "They are both hydrocarbons"—will rate you zero points in some other conversations.

It is tempting to accumulate more and more examples of selections from a repertoire in the light of what we think a situation requires. I shall, however, close with only one more example, taken from Hayes' discussion (Part V). Part of our response to any request, Hayes suggests, depends upon our model of the speaker. Age and experience may bring with them a variety of models, may bring varying degrees of belief that a particular adult is joking or means exactly what he says. Depending on our model of the speaker of the moment, we will choose or adjust our behavior accordingly.

Sources of Difficulty in Achieving a Match

At this point, I plan to adopt a suggestion by Bartlett (1958) about appropriate behavior. I have always liked his comment that intellectual skills are very much like athletic skills: Intellectually, you may have a knack for some games, but not for others. Skill is often a question of timing and of avoiding points-of-no-return; practice is necessary to avoid getting rusty. I also like, however, his comment that beyond a certain point, a list of similarities does not serve a very useful purpose. We need enough points to establish the analogy and then we should put it to work.

As a test of usefulness, I wish to ask: Does the idea of a range help us understand why it is sometimes difficult to achieve an effective match between the occasion and the performance?

Difficulty 1: A Narrow Band of Correct Answers. On any task, we may ask about the range and distribution of correct answers. On some tasks, all answers within a fairly broad range may be treated as equally correct, and answers on the edge of this range may be treated as "partially correct." On other tasks, however, the range of correct answers may be extremely small and everything outside this narrow band will be treated as "wrong." A "half-correct" answer, an interesting answer that is clearly thought out, and an absolutely wild answer are all equally "wrong."

These narrow ranges are easiest to illustrate from intelligence tests, tests that, as Sigel (1963) has nicely pointed out, do a great deal to limit our understanding of intelligence. Let me take one particular item from the Binet test for "verbal opposites" at age 6. One completion item is "an inch is short, a mile is——." "Plus" answers are "long" or "longer"; "minus" answers are "too long" or "long ways." The same kind of scoring occurs for the item: "A bird flies; a fish——." "Swims" is a "plus" answer, but "just swims around in the water" is minus.

As soon as one looks at items like these, one recognizes that the score of "plus" or "minus" may not reflect any difference in intelligence. The rule serves its purpose—it discriminates age or degrees of socialization—but it has also come to function like many other social rules designed to provide discrimination between groups. To repeat an earlier phrase, "not quite right" has come to have the connotation of "all-wrong."

This source of difficulty, I suggest, is not a trivial one. It takes explicit training and careful practice to achieve a type of performance where we can fit our answer to a narrow target quickly and spontaneously, i.e., without instructions as to what type of answer is being called correct. With enough such items, it would not be surprising to find that the Binet was a difficult test for children outside the population used as a standard. I, for one, would wish to know whether a narrow band of correct answers might account for race and class differences in Binet scores before assuming that such effects stemmed from some basic difference in learning styles (cf. Jensen, 1969).

Difficulty 2: Behaviors as "Good Things" in Themselves. By and large, we tend to think of development as the decontextualization of a general rule. In Piaget's theory, for example, development involves the ability to apply a range of operations across a variety of content areas and to interpret the data provided. Experiences may then be sorted out in terms of whether they provide familiarity with an operation in a single context or across several contexts.

This approach to development is extremely useful (cf. Goodnow, 1969a, 1969b). I would add, at this point, only the argument that some operations become so valued that they are applied indiscriminately: They become decontextualized to an absurd degree. Examples are not hard to find. Statisticians and editors are widely known to feel very strongly about the ritual quality of some analytic procedures. All of us need to be regularly reminded of the limits, along with the economies, that go with such favorite operations as labelling and categorizing. The sharpest set of examples, however, comes again from Arnheim (1969). In his view, our current scientific culture is obsessed with applying the operation of counting to every conceivable context, as if counting were the only way of estimating quantity and as if all other properties of objects were irrelevant. His analyses of some "new mathematics" programs provide some classic examples of the way a culture provides deliberate experience with an operation, experience to a point where it will be applied in any case of doubt about what to do.

Within our own theories of the development of skill, some of the commonest beliefs—the commonest suspensions of concern for the particular occasion—seem to cluster around questions of method. We all have, I suggest, quite definite values about "good" or "elegant" solutions, and about the occasions when certain types of "good" solution should be displayed. On a concept attainment task, for example, it is easy to believe that the "best" solutions are the ones achieved with no redundant questions, regardless of whether an extra question costs anything, and regardless of whether the individual has been told he should avoid redundant questions.

My own first approaches to such tasks were, I frankly admit, full of redundancies and a long way from conservative focusing. I tell myself that this is just a question of style, that, in any area where I know I can recover easily, I tend to wander around and get off the beaten path. In contrast, I seldom use such methods in driving through the city, where I have grave doubts about my ability to recover from a wrong turn or a shift in direction. I do know, however, that my poking about could easily be called "slopping around," "wandering aimlessly," or "being inefficient," and I am glad there are some intellectual counter-values such as "divergent thinking," "incidental learning," and the "importance of not being rigid." What is important, of course, is not the opposition of one way of working against another, but the recognition that most of us are capable of using several methods. The difficulties start when we display method X at a time when Y is called for, or when we insist that one method is always the best, forgetting to ask: Under what circumstances does redundancy help, hinder, or make no difference? Even this question may involve a misleading singleness of mind. I am not completely sure, for instance, that redundant choices are always intended, by the subject, to gather information. They seem sometimes to serve as ways of marking time, ways of underlining a phenomenon, or even ways of warding off distraction. If these purposes are involved, then "redundant" choices may be extremely useful.

Rules about allowable redundancy or allowable error are one form of rules about method. Another, one that has given me considerable trouble, has to do with the use of "action" versus "thought" (cf. Goodnow, 1969a). Rules about the necessity or the appropriateness of "doing" things in order to prove a point can differ between nations, as I think our Genevan visitors will agree. To put things in an extreme form, North Americans are inclined to regard European "proofs" as too long on logic and too short in experiment, as well as being entirely too cavalier about things like large samples, impeccable designs, and long statistical analyses. In contrast, Europeans are inclined to regard much of American psychology as excessively "busy," excessively caught up in the rule that "only seeing is believing," and almost timid, if I may stretch a point, when it comes to operating with logic only. Once again, I would like to suggest, the real question is not which method is best for all occasions, but which is best for what occasion. Once again, the difficulties start when we limit ourselves to one approach. An experiment by Hanfmann (1941) is an excellent example of this phenomenon: Ph.D.'s may have great difficulty with the Vygotsky task if they limit themselves to thinking, Rodin-style, and will not stoop to moving the blocks around.

Difficulty 3: Rules as Tricks of the Trade. One of the mysteries in children's matching of series is where they learn that a spatial interval can stand for a time interval and that this is the expected correspondence even though others are possible. The teaching appears to be implicit, the learning to be drawn out of a variety of experiences. The problem has led me to wonder how far other procedures or other equivalences are learned in similar fashion. I feel the question is worthwhile. To the extent that a rule grows out of some special experiences, or is learned "on-the-job" rather than being available for widespread teaching, we should expect large differences between age groups and social groups. A difference between ages may stem not as much from a difference in capacity as from the slow accumulation of on-the-job experiences. For some social groups, of course, the experiences may not accumulate at all.

Let me bring such possibilities down to earth with some examples. One of the problems that continues to intrigue me is the effect that going to school has on the development of cognitive skills. We know, for example, that urban Chinese children who are not going to school can do quite well on conservation tasks, but have a great deal of difficulty on tasks where they need to use the "trick" of holding one property constant while varying other properties in a systematic way (at least on tasks where they need to do all this "in the head") (Goodnow, 1962, 1969b). Now I think it would be a great mistake to assume that these children are not capable of "formal reasoning." They do not, it is true, spontaneously apply the rule of varying one thing at a time, but I hope Bärbel Inhelder will agree with me that this is only one aspect—perhaps just the most easily measured aspect—of formal reasoning. The real lack among these Chinese children is in the school experiences that bring the use of this procedure to a certain probability of occurrence. In fact, some recent data gathered by Susan Page at the Australian National University suggests that we may overdo our teaching of such methods: Dr. Page has observed school children who can, on tasks of combinatorial reasoning, apply the method of constants perfectly, but are not able to draw correct inferences from the data they have so impeccably generated (Page, 1971).

I would like to close with one last thought about "tricks of the trade." We often say, particularly with regard to the training of students for research, that they learn best—or we teach them best—by an "apprenticeship" system. I have puzzled over this. There are, after all, few other occasions when university faculty feel it necessary to provide on-the-job learning. And one of the possibilities that occurs to me is that we seldom, even in our "scientific" culture, explicitly teach people how to reason formally or how to solve problems. Most research workers recognize the heuristics or "rules of thumb" that Polya (1957) describes in his book on *How to Solve It* but few of us give our apprentices such books to read, or relate their learning experiences to explicit statements about the usefulness of breaking problems into steps, starting from both ends of a problem, isolating errors, setting up two hypotheses at a time, or borrowing models from other sciences. Part of the difficulty is that we have no readily available language to describe what goes on when we think, and we are reduced to working from examples, from such statements as "It's like the time we tried to do—."

What I am suggesting is the possibility that part of what we call "formal reasoning" may occur late in life—or never—because there are so few occasions when we can make the behavior sufficiently "out there" to work on and to discuss with one another. If that is the case, then development will be slowed down because there is little of the ingredient Piaget has described as critical for development, namely an exposure to provocative discrepancies between two occasions or two persons' points of view. What may also follow is that we may see in the near future some acceleration in the development of formal skills. The language of computers does provide a language for making explicit statements about the nature and effectiveness of rules, and, given sufficient exposure, children may progress at an earlier age to internalizing the rules made more explicit for them. My children, for example, have in their vocabulary such terms as "overload," "recode," and "that does not compute"—garnered from television rather than from school—and they apply these terms quite aptly to describe some of my instructions and their responses (not necessarily their under-standing). That may be a small beginning, but it is the beginning, I suggest, of a skill that we currently let develop only as a trick of the trade.

Bärbel Inhelder received her Ph.D under Piaget at the Institute of Psychology and Science of Education, at the University of Geneva. Her thesis was on reasoning processes in retardates, and applications of Piagetian theory to psychopathology—a continuing interest of Dr. Inhelder's that we sometimes lose sight of in this country.

Dr. Inhelder began her famed collaboration with Piaget in 1941 with the publication of a book, still untranslated into English, on the development of quantitative processes. In recent years, she has evolved a unique research style combining the sensitivity of the Piagetian *méthode clinique* with an objectivity and precision favored by American experimentalists. The result is a type of analysis that draws the Piagetian program firmly into an information-processing framework.

CHAPTER 6A

INFORMATION PROCESSING TENDENCIES IN RECENT EXPERIMENTS IN COGNITIVE LEARNING— EMPIRICAL STUDIES

Bärbel Inhelder

University of Geneva

Piaget's theory concerns cognitive development and developmental epistemology. It is therefore not surprising that such a theory is itself constantly developing. New problems are being raised, new methods are applied to deal with these problems, and explanatory models are refined and readjusted to account for new findings. Piaget showed that cognitive development has a direction, and proceeds toward increasingly better adaptation of the knowing subject to the reality that is the object of his knowledge. Through intensive and detailed study of the acquisition of various concepts (number, weight, volume, space, time, causality, probability, and others) it was possible to determine the underlying structures of thought that allow attainment of these concepts. Subsequently, it was possible to establish a hierarchy within these structures and to hypothesize their possible filiation. These structures have been formalized in algebraic form, as grouplike structures and semilattices for the preformal stages of thought, and as lattices and groups for the formal stage. The structures are atemporal and reflect the possibilities of a total system, but to locate the formative mechanisms that can explain the transition from one stage to another, we have to go beyond such structural models. Piaget and his collaborators have become increasingly interested in dynamic models, more specifically in self-regulatory mechanisms.

From a biological viewpoint, all regulations during development go beyond the mere maintenance of equilibrium. They originate through compensation for perturbations arising either in the organism or its environment, and result in new constructions. Similarly, in psychological development, incomplete systems or partial systems that conflict with one another are enlarged or integrated through regulatory mechanisms. An important aspect of such mechanisms resides in *post-hoc* corrections that modify action schemes.

Piaget calls his developmental epistemology "naturalist, but not positivist." Cognitive behavior is an outward sign of the assimilatory and accommodatory capacities of a living organism. The biological aspect of Piaget's theory is often difficult to grasp for those psychologists who believe that mental development is infinitely malleable (under favorable conditions and with adequate teaching methods) and who are convinced that what they think of as errors of growth can easily be corrected.

A biologically inspired theory that uses such concepts as assimilation, accommodation, and action schemes is very different from a learning theory that tries to account for cognitive development in terms of associations, connections, and conditioning. These latter types of mechanisms always suppose that two events are linked in the subject's mind because he has passively submitted to an outside pressure connecting the two. The concept of assimilation, by contrast, supposes that the subject actively assimilates a new event to existing structures. It is not a question of the subject's knowledge merely reflecting outside events, but of his own activity on the outside world, plus the feedback from this action which allows him to construct new concepts and action schemes.

Therefore, there is an interaction between the knowing subject and the objects that are to be known. It is true that Piaget has, until recently, emphasized the constructive role of the subject, and that comparatively little attention has been given to features of the objects favoring the attainment of knowledge. Objects can only be known, in closer and closer approximation, through the activity of the subject himself. The subject never attains complete knowledge of these objects; objectivity is the limit of these convergent processes. As knowledge of objects proceeds, the subject's activity becomes better and better organized. In a sense, this justifies Piaget's theoretical distinction between two types of knowledge—*logico-mathematical knowledge* and the *knowledge of the physical world.* From the Piagetian viewpoint, these types of knowledge result, on the one hand, from the organization of the subject's activities (logico-mathematical knowledge resulting from reflective abstraction) and, on the other hand, from the knowledge the subject gains about the object's properties (knowledge of the physical world resulting from physical abstraction).

From the viewpoint of developmental psychology, the relations between the two abstraction processes and their reciprocal influence have not yet been sufficiently studied. Among our ambitions is to explore these relations through learning experiments. We suppose that what the child learns about objects influences the way he organizes his own activity (and vice versa) and that in this link resides one of the dynamic factors of development. Learning experiments seem particularly apt to help us observe transition mechanisms at work. By inducing the elaboration of a concept, and by working with the child in several (sometimes as many as six) sessions during 2 or 3 weeks, we may observe, or even induce, some of the crucial moments where "something happens." Evidently, we can never observe the mechanisms, but only the behavior that is their result.

We hope that with new facts obtained from the learning experiments, we will be able to get some ideas as to the possible form of a dynamic model of transition mechanisms. In order to study as closely as possible the mechanisms at work in the transition of one substage to another, we chose to conduct learning experiments on the well-explored problems in conservation and class inclusion (just to give you these two examples among many others). As I have already said, developmental psychology aimed first of all at establishing a hierarchy of underlying structures. Conservation principles and class inclusion operations are important indicators of the existence of a grouplike structure. Logically speaking, an operation transforms a state A into a state B, while its inverse transforms B back into A. Through these transformations some quantitative property is kept constant, and this invariance can exist only in a coherent system of operations. It is for this reason that when a child understands that (for instance) the weight of a plasticine ball does not change when the ball is transformed into a sausage or a pancake, we can interpret his understanding as an indicator of the existence of a coherent system of operations. Though the underlying structure of operations may be the same in many concepts of conservation, it is well known that in development they do not all appear at the same time, but become established successively over a number of years. One of the very first, attained by most children around the age of six, is that of numerical quantity. At that age, children know that a change in the disposition of a set of discontinuous elements does not change its number. Younger children, when presented with two linear arrangements of discontinuous elements in optical one-to-one correspondence, of which one is then spread out, think that the spread-out elements, because they *go further than* the other elements, are *more* in number.

One of the questions we hoped to elucidate by learning experiments was how do children construct more difficult conservation concepts once the conservation of numerical quantity is attained? Since the different conservation concepts have been extensively studied, both cross-sectionally and longitudinally, they appeared to constitute a privileged case in which we might be able to observe supposedly general transition mechanisms in action.

In one of our experiments designed by M. Bovet (Inhelder, Bovet, & Sinclair, 1967), we tried to lead children who showed (in pretests) an incipient notion of numerical conservation, to a grasp of the conservation of continuous quantities (normally acquired some 3 years later).

The children had to succeed in a test of numerical conservation, consisting of the following items:

(a) Two identical glasses, A and B, are filled with large beads (where the experimenter and the child simultaneously drop beads, one or two at a time into the glasses). Glass B then is emptied into a narrower glass (N), or into a larger glass (L). The conservation question is asked. The beads in glass N (or L) are then poured back into B.

(b) The beads in glass A are poured into L, and those in B are poured into N at the same time. The conservation question is asked again.

Children who passed the pretest then participated in the experiment. Without going into the details of the procedure, the following types of situations were used. In a preliminary situation, toy houses glued onto matchsticks are first set out in two rows, in one-to-one-correspondence. Then houses in the second row are displaced (see Fig. 6.1).

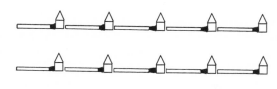

Fig. 6.1. Toy houses, glued to matchsticks, used in conservation experiment.

Questions are asked, first on conservation of the number of houses ("Are there as many green houses as red houses? or more? or less? How do you know?") and then on the length of the paths ("Is one of the paths just as long as the other?").

In other situations, the child himself has to construct paths with matchsticks. Both experimenter and subject have a number of matches at their disposal, but the subject's matches are shorter than those of the experimenter and a different color (seven of the subject's red matches add up to the same length as five of the experimenter's black matches). The experimenter constructs either a straight or a broken line (a "path") and asks the subject to construct a line of the same length ("just as long a path"; "just as far to walk," etc.). Three such problems are presented.

1. The first problem-situation is the most complex: the experimenter constructs a sort of zigzag line and the subject has to construct a straight line of the same length directly underneath (Fig. 6.2).

2. In the second situation, the subject again has to construct a straight line of the same length as the experimenter's zigzag line, but no longer directly underneath (Fig. 6.3).

3. The third situation is the easiest, since the experimenter's line is straight and the subject is asked to construct a straight line directly underneath it (Fig. 6.4).

The experimenter uses the same number of matches (five) as in problem situations 1 and 2, so that this third situation (seven of the subject's matches are needed to make a straight line of the same length) suggests a correct solution to situations 1 and 2 by transitivity.

The three problem-situations remain before the subject. After he has given his first three solutions, he is asked to give explanations and eventually to reconsider his constructions, while the experimenter draws his attention to one situation after another.

In this experiment, we interviewed a group of children (mean age, 6 years) who without having the concept of conservation of length had to succeed in a test of numerical conservation (Piaget & Szeminska, 1952). Of course, not only must the subjects give consistent numerical conservation answers, but they must also be able to justify their answers. Some typical examples of solutions to problems 1, 2, and 3 are as follows.

In problem situation 1, the most elementary solution is to construct a straight line with its extremities in coincidence with those of the experimenter's zigzag line. The child is convinced that the two lines are the same length, although his line is made up of four short matches, and the experimenter's line of five long matches.

In situation 2, the child finds no ordinal point of reference, since he has to construct his line at some distance from the experimenter's line, and so he uses

Bärbel Inhelder

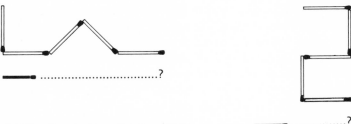

Fig. 6.2.The first problem-situation: Child
must construct a straight line equal in length
to the zigzag line.

Fig. 6.3. The second problem-situation.

Fig. 6.4. The third problem-situation.

the numerical reference: He constructs his line with the same number of matches
the experimenter has used, regardless of the fact that his matches are shorter.
When the experimenter now goes back to the problem situation 1, the child will
notice—with some embarrassment—that there he has constructed a line, which he
judged to be of equal length, that does not have the same number of elements as
the model line. At this point, we often see amusing and original compromise
solutions. For instance, in situation 1, the child may break one of his matches in
two, thus creating a line with the same number of elements without destroying
the ordinal correspondence (see Fig. 6.5).

Another solution, again clearly indicating the conflict between ordinal and
numerical references, consists of adding one match, but placing it vertically
instead of horizontally (Fig. 6.6).

When the child then is asked to construct his line in situation 3, he starts by
using the same number of matches (five) as the experimenter has used for his
line. Since this time both lines are straight and the child's line is directly under
the model line, he sees immediately that this does not give the right solution.
Because his matches are shorter, his line is not as long as the model line (Fig.
6.7).

It is not the purpose of this paper to discuss in detail the purely psychological
results of these learning sessions. We intend to use this experiment as one of the
many examples of the intricate coordinations and differentiations that take
place when a new concept is formed, and of the nature of the processes that
make this progress possible. In fact, in many other experiments we observed the
same type of progress, and we feel justified in generalizing from this particularly
clear instance.

Fig. 6.5. A child's attempt to integrate ordinal and numerical references–by breaking a match. [Inhelder later describes this as the third stage of the construction process–ED.]

Fig. 6.6. Another attempt to integrate ordinal and numerical references.

Fig. 6.7. In the third problem-situation, the child may discover the inadequacy of his counting solution.

We were able to observe that our subjects not only made considerable progress, but that there were qualitative differences in this progress, dependent upon their developmental level at the beginning of the learning sessions. A good proportion had clearly mastered conservation of length at the end of the sessions. Another group went part of the way. Some subjects progressed only a little or not at all, thereby making explicit a number of obstacles that the more advanced or brighter children overcame so quickly that we might have missed their significance.

At the outset of the experiment, as was mentioned previously, all our subjects were capable of conserving simple numerical quantity, which implies they had already coordinated the initial way of judging quantity by an ordinal relation ("going beyond" or "starting and finishing at the same point") with a way of judging based on one-to-one correspondence. It could therefore be supposed that the attainment of conservation of continuous length is a simple result of what, in associationist theories, is called *generalization.* Nonconservation of length shows that the obstacle is, again, an ordinal or topological way of judging by "going just as far" or "going further than." By presenting lengths constructed from separate, but contiguous elements, a "transfer" would take place and the problem of transition mechanisms would have been solved in a simple, but, for our purpose, uninteresting way. A first result of our analysis of the subjects' behavior showed clearly that this was not the way in which the transition took place.

Essentially, it was possible to distinguish four successive steps in the construction process. Those subjects that made hardly any progress at all showed us the importance of the *first step.* In the preliminary situation with the toy-houses glued to matchsticks (all of equal length) one asks questions of the number of houses and the length of the path. These children answered correctly the number of houses question. They counted the houses, and did not talk about one set of houses "going further" than the other. However, as soon as they were asked a question about the respective lengths of the paths, they did not thi k of counting the elements, or of going back to the one-to-one correspondence. They answered incorrectly, judging according to the going-beyond criterion. In this way, it became clear that one or another of two (or more) different systems of evaluation could be solicited, both being, in a sense, pertinent to the question, but neither were sufficiently developed to allow their integration. There was successive activation of two separate systems, and no contradiction was felt by the subject.

A *second step* in the construction process follows very soon afterward. Instead of the two evaluation schemes arising separately, according to the question asked, both seem to be present practically simultaneously. For example, when the subjects had to construct a path "just as long" as, and parallel to the experimenter's, but with shorter matches, they would start off by counting the elements [scheme activated by problem situation (2)] and build their path with the same number of elements. However, no sooner had they finished their construction, than they noticed that one path "went further" and they found their solution no longer acceptable. They could then turn to the other solution, but on noticing that despite the coincidence there were more small matches in the one path than long matches in the other, they went back to their first solution. Neither could satisfy them and they could not conceive of a new solution taking both the preceding ones into account, though they were conscious of the contradiction.

The *third step* did not appear in all the different experiments, but it is perhaps the most significant one. It consists of an inadequate effort at integration, and is visible in what we have called compromise solutions. As we have already mentioned, the child will break one of his matches in several pieces and thus obtain the same number of matches and still not have a path that "goes beyond." Either that, or he will ignore the instruction that he has to make a straight path and put one of his matches vertically instead of horizontally. In this way, he fulfills both his exigencies in a solution that, at least temporarily, satisfies him.

From here, the *fourth step* in the construction process follows for many subjects. Instead of one scheme operating a *post-hoc* correction on the other, we now see a *reciprocal adjustment* whereby the criterion of coincidence (sufficient provided the two paths are parallel) and that of numerical equality (sufficient provided all matches are of equal length) are successfully integrated into a coherent system which allows the child to solve problems of length in all generality, and no longer only in special cases. Now the different schemes can be integrated, which gives a new impetus to the search for necessary and sufficient conditions for equality of length. This results in a complete understanding of the compensation involved. The children explain, "You need more matches when they are smaller" and "The path goes less far but it has zigzags."

Development takes place in a very similar way in all the processes that have come to light during our training experiments. There is however, one essential difference, namely: With logical operations (in the strict sense of the term), the regulatory mechanisms which sooner or later lead to an awareness of contradiction are not followed by compromise solutions in the form of partial compensations, but are immediately followed by complete logical compensations which later result in correct solutions. A particularly striking example is that of the acquisition of logical quantification (Piaget & Szeminska, 1952; Inhelder & Piaget, 1964).

The problem of class inclusion concerns additive compositions. For instance, if B is the general class and A and A' the subclasses, the following operations obtain: $A + A' = B; B - A' = A$ and $B - A = A'$. From this it can be deduced that if both A and A' are nonempty classes, B is larger than A'. The inclusion of class A in class B provides the relationship which proves the statements "all A's are some B's" and "A is smaller than B." Certain subjects can agree with the first statement even though they do not understand the second. Complete understanding of the concept of inclusion implies the understanding of the link between the operation $A + A' = B$; and the operation $B - A' = A$. This link takes the form of logical compensation. It is only at the level of concrete operations that the child becomes capable of working simultaneously on a general class defined by a general property (e.g., flowers), and on subclasses of this general class that are defined by a more restrictive property (e.g., roses). At the pre-operatory level, the child does not conserve the whole when he has to compare it to one of the parts. His mistake is that, when he begins by mentally evaluating A, he isolates it from the whole B and can only compare it with A' and not with B. When faced with a bunch of flowers containing a great many roses and a few tulips, and asked if there are more roses or more flowers, the child replies that there are more roses. If he is then asked "more than what?" he often answers "than tulips." The main difficulty lies in the fact that the child is asked to compare within only one collection the logical extension of a subclass A with the logical extension of the total class B.

Dr. Sinclair constructed a learning procedure in which the children had to construct by themselves two collections within which the subclasses varied in comparative size while the total collection was kept constant (Inhelder & Sinclair, 1969).

The experimenter gives to one girl doll six pieces of fruit, for example four peaches and two apples (PPPPAA). The child is asked to give the other (the boy doll) "just as many pieces of fruit, so that they have just as much to eat, but more apples, because he likes them better than peaches." The instruction is repeated as often as necessary, in different forms. The situation can be varied, made easier, or more difficult.

Let me just mention one typical example. At the beginning of the learning sessions, a child asserts that the experimenter's instructions cannot be complied with: "It can't be done." He finally gives the other doll an identical collection: four peaches and two apples.—"Can you remember what I just said?"—"*He is to have the same thing as the girl.*"—"The same thing as what?"—"*The same thing of the other fruit.*" He thus refers to A' and not to B in classes $A + A' = B$, which corresponds to the second step in the construction process in the preceding experiment.

The experimenter's instructions: "Give the other doll more apples, but just as many pieces of fruit" contains two conditons: *more apples,* referring to the subclass; *just as many,* referring to the total class. In his interpretation of these instructions, the child seems to be incapable of simultaneously taking into account the four components, namely: the *same, more, total class, subclass.* At first he mentions only the condition referring to the total class ("*the same thing as the girl*"), but when the experimenter asks him about the first part of the instructions he disconnects this condition from the total class and applies it to the subclass (*"the same thing of the other fruit"*). When the other condition is stressed (more apples) the child applies it correctly, but then neglects the first one. He says *"We've got to add some then"* and proceeds to add two apples to the whole collection (four peaches and four apples). When he is asked if he is satisfied with his solution, he says *"No."* When we repeat the instructions, he takes away all the fruit he had given the boy doll, ponders, and then seems to make a real discovery. *"We've got to give just apples then?"* and gives six apples. This solution actually does solve the conflict among the conditions. It does satisfy all the conditions, but vacuously. That is, he solves the problem of including one class in another by identifying the total class with one subclass. He identifies the part and the whole without going through the trouble of having to make compensations for the members of the complementary subclasses. (Compensation means: taking away one A' whenever one A is added).

This kind of solution is functionally similar to the *third step* in the construction process in the preceding experiment: the compromise solution between ordinal and numerical schemes, but here the compensation is immediately complete because it happens to be a special case of the solution. It is specific to logical problems in the strict sense where the ordinal and extensional aspects of quantification are nondifferentiated.

That this is a special case and not a general logical solution is clearly demonstrated by the fact that when the experimenter's questions reintroduce the two aspects, the child again decomposes his solution into his former disconnected categories.—*"Now he's got more apples than the girl."*—"Right. Do they have the same number of pieces of fruit?"—*"No, one's got more: the boy. I gave him two extra apples."*—"How many pieces of fruit has he got then?" (Without counting)—*"He's got eight."*—"Count them carefully." (Surprised)— *"He's got six too!"*

This particular child, who started at the lowest operative level was not able to go further. However, children who were more advanced at the beginning of the learning sessions resolved the contradiction by a very adequate, complete compensation of logical operations and acquired full understanding of class inclusion, not only in situations involving two collections, but also in the more difficult one-collection situation. Finally, for all these children, training in class inclusion had a unexpected positive effect on progress in conservation problems.

These two examples among many of our learning studies seem to lead to the following conclusions. Instead of a more or less straightforward type of development, with differentiations becoming more and more refined (in the form of a treelike diagram), the interactions between different subsystems appear of the greatest importance. As the first example has shown, interactions between numerical and ordinal ways of dealing with problems of judging or constructing lengths lead to a conflict. It is this conflict which will trigger the process leading to the final resolution, through reciprocal assimilation of the two different subsystems that do not necessarily belong to the same developmental level. The emergence of conflicts can explain the frequently occurring regressions in the subject's overt reasoning—they are only apparent regressions. In fact, they are observable symptoms of an internal event announcing the beginning of a structuration of a higher order.

It now seems necessary to relate such a dynamic model to the classical Piagetian structural model. In the first place, the different systems of judging or constructing are internalized schemes. As to their appearance and their possibilities of being integrated into others, these schemes are determined by the general structure of the corresponding level of development.

In the second place, the hierarchical structures are in part common to both types of knowledge—logico-mathematical on the one hand, and knowledge of the physical world on the other. During the four successive steps in the construction process exemplified in the preceding experiments, either the apprehension of the properties of the subject's own actions, or the apprehension of the actual properties or features of the objects may be preponderant at one time. The epistemological nature of their interplay only becomes clear in the structural model.

From our point of view, it is illusory to try to establish process models which are not closely linked to structural ones. Since we are concerned with the specific Piagetian perspective, it would appear that the structural model, since it is based on a developmental hierarchy of structures, can absorb the process one. In fact, if we want to find the components that are common to both, we should think of the all-important concept of *compensation.*

The structural model uses, for each different level of development, specific types of compensation—for instance, the cancellation of a direct operation, or reciprocity in the case of the logic of relations. Psychologically and even biologically speaking, disturbances always give rise to a reaction on the part of the organism, but this reaction is not a passive submission to the environment. On the contrary, it leads to recombination of already existing capacities, in order to reestablish the destroyed equilibrium. In this sense, the reestablishment of an equilibrium involving a novel construction is also a compensation. The process model would therefore comprise compensations in the psychological sense. We have seen the example of first *juxtaposition,* then an *opposition,* then a *compromise,* and finally an *integration* of different schemes. The final integration, as we have also shown, gives rise to a new set of compensations.

In biology, new combinations only take place inside what are called *reaction-norms.* Similarly, we propose that in cognitive development, these new combinations can only occur inside what may be called narrow zones of assimilating capacities. The structural levels are at the root of the generation of new combinations, but simultaneously they impose limits on the novelties that can be produced. The compensations in the structural model would thus find their dynamic explanation in the process model; and the way these new combinations act will find their explanation in the structural model.

Guy Cellérier received his first degree in the foundations of law from the University of Geneva. In conversation with a friend about causal implications in law and psychology, Dr. Cellérier first heard the name of Piaget, read Piaget's book on causality (Piaget, 1930), began to attend Piaget's courses, and finally took another doctorate with Piaget in biology and epistemology. During that period Seymour Papert (Minsky & Papert, 1969) acquainted him with information processing theory, and codirected his thesis.

At present, Dr. Cellérier is Piaget's research associate at Geneva, and upon Piaget's retirement will take over his course on epistemology. His theoretical objectives concern the integration of process and formalization in Piagetian theory. In the following paper, he raises a number of philosophical issues that must be faced by model-builders. As general background for this closely written paper, Piaget's book *Structuralism* (1970a) is recommended.

CHAPTER 6B

INFORMATION PROCESSING TENDENCIES IN RECENT EXPERIMENTS IN COGNITIVE LEARNING—THEORETICAL IMPLICATIONS

Guy Cellérier

University of Geneva

Professor Frijda is reported (by Gascon, 1969) to have said, in an unpublished conference that "Piaget's theory is easier to program than any other existing theory of intelligence." However, my impression is that Piaget's central concepts are not sufficiently specified in their present form to be programmable. His experiments are programmable, but their simulation should only be considered as a means to elucidating the nature of these constructive processes. This is what I wish to submit to a discussion here.

Frijda goes on to say that "programming Piaget does not give rise to problems of principle, but only to practical ones." His examples of practical problems are: how to simulate the processes of abstraction and equilibration; how to make the proper operation and concepts available to the program at the right time; how to formalize the child's environment. If these represent practical problems for the programmer, they also happen to be fundamental problems in Piaget's theory as it stands today. Furthermore, these types of problems would seem to arise whenever we try to convert a structural theory into an information processing one. I would like to add straightaway that I strongly agree with Frijda that all the problems he mentions are fundamental to this conversion. I would only add simulation of *reciprocal assimilation* (the process that coordinates schemes) to his list, and reorganize the list somewhat so as to make it reflect the interdependencies that exist between the problems it mentions.

Piaget himself has never explicitly formulated his views on simulation, so as a first approximation to coordinating his structural approach with simulation problems, I will try to relate this question to Piaget's general position on the nature of explanation.

In Piaget's view, to explain a physical phenomenon (say the expansion of a gas when it is heated) we first discover regular relations between selected properties (pressure, temperature, volume in this case). This is a problem in pattern *recognition*. Then we express these regularities in terms of our own operations (Boyle's equation). This is not an explanation, it simply recodes under the guise of a physical law, a great number of possible experimental situations. This description, however is stronger than the first because the rule allows us to compute what the object will do. We have reconstructed the extension of our experiments and extended it hopefully to all possible experiments. Our new description now allows us to do pattern *generation*. It has, in some sense, captured the *structure* of the task environment—the structural constraints that force it, when it moves, to do so in certain regular paths.

If we now go on to inquire how the object manages to do this computation, we start to move in the direction of explanation. We generally try to discover elementary behaviors of the object (or of its parts) that can be said under some interpretation—again in terms of our operations—to do analog computation of our digital ones, or of their decomposition. Then we show that specific interactions or composition of these elementary behaviors—which may or not be verified experimentally—*necessarily* result in the observed laws and explain them deductively. We now have a process that implements and animates the structure defined by the laws, and we can attribute these lower level operations to the interaction of objects.

The first part of this process—the establishment of structural laws—would describe Piaget's central preoccupation in psychology. He has often compared his representation of the child's stabilized use of rules and concepts to the mathematician's axiomatic representation of an underlying intuitive theory. His succession of *logico-mathematical structures* reflects the succession of implicit intuitive theories the child evolves about such concepts as space, time, number, and perhaps truth and its conservation in deduction. This sequence is open at both ends. At the lower end elementary logical operations have their root in psychological actions on objects or concepts, these actions having their own roots in biological adaptation. At the upper end the last of the child's structures merge with the first of the adult mathematician's. The child's largely implicit reflective abstraction evolves into the adult's explicit formalization procedures. Moreover, the sequence of mathematical abstractions does not seem to have an upper bound.

This structural approach was dictated, it seems to me, by two main factors in Piaget's thought—one essential, the other somewhat accidental. The first is his fundamental preoccupation with epistemology. He often uses psychology to provide counterexamples to philosophical views on the nature of knowledge. More importantly, however, Piaget's grand design may be characterized as the reconstruction of the Kantian *a priori* categories of knowledge—as developmental necessities. To do this, structures were excellent building blocks. Structures are, in a sense, microcategories. They acquire their normative properties (the quality of deductive necessity) only *a posteriori* through development. Although this developmental aspect refutes the Kantian hypothesis, the Kantian criteria are nevertheless satisfied. Compositions of the structural microcategories generate the Kantian categories. For example, the coordination of class inclusion and seriation generates the concept of number—with all of its Kantian attributes.

The second factor is related to the state of the art in mathematical formalization as it was accessible to the layman (as opposed to the professional mathematician) when Piaget was doing his main work on *groupments* (the INRC group, etc.). The prevalent formalization procedure at the time was what Hilbert called *the postulational method*: we postulate a set of entities, define the operations—i.e., rules for combining them—by their effects on these objects and hopefully proceed to discover and prove interesting properties of these objects and operations. The interesting properties should at least include the intuitive properties attached to the concepts of the underlying (intuitive) theory we are formalizing. This is achieved through an interpretation of the abstract symbols in terms of these underlying concepts and actions.

This type of representation is at least twice removed, in its degree of abstraction, from the actual actions and situations with which the child or the adult deals. The situations or their internal psychological representations (concepts, equivalence classes of situations, etc.) are first coded into abstract symbols, elements of a set, and thus divested of their content. The actions (external or internalized) that transform one situation into another are coded into operators that do the same on the symbols. More often than not in Piaget's formalizations, the resulting structure is then defined on the *compositions* of these operators—these compositions reflecting the general coordinations of actions. By way of consequence, the relation of action to situation is also divested of its psychological means-end dimension. The main point here is that action itself also loses its content in some sense. As it is only defined by its effects or a given extension, the definition of an operator need not incorporate a description of how this result is produced. The operator becomes a black box. The symbol "+" represents addition, but does not specify its algorithm.

In brief, I believe these two factors—Piaget's interest in the structure and evolution of concepts, and his use of a postulational method—suffice to account for what has sometimes been called his "sublime disregard of process" in his epistemological analyses. However, it would be grossly misrepresenting his theory to say that process has no place in it. Piaget's insistent characterization of intelligence as an extension of biological adaptation, and of schemes as the organs of this adaptation are obvious counter examples.

Definitions of the scheme as goal-oriented sequences of conditional actions and perceptions sound very TOTE-like (Miller, Galanter, & Pribram, 1960) nowadays. I am tempted to speculate that if the genetic or constructive approach to formalization (in Hilbert's terminology), with its representation of processes and its accent on explicit rewriting rules, had been as developed and accessible as it is now, Piaget would have expressed the regularities he observed in behavior in terms of systems of formalized schemes and not of structures. These systems would certainly be easier to simulate, because they would embody the rulelike components of cognition. However, we would still be left with the problem of relating their output to the situation or state-description aspect of knowledge, that is, of interpreting this output in terms of the observed intuitive concepts and representations, as well as of their relations. This would mean constructing a structural theory.

Structure- and scheme-based representations are therefore just two different ways to describe the same observable regularities. Actually, they are not trivially equivalent. Their relations are very similar to the ones we find in many mathematical systems. The same set of strings of symbols can be described as a Boolean algebra in the classic postulational approach, or as "cranked out" by a formal system. Automata have associated semigroups, recurrence relations sometimes have equivalent algebraic forms, and there seems to be no simple way to convert one type of representation into the other. Such a conversion always entails some amount of invention and discovery. Furthermore, the relation is not necessarily one-to-one. We can find an instance of two automata with the same semigroup that cannot be called identical under any reasonable definition of machine homomorphism.

It is quite clear that programming Piaget in the sense of simulating all Piaget-type situations would not be programming the essential Piaget, i.e., the *development* of intelligence. These experimental situations do not cover the whole scope of intelligent behavior in children. Even if they did, we would be left with a juxtaposition of independently evolving programs with no central unity. We would be left also with the job of writing the central coordinator program. However, Piaget's recent experiments on conceptualization of schemes, and on conflicts between schemes, show a significant trend towards a more detailed observation and representation of processes. I think a formulation of these observations in a completely specified algorithmic form is a necessary condition for the realization of this goal.

Nevertheless, these complementary approaches are only descriptive. If we now turn to the second component of explanation—namely, to showing how the observed regularities are produced and implemented by the child—we find the same problem.

In Piaget's language, the succession of stabilized behaviors in seriation gives rise to a sequence of structural representations of concepts, these concepts and their structure evolve. In Gascon's (1969) simulation, the formulation would be: The child uses different rules or algorithms for seriation, that also evolve with age. Furthermore, to each structure in the sequence corresponds a related algorithm—i.e., the sequence of stages is identical in both cases. The remaining problem is also identical: It is to specify what *produces* these successions of rules and concepts. Gascon achieves the simulation of evolution simply by modifying parameters of the program. The main one is the number of relations that must be known about one element of the series before it is put in final position. If this number is one, the program generates a juxtaposition of ordered couples. At the other extreme, if it is six (there are seven blocks to be ordered) it generates a seriation. The formative mechanism that produces the transitions from one extreme to the other is clearly not simulated in any way attributable to some existing mental process in children.

The process of generating uncoordinated couples can be conceptualized in terms of rules: Piaget's *rule of couples*. In terms of structure it is a *classification* into heavy and light blocks. The corresponding conceptualization is that of weight as an absolute, nonrelational property of objects. During the intermediate stage, (not simulated by Gascon) the rule of couples may enter into conflict with itself: If $A < B$ is established and by some combination of design and bad luck B is again evaluated to establish $B < C$, A and C can still be classified, but now B cannot be, so the classification is refined and B becomes a medium element. However, now the rule must be changed to accommodate the insertion of any new element into one of *three* classes. This may be done in many ways, but it seems the new stabilized concept emerging from these empirical explorations is that of weight as a relation.* This is linked to the emergence of the rule of *local maxima* as an extension of the rule of couples: $[\max (a,b) = a] \Leftrightarrow (a > b)$ to triples. However, on triples, this entails the empirical discovery of the rule:

---

*In other words, the two nonrelational properties "a is heavy," "b is light" are integrated into the single relation "a heavier than b"—ED.

max $[\max(ab), c] = \max[a, \max(bc)] = \max(abc)$.* The extension of this rule to the whole sequence, followed by its systematic repetition, then generates a decreasing series of local maxima (this is the operatory algorithm "determine the heaviest of all, then the heaviest of the rest, etc". . .).

If we now ask: "How do the new rules and concepts appear," this experiment and many others seem to show the results of a common process. Piaget (1970b) defines it again in a postulational manner, by its effects on the elements—schemes and concepts—it acts upon: *"Reflective abstraction* extracts from the lower structures what is needed for the construction of higher structures. The ordering process in seriation is abstracted from elementary forms that appear in the local orderings of couples, triples or empirical series." To complete the picture, one must add, that the origins of these local orderings can themselves be traced in the general coordinations of sensorimotor actions—i.e., in their sequential character. The second stage of the abstraction process consists in recombining the elementary processes and coordinating them into a new synthesis. The final stage consists in systematizing the coordination process itself, and in extending it to all possible cases. "The self-regulation of the coordination process results in the equilibration of the connections following the two directions (direct and inverse) of possible constructions." The example in seriation would be descending and ascending methods producing decreasing and increasing series, respectively. The achievement of equilibrium produces the *novel* properties of the system compared to the preceding one, their operatory reversibility, for instance. It also preserves some of the essential properties of the lower system as particular cases of the novel one. Piaget's classical example is that of the successive extensions of the concept of number from integers to complex numbers.

What would be the elements of a constructive formulation of the abstraction process? The main idea seems to be that the new rules and concepts arise from recombination of the ones that are present. This recombination relies heavily on the existence of a general purpose representation system that can code both actions and situations, and of a pattern recognition device that acts on these representations to produce rules and concepts—that is, higher order entities such as prescriptions and descriptions. This means the representation system must have some capacity to accommodate new types of input: it must itself be adaptive. Finally, there must exist a decomposition and recombination device that acts on these descriptions and prescriptions to generate new ones. The actual choice of which combinations should be generated would have to be based on the construction of a succession of partial, reorganized representations (structured models) of the relationships between prescriptions and descriptions,

---

*In a series of more than two, the child must discover the associativity—i.e., that the order in which the blocks are chosen for comparison does not matter—through experience—ED.

and of techniques for transcribing one into the other, thereby linking the structural and process descriptions. The selection of the adapted combinations would depend on an evaluation of their effects on the (external) problem environment, this evaluation being used to update the internal model and start a new recombination sequence.*

This cyclic chaining of external observations and internal coordinations is emphasized in Piaget's recent reformulation of the equilibration model. By generating the extension of certain rules, new properties of the environment can be discovered. These new properties serve to invent new rules that can then be used to discover new properties. The cycle stops when nothing new is generated, under a given definition of the problem environment. The constructive interaction of rules and concepts through their extension is already very striking in the seriation experiments.

This type of analysis gave rise to a picture of cognitive development as a parallel evolution of cognitive categories, each composed of a neat filiation of progressively stronger structures. It has been recently complicated by the discovery that many different schemes and concepts may be applied by the child to the same problem, and that the different cognitive categories seem to evolve at slightly different rates. The net result is that lateral interactions between precursors appear at the decomposition and recombination level. These interactions (Piaget describes them as reciprocal assimilations between schemes, resulting in new coordinations) take place between elements that are heterogeneous in two ways: (1) They originate from different categories; and (2) their degrees of completion are not necessarily the same. Thus, Piaget's picture of development now incorporates *vertical* relations (intracategory filiations) *horizontal* ones (intercategory lateral interactions), and *oblique* ones (interactions between elements of different operatory levels).

Professor Inhelder's new line of experiments is partly responsible for this change in the model and will help to elucidate the following aspects of the problem at hand:

(1) Their initial diagnostic phase should produce an inventory of the possible precursor elements that the abstraction and coordination act upon. By repeating this analysis on the precursors themselves, and doing this on elements from different categories, we may find a set of elementary precursors that belong to the ancestry of a wide variety of structures. For instance, I believe some kind of elementary *contiguous composition* scheme is implemented throughout the various *groupments*. Its actualization on a given problem will depend on the coding of the problem's particular elements (e.g., logical, topological) in a form acceptable by the composition routine. By *contiguous*, I mean the result of the

*An example of such a "general purpose representation system" may be found in Klahr and Wallace, Part IV of this volume—ED.

first action must—in some way depending on the child's descriptors—resemble the initial conditions of the following one. For instance: $A \rightarrow B * C \rightarrow D$ is defined only if there is some XY such that $(A \rightarrow B * X \rightarrow Y) = A \rightarrow C$. The converse decomposition scheme would also be a frequent common ancestor. An instance of this would be professor Inhelder's example of practice on inclusion of classes favoring acquisition of conservation. The common decomposition scheme being activated would be the commutative partition $A + A' = B = A' + A$ generalized to any partition of B, and extended to the assimilation of continuous objects.

(2) The actual learning experiments should allow us to observe not the coordination process itself, but a close series of snapshots of its effects—how the schemes are decomposed, what are the successive recombinations that are generated and tried out, what are the guiding constraints their generation is subjected to. This last aspect is already remarkably illustrated in Dr. Inhelder's paper by the conciliation solutions of the children who construct equal paths, but who break up their units to preserve numerical equality.

To sum up and conclude, I believe structural and process models are not just theoretically complementary descriptions of the same phenomena, but that they reflect—in a perhaps too stylized form—the constructive interplay of rules and concepts in actual thought. Children, or adults for that matter, use structured representations of their task environment to "compute out" on them possible courses of action. We call this process *thought.* It is not a random walk through a faceless maze, but more like the choice of a path through a somewhat uncharted one. Moreover, our rules of choice and the chart itself are constantly being updated by the discoveries we make not only on the maze, but also on our own methods of exploration. When we divest our representations of their contents, and our computations of their objects, we may, *a posteriori,* project thought on the two dimensions of structures and formal deduction systems.

Furthermore, I suspect the formative mechanisms Piaget defines, are not mere artifacts of the theory, but reflections of the processes that actually weave the two dimensions of our models into a functional performing system. I do not believe our representations are stored as permanently organized cognitive maps, but rather that we actively reconstruct the maps from sets of stored cues whenever we have a specific problem to solve in detail. When we do this, we integrate the relevant cues we may have accumulated since our last reconstruction. It is at this point that the final product—our cognitive maps—come closest to being models of the psychologist's structures. With practice, we may become better at the reconstruction of itself—that is, our rules for representation evolve. In this sense, structures are only *a posteriori* descriptions of the results of an evolving process.

In the same manner, schemes should not be conceptualized as fixed, stored programs or subroutines, but as being reinvented more or less completely whenever they are called in on a specific problem. There again the final product may *a posteriori* be described as a formal system. In both cases, what we call *development* is the result of change in our reconstruction rules. How this change occurs is therefore the central problem in both structural and process theories. My conjecture is that it can only be solved by a synthetic approach describing a functional progressive reequilibration that would somehow avoid infinite regressions into metarules and metaconcepts by incorporating a cycle of alternating constructions of the metalanguage of one category in the language of the other.

Allen Newell was graduated in physics from Stanford University in 1949. Following a year of graduate work in mathematics at Princeton, he joined the RAND corporation, and pioneered the study of formal human organizations using simulated environments. Since 1955 he has been concerned with artificial intelligence and the psychology of human thinking. His initial work resulted in the construction of the first computer program to prove theorems (LOGIC THEORIST), and resulted in the development of the technique of list processing and list processing languages. Following this in 1959, the GENERAL PROBLEM SOLVER was developed, the first program to provide detailed simulations of human problem-solving behavior in a range of tasks. His extensive work with Herbert Simon is summarized in their new book *Human Problem Solving*. In 1957, Dr. Newell picked up his Ph.D. from Carnegie-Mellon, and is currently our University Professor.

The concepts of structure versus process are critical to developmental theory. No one understands their information-processing implications better than Allen Newell. This paper was written, at the editor's request, especially for this volume.

CHAPTER 7

A NOTE ON PROCESS-STRUCTURE DISTINCTIONS IN DEVELOPMENTAL PSYCHOLOGY

*Allen Newell**

A child comes into the laboratory and is given a series of tasks. For example, on a table is a rough line of blocks of various colors and shapes. The child is told to point to the green blocks, and then to point to the square blocks. He is asked: "Do the green blocks include the square blocks?" Other tasks vary in wording, materials, instructions, and complexity. All are designed to be solvable if the

*I appreciate the extensive criticisms on an earlier draft provided by Sylvia Farnham-Diggory, G. Groen, D. Klahr, H. A. Simon and R. Young. This research was supported by Research Grant MH-07722 from the National Institutes of Health.

child has the concept of class inclusion and to fail in characteristic ways if the child does not yet have the concept. It is from such experiments, then, that we try to pin down scientifically the course and causes of child development.

Distinctions between process and structure occur throughout our attempts to describe this development. Within this volume, the paper by Cellérier is most explicitly focused on such distinctions, but several other papers also reflect such a division, e.g., the Klahr and Wallace paper and some of the introductory remarks by Simon. Similar theoretical distinctions occur in other scientific domains, although we restrict ourselves here to the study of human behavior.

In describing the child, we talk about his cognitive structure and his attainment of various structures; we talk about the processes he uses to perform the tasks and his processes of development. Structures appear to be something static, permanent, and object-like—what is. Processes appear to be something dynamic, transient, and transformation-like—what happens.

The concepts of process and structure, and the distinctions between them, are as ancient, venerable and pervasive as the atoms of Democritus and the flux of Heraclitus. I wish neither to enter upon a general discussion of the concept nor to touch upon the positions held and traditions furthered by all who have had their say upon this matter.* My aim is more limited and can be summed up in two related points:

> In a developing information processing system (such as the child) many things can play the role of structure and many can play the role of process. It is important to know which of these—if any—is being talked about.

> This diversity represents empirical possibilities for the nature of the developmental system.

In a sense, I wish to engage in a necessary multiplication of entities, which proliferation, I believe, is a necessary preliminary for thinking about developmental systems.

In support of the preceding two points, a collection of distinctions will be displayed that contrast structure-like aspects and process-like aspects of information processing systems. The distinctions are all familiar ones, at least in computer science, where they have been found useful and even necessary to the conduct of business. The purpose, then, is not so much to establish these distinctions as to illustrate them clearly. To this end we will proceed mostly by a sequence of elementary examples.

The Material-Activity Distinction

If we open up an automobile, we call the various parts we see inside the structure—e.g., the carburetor, the distributor, the block, etc. We call the

---

*For at least one recent effort to touch on many of them, see Piaget (1970a).

running motor a process—a transformation of fuel into motion. The structure provides the necessary arrangements for the process to occur upon occasion.*

Applying the same view to the child while performing a laboratory task leads to distinguishing the various anatomic parts as structure—e.g., the cerebellum, the cortex, and the limbic system. It leads to calling the *child-while-performing* a process. The whole picture, however, is most unsatisfactory, even when pressed to the finest detail currently possible. The difficulty is not with the view per se, but with the empirical fact that we obtain none but the weakest correspondences between the system's structure and the details of its processing, i.e., why it functions as it does. Still, this view that identifies the structure with the material aspect of the system and the process with the activity must stand as a primary reference point.

In this division into structure and process, the structure is identified as that which is static and immutable. Someone is sure to note that such is not the case—the metal in the car wears away (and indeed that this wearing may be an essential part of the cars functioning, as in the bearings). We are forever being told that the bones and the teeth—the most structure-like parts of our anatomy—completely replace themselves as material entities every so many years. Thus, what was structure becomes process, and what seems a clear distinction becomes muddied.

Clarity can be regained by attending to the *time constants* with which change occurs in relation to the time constants employed in observing or measuring the system. This can be illustrated by Figure 1. All things that we can measure about the system change over time. However, if our measuring instruments have only a time grain of Δt, and a measurement grain of Δm, then changes that are fast compared to Δt will never be seen by us, and we will measure only an integrated effect (curve X is seen as a constant). Similarly, all changes that are slow (within Δm) with respect to the total duration over which measurement occurs ΔT, will appear constant to us at their instantaneous value (curve Z is also seen as a constant). This we call "structure," for it appears changeless. The parts of the system we call "process" are those characterized by measurements whose changes are not too fast and not too slow (curve Y). If we change our instruments, or our viewpoint, then what was structure quickens into process or what was process freezes into structure. All things appear as process or structure, depending on the viewpoint.

So it is with our child. What is structure-like and what is process-like depends on our viewpoint. Given that our attention is ultimately focused on the questions of development (measured in years), whereas the experimental situation used for measurement has a duration of hours or sometimes minutes,

---

*The total description is not complete without giving other necessary ingredients: the fuel and the controlling devices, such as the accelerator setting, which determine whether the occasion will in fact occur. But these are secondary matters.

Measurement

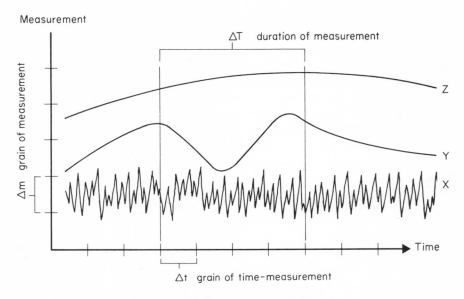

Figure 7.1 Measurement possibilities

the span over which our viewpoint roams is wide indeed: from development, to learning, to adaptation and assimilation of a particular experimental task, to the moment-by-moment processes accompanying performance.

Program-Data Distinction

In all attempts to describe machines capable of general action, there arises a separation between the machine and that on which it works: its input and output. In information-processing systems, the distinction is usually termed that between "program" and "data." It is familiar enough, e.g., the analysis of variance program as distinct from the matrices of numbers on which it works.

Let us illustrate this concretely by a simple example:

Program	Data	
	Set 1	Set 2
Take X	$X = 7$	$X = 9$
Subtract Y	$Y = 4$	$Y = 5$
Add Z	$Z = 1$	$Z = 2$
Print result		

On the left is a program for a simple arithmetic calculation and on the right are two sets of data (out of an infinite range of possibilities). The total system behaves differently, depending on which set of data is used (printing 4 or 6, respectively).

The program plays the role of process—producing the behavior and representing the dynamics. The set of data, then, plays the role of structure—being inert and static. This may seem somewhat odd. Calling it *content* rather than *structure* might appear more to the point, for the data seem to be transient and variable. But the structure-like character of data becomes apparent if we shift from a system whose data part is small and simple to one whose data part is large and complex. To revert to our original example, suppose our child could be conceived as the following system:

Program	Data
Inference system for deriving answers	Factual knowledge about sets and relations of sets to each other.

We would be likely to refer to the data as the cognitive structure of the child and the inference system as the process whereby that cognitive structure becomes manifest in behavior.

The Interpreter-Language Distinction

A confusing factor in the example just presented is that the program itself is a structure that specifies the dynamics to be carried out. It does not behave directly. Indeed, as we are all aware, programs are put into the memories of digital computers in order to produce real behavior and get real results. The computer provides an *interpreter,* which is a process that takes a program (such as the previous examples) as data and produces as output the sequence of operations commanded. These, in turn, work on the input data to produce the actual output desired. We can show this as follows:

Process	Program	Data
Interpreter	Take X	$X = 7$
	Subtract Y	$Y = 4$
	Add Z	$Z = 1$
	Print result	

process	structure

process	structure

Now the program is either process or structure, depending on which view we take, i.e., on which way we group the parts of the total system.

The preceding illustration is only the start. For one can construct programs that interpret languages. Indeed this is a favorite occupation in computer science, in order to use a programming language other than the one designed into the machine. Thus, we could have

Process	Program	Program	Data
Interpreter	Interpreter for higher level language	$W \leftarrow X - Y + Z$ Print (W)	$X = 7$ $Y = 4$ $Z = 1$

Now each program can play several process and structure-like roles. The expansion could be extended indefinitely and on occasion in computer science research goes another level or two.

What is true of the child? The question is not to be settled by fiat, for these are actually differently structured information-processing systems and nature could, in principle, have evolved man in many different ways. A given level of program organization can be interpreted directly by a process or by another level of program (i.e., by a programmed interpreter) without leading to any qualitatively distinguishable behavior on the part of the total system. For example, are the production systems in the Klahr and Wallace chapter a representation of actual process or are they interpreted?

The Grammar-Recognizer Distinction.

In modern formal studies of linguistics, a language is represented by a set of sentences formed out of some given alphabet of characters. For example, we might take the alphabet as consisting of all the Roman capital letters, A,B . . .,Z. The possible expressions are strings of these letters, ABBC, PDQQ, WORM, ... A particular language is a particular (possibly infinite) subset of all these expressions. Again to be concrete (and very simple) we might take the language to consist of

AC, ABC, ABBC, ABBBC, ABBBBC, . . ., AD, ABD, ABBD, ABBBD, ... To define this language precisely we introduce a *grammar*, which is a set of rules for describing expressions:

Grammar:

$$\langle \text{expression} \rangle : = A \langle \text{kernel} \rangle \langle \text{terminal} \rangle$$
$$\langle \text{kernel} \rangle : = \phi \mid B \mid \langle \text{kernel} \rangle B$$
$$\langle \text{terminal} \rangle : = C \mid D$$

This is to be read as: An expression is an A followed by a kernel followed by a terminal; a kernel is either null (ϕ) or a B or a kernel followed by a B; a terminal is either a C or a D. If one generates the specific strings of letters according to these rules one gets exactly the strings above. For example, ABBBC is an A followed by a kernel (BBB) followed by a terminal (D); and BBB is a kernel because it is a kernel (BB) followed by a B, where BB is a kernel because it is a kernel (B) followed by a B.

To make use of a language requires that it be recognized, that is, that a process exist that can determine whether a given presented expression belongs to the language or not. Given AB it should say no: given AC it should say yes; given ABBBBBBBBBBBBBBBBBBBBBBBBBBBBBBBBBBBBBBBBBBD it should say yes. One can write a program for the recognizer:

Recognize:

        Test first letter,
          if not A stop and print "not legal";

Loop: Test next letter,
          if B go to Loop;

        Test next letter,
          if C go to End,
          if D go to End,
          otherwise stop and print "not legal";

End: Test next letter,
          if exists stop and print "not legal,"
          otherwise stop and print "legal."

If you take any string and follow the program above you will find that it prints "legal" if and only if a string is an expression in our language and it prints "not legal" otherwise.

Neither the grammar nor the recognizer *is* the language, which is defined extensively as the set of legal expressions. But each characterizes the language completely, by determining the exact set of expressions that form the language, and thus all of the properties of the language. In just the same way either $3 + 1$ or 2×2 characterizes the number 4 completely. The grammar may be taken as a structure characterization of the language and the recognizer as a process characterization.

The complexity of languages is reflected in their grammars. Questions of the context required to analyze an expression, of the embedding of phrases within phrases permitted in an expression, and of the types of transformations necessary to decode an expression all are reflected in the grammar. An important part of the basic scientific progress in formal linguistics has been the development of a hierarchical classifaction of grammars that captures these several notions of language power and complexity. This classification is in terms natural to the grammar—that is, in terms of the types of grammatical rules permitted in writing the grammar.

Because recognizers also characterize a language completely, these same notions of linguistic power and complexity should be reflected somehow in the structure of the recognizers. Not only is this so, but the corresponding classification of recognizers is a natural one in process terms—in terms of the kinds of memory required by the recongizer. Simple languages (so-called finite-state languages) require only a finite amount of memory; so-called context-free languages (those expressible by the notation we used in our example) require an unbounded amount of memory, but of a simple kind called a push-down list; more complex languages require a completely general memory.*

Thus, there are two corresponding hierarchies, one concerned with grammars (structures), one concerned with recognizers (processes), each a natural classification. The development of these classifications and the proving of their correspondence has been one of the small elements of beauty in mathematical linguistics. It implies that there is a duality between structure and process. One can look at a given phenomena (language) from either viewpoint—structure or process—and obtain fundamentally the same knowledge.

Competence-Performance Distinction

The current conception of a distinction between competence and performance is due to the transformational linguists generally, and Chomsky (1965) in particular. It provides another variation on our theme. Consider the language we defined above. We wrote a particular recognizer for it. But that is not the only recognizer for the language, even though it is a complete characterization of the language. For instance, we might have the following recognizer:

Program	Data
Parser	(expression) := A (kernel) terminal) (kernel) := ϕ | B | (kernel) B (terminal) := C | D

The parser is a general program that takes as input any grammar expressed in the above notation. The total recognizer itself has a process part (the parser) and a structure part (the grammar), just as in the earlier example of programming language interpreters.

*See Hopcroft and Ullman (1969) for an elegant, but not elementary, exposition.

These two recognizers do not exhaust the possible ones that could be constructed. There are an infinite number of them varying in many different ways. For instance, we just varied the recognizer in terms of the division between program and data. But there can be variations due to the underlying processing system (i.e., in hardware, so to speak). Suppose, in our little example, the basic hardware automatically recodes all repeating letters on input as the letter followed by a count before giving them to the parser. For example

Input expression	Actual input to recognizer
AC	AC
ABD	ABD
ABBD	AB2D
ABBBBBD	AB5D
ABBBBBCCC	AB5C3

The recognizer for the sentences would be quite different from either of the recognizers above.

Thus we can separate the assertion that the entity knows the language—i.e., has competence—from the assertion that it contains a particular recognition process. To exhibit this competence—to perform— requires *some* process, but its exact nature can be ignored while attempting to ascertain the competence. If we consider that processes may be imperfect, so that the performance will not agree entirely with the output of any error-free recognizer, then the separation of performance from competence becomes even more important.

The distinction between competence and performance is akin to the distinction between structure and process. Competence appears to reflect the essential knowledge that the subject has—his cognitive structure. The system that puts that knowledge into action is clearly process. However, the distinction is different from that expressed in data versus program; the competence is not a part of the system (as is the data). It exists nowhere at all, being rather an abstract description of what the processes that constitute the actual system are capable of doing.

In particular cases, of course, it is possible to construct a system such that its data part is also an adequate expression of its competence. The preceding case, where we took the grammar itself to be the data and provided a general parser as the program, provides a concrete example. But this is not the usual affair. Indeed, it has been often noted that the amount of processing required by current transformational grammars of English, if done in the manner above, is far in excess of human processing capacities (e.g., Fodor & Garrett, 1966).

We have drawn the competence-performance distinction with respect to language, partly because appropriate concrete examples were at hand, and partly because the distinction has achieved great play there. But the same distinction arises in connection with all cognitive behavior, and especially with that concerned with development. For example, the structures posited by Piaget that characterize the developing child are characteristically expressions of competence. Their distance from detailed data, which has been so often remarked, is very like the distance between the grammars of the linguist and actual linguistic performances of native speakers.*

Process and Structure in Development

The distinctions we have made so far generally refer to a system at a given moment in time. Only in discussing the material-activity distinction did we introduce a time perspective, and then only to note that what is seen as changing and what as fixed depends on the viewpoint and the measuring instruments. When, as in the development of the child, we focus attention on change and how that change comes about, the question of what can play at being process and what can play at being structure becomes much more complex.

It would seem simplest to cling to the notion that the state of the system at each point of time is its structure, and whatever changes that state is process. But since, from a developmental perspective, the state of system at a point in time is still a *performing* system—e.g., it is our child performing in a class inclusion experiment—that momentary structure can itself be viewed as partly process-like and partly structure-like. It consists of various material parts whose activity constitutes performance; these material parts are distributed into those having to do with program and those having to do with data; these layers of program and data realize some hierarchy of interpreters and languages; and the whole may be seen as realizing a certain competence, which informs the particular performance that we witness on an experimental occasion. When we ask what changes and what causes the change, the possibilities grow almost combinatorially.

Nothing is to be served by enumerating all these possibilities. However, considering a few of the options will be revealing. Consider the child in the class inclusion task at performance time (i.e., at the moment when the task is being accomplished successfully). Then the child's performance system could be (at least) any of those shown in Table 1.

In the top case, the knowledge about inclusion is given as an assertion about a property that inclusion has. Remember, we are to view such knowledge as a data expression somehow represented in the child's head. Thus, to use this knowledge to solve a particular task—e.g., "Are the green blocks included in the square blocks?"—a process must derive the consequences of this abstract knowledge and apply it. We can call such an interpreter a *consequence-deriving interpreter*.

---

*It should be noted that neither Piaget (1970) nor Cellérier in the present volume apparently sees the issues in quite these terms.

In the next case, there exists a general program for all such inclusion problems. To apply this program to the task at hand, the parts of the program must be identified with corresponding elements of the actual task. This applies not only to variables, such as X and Y, but to processes such as *generate* and *test,* which are left unspecified in the program. Thus the interpreter must continually bridge the gap between the generalized terms of the program and the specifics of the concrete task. We can call such an interpreter an *instantiating interpreter,* since it reduces the generalized terms to specific instances.

In the third case, there is a highly specific program. However, the program is for the inclusion problem in a different task environment. Thus, the interpreter, called here the *analogizing interpreter,* must make the mapping from the old task to the new one.

In general, little can be said about whether it is easier to instantiate from a general form or to work analogously from a concrete, but different, instance. It clearly depends on many things, such as how many distracting features are in the analogous task and how abstract the general form is. The point is not to evaluate one or the other, but to realize that a performing system could be constructed in either fashion for a specific task.

The fourth case is one where the identifications have all been made for the specific task at hand. The interpreter, now an example of a familiar *program interpreter,* must follow the program and execute the primitive information processes contained therein. It has none of the extra tasks of consequence derivation, instantiation or analogizing.

The fifth and final case is the process that has no division into an interpreter part and a data part, but simply represents a totally assimilated scheme for accomplishing the specific task. Examination of the system would reveal no subpart that could be identified with program and no subpart that could be identified with the interpreter. The production schemes described by Klahr and Wallace (Chapter 8) provide examples (if we do not view productions as being interpreted by still another interpreter).

How might one of the performance systems of Table 1 come about? Being concerned with development we should, perhaps, look to what could give rise to the program that is within the child when some years younger. But genesis must occur from somewhat closer in time. For the present experimental situation is existentially new to the child. No matter how similar it is to other, prior situations, the current situation must be assimilated and accommodated in order to produce a performance. At instruction time, then, the child must have some sort of system for doing the task. During the course of the instruction the subject organizes himself, so that at performance time, he has attained one of the organizations we have listed. (Actually, of course, we have not listed all the organizations that would solve the task. For instance, it could be solved by trial and error, meaning by this that the subject manipulates the situations until he recognizes—or the experimenter recognizes—that the problem is solved.)

TABLE 1

Possibilities for Performance in Systems for Class Inclusion

Interpreter	Program-Data	Example
Consequence-deriving interpreter	Knowledge about class inclusion	Set X is included in set Y if and only if for every x in X, x is in Y.
Instantiating interpreter	General program for class inclusion problems	Generate members of set X (call them x), if no more stop and report "X included in Y"; Test if x is a member of Y, if not stop and report "X not included in Y"
Analogizing interpreter	Specific program for class inclusion on different tasks	Put finger on the leftmost toy soldier; Test if the toy soldier belongs to me, if not stop and report "Toy soldiers don't all belong to me"; Move finger on next toy soldier to the right, if find one go back to Test, otherwise stop and report "I own all toy soldiers."
Program interpreter	Specific program for class inclusion on this task	Look at the leftmost green block; Test if the block is square, if not stop and report "The greens are not included in the squares"; Look at the next green block to the right, if find one go back to Test, otherwise stop and report "The greens are included in the squares."
Uninterpreted process	(No data-like component)	

The assortment of organizations we have posited at performance time provides also a good description of what might be available at instruction time (after all he is still the same organism), though we need to augment the list with a condition of unpreparedness. Thus, we can draw a diagram for the possible acts of genesis in which the subject arrives at instruction time in one of the five possible conditions shown below and has developed by performance time one of the four possible organizations. (We ignore the case where the subject remains unprepared—we are considering successful performers.)

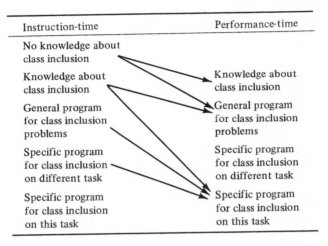

The lines indicate the plausible short-term developmental transformations. In general it is not plausible that acts of genuine induction or generalization take place at instruction time. Consequently, all of the transformations run down hill toward greater specialization to the task. To keep the diagram uncomplicated, the horizontal lines (indicating that no actual development took place) are not drawn in.

It is worth recalling that we get successful behavior at performance time only when we combine the organization, as just given, with an appropriate interpreter. These interpreters are content free. That is, they do not contain specific information about the class-inclusion task. A child need not have a given interpreter, and if he does not, then the corresponding data organization (as given) does not provide an effective basis for performance. For example, below a certain age a child has no interpreter for taking general knowledge about a task (here, the knowledge about class inclusion) and deriving from it the behavioral consequences that permit the child to perform the task. Thus, the existence of the interpreter is necessary for a type of performance system. We can assume that no creation of these interpreters can take place in the interval between instruction time and performance time. They are, however, developed over some longer duration, and the question of their genesis is as important as the questions of genesis being raised here.

There are seven transformations represented in the preceding figure. They represent four different sorts of functional processes:*

Induction:	Formulating generalized knowledge on the nature of the task from imperfect information given during the instructions. No knowledge → knowledge
Assembly:	Constructing a program out of component primitive operations given general knowledge of the task to be performed. No knowledge → general program No knowledge → specific program Knowledge → general program Knowledge → specific program
Compilation:	Obtaining a program that is specific to a task from a general one. General program → specific program
Adaptation:	Obtaining a program by adapting another analogous program. Analogic program → specific program

These varieties are not equally probable, given a particular setting, e.g., given a child of a given age and prior abilities. Furthermore, they are not ordered. Thus, no one kind of developmental transition is uniformly easier to accomplish than others.

Considering this piece of microgenesis directly, the slices taken of the system at given points in time reveal its structure, and what propels it from state to state reveals the processes of which it is capable. Thus, the listed items—from knowledge down to specific program—appear as structure; the schemes of induction, assembly, compilation, and adaptation appear as process.

But within the several alternatives for structure some are highly structure-like (the knowledge) and others are highly process-like (the programs). Furthermore, the source of ultimate process (a program at performance time) may be something that is process-like, rather than structure-like. Still further, the actual ultimate process may be something constructed only for the moment, and not existing beyond the confines of the local task situation. Thus, what the system contains when not performing can be a process-like object which really plays the role of structure (as source for the ultimate process) when the time for performance comes.

We have focused on the immediate genetic situation, not to deny the larger

---

*Additional discussion on these possibilities for the creation of processes can be found in Newell and Simon (1972), Chapter 14.

changes in the organism that occur on the scale we term learning and development, but to illustrate the complexity of process and structure that one must be prepared to deal with even within the immediate situation. Considering the longer reaches, what is to be created and developed is not only the types of structure shown, but also the interpreters and the processing systems called here induction, assembly, compilation, and adaptation.

Conclusion

At the very beginning of this chapter, I claimed to make two points. The first point was that in a developing information-processing system many things can play the role of structure and many can play the role of process—and that it was important to know what was being talked about. I hope this point has been amply illustrated. Despite their multiplicity, these illustrations should not have caused confusion; for each of the distinctions is both important and useful. Rather, they should have shown that a richer and more precise network of concepts is necessary in order to discuss developmental systems. The terms, "structure" and "process" serve only a general umbrella-like function.

The second point made at the beginning was that the diversity represented mainly empirical possibilities about the nature of the developmental system, and not just alternative viewpoints. This was especially true in the last section, where I laid out one set of possible mechanisms whereby the child could organize itself for the imminent experimental task. We do not know enough about the information processing done by children (or by adults either, for that matter) to close the door on very many possibilities. We certainly do know a little about the limits on the processing capacity of children and a little about their processing organization (see the comments in Simon's introduction). But these are not yet enough.

The diversity generated in this chapter cannot be removed by any exercises in terminological clarity or operationalism. Simplicity will come only by the pursuit of detailed empirical knowledge about the child's performances against the explicit background of the specific sorts of information-processing systems that might have given rise to those performances.

PART IV

COMPUTER SIMULATION

David **Klahr** received his B.S. from MIT and his Ph.D. from Carnegie-Mellon's Graduate School of Industrial Administration (GSIA). After a faculty sojourn at the University of Chicago, Dr. Klahr returned to Carnegie-Mellon as GSIA's director of educational research and development, a post designed to permit him to further his interests in educational technology and the organizational analysis of educational systems.

In 1968-1969, Dr. Klahr was a Research Fellow and Fulbright Lecturer in the British Isles. It was then that he began his collaboration with Dr. Wallace at the University of Stirling, in Scotland. The collaboration has emphasized the application of information-processing analytical and simulation techniques to the study of cognitive development. The first two papers of the Klahr-Wallace series have recently appeared in the *British Journal of Psychology* and in *Cognitive Psychology*, (Klahr and Wallace, 1970a, 1970b).

J. G. Wallace received his M.A. and M.Ed. degress from the University of Glasgow and his Ph.D. from the University of Bristol. After completing an extensive survey of research on conceptualization (Wallace, 1965) he moved to the new University of Stirling for an eventful three years before taking on his present post in the Department of Education at the University of Warwick.

CHAPTER 8
CLASS INCLUSION PROCESSES*

David Klahr   *and*   *J. G. Wallace*
Carnegie-Mellon University   University of Warwick

During the last decade, two fundamental problems have dominated the area of cognitive development. The first is that of determining the developmental relationships among particular cognitive skills. The intractable nature of this problem is exemplified in the steady stream of studies dealing with the Piagetian concept of a stage in intellectual development and with the stage of concrete

*This work was supported in part by a grant to Dr. Klahr from the Ford Foundation and to Dr. Wallace from the British Social Science Research Council. We wish to thank our colleagues Guy Groen, Allen Newell, Don Waterman and Richard Young for many stimulating discussions about production systems and cognitive development. We are further indebted to Allen Newell for his careful critique of an earlier version of this paper.

operations in particular, (Flavell & Wohlwill, 1969; Pinard & Laurendeau, 1969; Flavell, 1971). The second, equally complex problem is to determine the transition rule in cognitive development, i.e., the mechanisms or processes which govern the child's movement from stage to stage through the developmental sequence. The difficulties which characterize research on this theme are illustrated in the conclusion, drawn by Laurendeau and Pinard (1966), that an overview of the results of the studies to date provides grounds for pessimism about the outcome of an experimental approach to the transition problem.

In this paper we outline an approach to the problems of stage and transition which we believe has the merit of circumventing some of these methodological difficulties. Rather than attempting to deal with the issues *in extenso,* we shall discuss them in the context of a single specific area: class inclusion. The class inclusion (CI) task originated with Piaget (1952) in his study of the concept of number and was systematically investigated by Inhelder and Piaget (1964). A typical example of the task involves confronting a child with a collection of objects, say six primroses and six other flowers, and then asking, "Are there more primroses or more flowers?" The prominence accorded to class inclusion by Piaget (1952) indicates that it represents the quintessence of the stage of concrete operations. Furthermore, the empirical results obtained by presenting children with class inclusion tasks afford striking, but typical examples of complete changes in performance with development. Any suggested solution to the transition problem must account for such changes.

Theoretical Views

The position adopted by Piaget and Inhelder (1969) is still the dominant theoretical view of class inclusion:

> If, for example, in a group B of 12 flowers within which there is a subgroup A of six primroses, you ask the child to show first the flowers B and next the primroses A, he responds correctly, because he can designate the whole B and the part A. However, if you ask him, "Are there more flowers or more primroses?" he is unable to respond according to the inclusion $A < B$ because if he thinks of the part A, the whole B ceases to be conserved as a unit, and the part A is henceforth comparable only to its complementary A'. He may reply, therefore, "the same," or, if there are a clear majority of primroses in the set, he may say that there are more primroses. The understanding of the relative sizes of an included class to the entire class is achieved at about eight and marks the achievement of a genuine operatory classification [p. 103].

Thus, according to Piaget and Inhelder, failure on the CI task comes from the child's inability to think of the whole B while thinking of one of its parts A. It is only later that the child develops the requisite representations and processing capacity such that "the whole B continues to exist even while its components A and A' are separated in thought" (Inhelder & Piaget, 1964, pp. 103-104.)

Empirical Studies

While there has been little development on the theoretical plane, a considerable amount of empirical data on variants of the CI task have accumulated in the past decade, (e.g., Blair-Hood, 1962; Kohnstamm, 1963, 1967; Smedslund, 1964; Kofsky, 1966; Wohlwill, 1968; Ahr & Youniss, 1970). Although some investigators have chosen to use CI as a "standard" measure of cognitive development (e.g., Jennings, 1969; McGhee, 1971), this may be somewhat premature, for the results of these studies (as indicated later) exhibit the degree of variation and inconsistency that is characteristic of investigations of concrete operations. This has prompted attempts to produce both methodological refinements (Smedslund, 1964, 1966a,b), and theoretical revisions (Flavell & Wohlwill, 1969; Flavell, 1971; Wallace, 1971).

In this section, in addition to the Inhelder and Piaget study, we shall review four investigations of performance on the CI task. In one of them, the CI task appears in the context of a range of other tasks directed toward the study of the emergence of concrete operational skills (Smedslund, 1964). In the second, the CI task is the postulated terminus of a series of logically prior tasks (Kofsky, 1966). The other two are experimental studies of the CI task *per se,* and seek to determine the effect of specific procedural variations upon task performance at different ages (Wohlwill, 1968; Ahr & Youniss, 1970). None of these studies is longitudinal, although for any specific study the subjects are relatively homogenous, usually from the same school and socioeconomic class.

Summary descriptions of all the studies are presented in Table 8.1 and Figs. 8.1 to 8.4. Table 8.1 shows the major characteristics of the conditions under which the CI question was posed, and Figs. 8.1 to 8.4 show either the percentage of children in each age group passing the task or the mean percentage of correct answers in each age group. We present the relevant procedural variations and the results for each study below, and then in the following section we discuss the interpretations of these results.

1. Inhelder and Piaget*

Inhelder and Piaget presented the class inclusion question in the context of a full range of classification problems. These included: spontaneous classification; general questions on inclusion ("if you make a bouquet out of all the primroses will you use these [blue primroses]?"); and four questions bearing on the quantification of inclusion:

    (*i*) "Is the bunch made of all A bigger or smaller or the same as the bunch of all B?"
    (*ii*) "Are there more A or more B?"
    (*iii*) "If you take all the A's, will there be any B's?"
    (*iv*) "If you take all the B's, will there be any A's?"

*See Inhelder and Piaget (1964, pp. 101-116).

TABLE I

Summary of Class Inclusion Experiments

---

1. Inhelder and Piaget (1964) (IP1, IP2)
   a. Items: pictures of flowers mixed with pictures of other objects
   b. Distribution: 4 yellow primulas (A), 8 primulas (B), 16 flowers (C), 20 objects (D)
   c. Subclass ratios: IP1 A/A' = 4/4; IP2 B/B' = 8/8
   d. Question form: IP1 = "more B or more A?"; IP2: "more C or more B?"
   e. Mode: pictorial, some reference to external world (e.g., flowers in the woods)
   f. 50% age: IP1, 7 yrs-8 yrs; IP2, 7 yrs-8 yrs

2. Inhelder and Piaget (1964) (IP3, IP4)
   a. Items: pictures of animals partitioned by boxes
   b. Distribution: 3-4 ducks (A), 6-9 birds (B), 11-14 animals (C)
   c. Subclass ratios: IP3 A/A' = 3/3 to 4/5; IP4 B/B' = 3/5 to 5/5
   d. Question form: IP3: "more B or more A?"; IP4: "more C or more B?"
   e. Mode: pictorial, some *in extenso* references
   f. 50% age: IP3, 9 yrs; IP4, 8-9 yrs.

3. Smedslund (1964) (S)
   a. Items: Geometrical two dimensional objects (pieces of linoleum)
   b. Distribution: 10 red round pieces, 13 red pieces (B)
   c. Subclass ratios: A/A' = 10/3
   d. Question form: "more red ones or more round ones?"
   e. Mode: objects actually present, but covered immediately prior to question. Then uncovered and question repeated.
   f. 50% age: 6 yrs
   g. Subjects: 160, upper middle class, university town, public school, Boulder, Colorado

4. Kofsky (1966, 1963) (K)
   a. Items: small wooden blocks (2" × 2" × 1")
   b. Distribution: 3 red triangles, 2 blue triangles, 4 blue squares
   c. Subclass ratios: For K1 A/A' = 3/2; for K2 A/A' = 4/2
   d. Question form:
      K1 - "More triangles or more reds" or "More reds or more triangles"
      K2 - "More blues or more squares" or "More squares or more blues"
      K3 - "More blues or more triangles"
   e. Mode: objects actually present
   f. 50% age: 8-9 yrs (Scoring: correct only if K1 and K2 correct)
   g. Subjects: 122, above average intelligence, nursery and elementary school, Rochester, New York

5. Wohlwill (1968) (Experiment 3)
   a. Items: pictures of common items
   b. Distribution: 12 different collections, ranging from drums and guitars to ball players and cowboys. Three conditions:
      A. identity within and segregation between subsets
      B. similarity within and intermingling between subsets
      C. As in B, plus two extraneous objects
   c. Subclass ratios: from 6/2 to 5/3
   d. Question form: "more A or more B?" or "more B or more A?"
   e. Mode: pictorial mode: stimuli present
      Verbal mode: Entire set generated verbally, e.g., "Suppose I had six jackets and two hats, would I have more jackets or more things to wear?"

TABLE I *(Cont.)*
Summary of Class Inclusion Experiments

---

  f. 50% age: not reached in this group.

  g. Subjects: 54, lower middle class public school, Worcester, Massachusetts

6. Ahr and Youniss (1970) AY (Experiment 1)

  a. Items: paper cutouts of cats and dogs, and red flowers and yellow flowers

  b. Distribution: 8 objects, presented in horizontal row with subclasses integrated

  c. Subclass ratios: systematic experimental variation, from 8/0 (eight cats, no dogs) to 4/4 (four cats, four dogs)

  d. Question form: systematic experimental variation: "more A or more B?" or "fewer A or fewer B?"

  e. Mode: pictorial, objects always present, no *in extenso* references

  f. 50% age: 10 yrs

  g. Subjects: 60, grades 1,3,5 middle class parochial school, Washington, D.C.

The second of these four is what we are calling *the* CI task.

The collection of objects used (see Table 8.1) comprised four nested sets, $A < B < C < D$ and the results reported are for $A < B$ (labeled IP1) and $B < C$ (IP2). Although the referent for the questions was usually the particular set of objects placed before the child, there were occasionally broader references (e.g., In the woods are there more flowers or more primroses?).

Inhelder and Piaget repeated this procedure with pictures of animals instead of flowers (labeled IP3, IP4), reasoning that classes of animals are "more remote from everyday experience and therefore more abstract [than classes of flowers]." The implication is that the ability to manipulate more abstract classes lags behind the ability to manipulate concrete, familiar classes, because the child "is compelled to rely far more on purely linguistic concepts and he may need to structure and develop these in the course of the actual experiment." (pp. 110-111)

The results for the four task variants are shown in Figure 8.1. The task dealing with flowers (IP1, IP2) is obviously easier than the task dealing with animals (IP3, IP4). Furthermore, the questions referring to the smallest class and its immediate superordinate class ("more B or more A?", IP1, IP3) are generally more difficult than the questions about the second smallest subclass and the class immediately above it, ("more C or more B?" IP2, IP4).

2. Smedslund (1964)

Smedslund devised an extremely careful procedure for establishing a context in which to pose the class inclusion question. He started out with 13 red pieces of linoleum of which 10 were round and three were square, and six white pieces of which three were round and three were square, distributed irregularly over a small black square supporting background. The child was first given a set of nine preparatory questions and corrected after each error until the correction

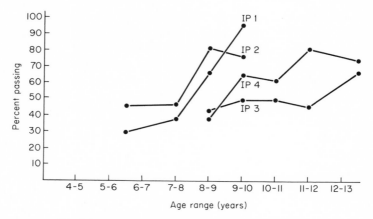

Fig. 8.1. Inhelder and Piaget results on class inclusion.

was remembered, then he was given the class inclusion question. The sequence of questions and experimenter operations were:

a. Experimenter points at a red round piece:
    1. "What color is this?"
    2. "What shape does it have?"

b. Experimenter points at a white square piece:
    3. "What color is this?"
    4. "What shape does it have?"
    5. "Can you place all the white ones over here?"

c. Experimenter removes all the white pieces and points at the remaining red ones:
    6. "Are all these red?"
    7. "Are there more round ones or more square ones here?"

d. Experimenter covers the objects so that the subject cannot see them, and he points to the cover:
    8. "Are all the pieces under here red?"
    9. "Are there more round ones or more square ones?"

e. Now *with the objects still hidden from view,* the experimenter poses the class inclusion question.
    10. "Are there more *red* ones or more *round* ones?"
    11. "How do you know that?"

f. Finally the objects are uncovered by the experimenter:
    12. "Now, look at them. Are there more *red* ones or more *round* ones?"
    13. "How do you know that?" (Omitted when responses to 10, 11, and 12 were correct.)

As a second subitem, the procedure was repeated with a similar set of materials and questions in which red and white were exchanged and round and square were exchanged in the materials and questions listed previously.

The procedure meets Smedslund's criteria for testing concrete reasoning (or inference). He defines an inference as being concrete if and only if:

> It involves symbolic processes, i.e., processes which *represent events*; and the events represented by the initial states have been *perceived* by the subject; and the structure of the inference is isomorphic with a *logical structure* (p. 3).

Thus, the CI task, (as well as the others reported in Smedslund's monograph) has the following characteristics:

> The initial events are perceived by the subject and are then removed. The initial events have one necessary conclusion. If the subject arrives at this conclusion, he is, in this situation, capable of concrete reasoning. If he does not arrive at this conclusion, he is, in this situation, not capable of concrete reasoning (p. 4).

Figure 8.2 shows the percentage of children in each age range who gave a correct response to question 10 mentioned previously (Class Inclusion, objects covered) on either or both of the subitems. Smedslund notes that adequate or inadequate explanations (questions 11 and 13) almost always accompany correct or incorrect answers to 10 and 12 respectively. The effect of covered versus uncovered objects is almost nil except for the youngest children (age 4:3 to 6:2) of whom almost 15% failed when the objects were visible (uncovered) and passed when they were not.

The Smedslund results seem to indicate a rapid onset of the ability to pass the CI task: from total failure before age five to almost total mastery after age seven.

3. Kofsky (1963, 1966)

Kofsky translated Inhelder and Piaget's (1964) account of the development of CI into a series of 11 partially ordered steps. Each of these steps was further translated into a task that was designed to diagnose the stage of the child in his development toward an understanding of class inclusion. The last task in the postulated developmental sequence is, of course, the CI task itself. The objects were small wooden blocks: three red triangles, two blue triangles, and four blue squares. Three questions (with associated commands) were asked, in random order:

a. "Are there more blues or squares? Count the blues. Count the squares."
b. "Are there more reds or triangles? Count the reds, count the triangles."
c. "Are there more triangles or blues? Count the blues. Count the triangles."

Notice that in Question a the superordinate class is blue, with subclasses

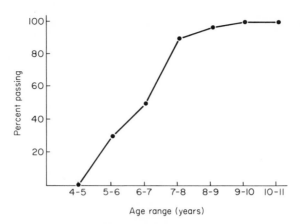

Fig. 8.2. Smedslund results on class inclusion.

defined by shape, while in Question b the superordinate class is triangle, with subclasses defined by color. For Question c, the relevant sets intersect, and no inclusion relation exists. A child was scored as passing CI if his responses to both Questions a and b were correct. The results are shown in Fig. 8.3.

4. Wohlwill (1968)

Wohlwill presented the CI task in two forms, pictorial and verbal. In the pictorial form pictures of common objects, such as hats, children, dogs, etc., were presented to the subjects and the standard CI question was posed. Three conditions of subset homogeneity were used (see Table 8.1). In the verbal presentation, the only stimulus was the verbally posed question, e.g., "Suppose I had six jackets and two hats, would I have more jackets or more things to wear?" The same subset variations were used in the verbal condition as in the pictorial condition. In three of the four reported studies, Wohlwill found a significant verbal facilitation effect.

5. Ahr & Youniss (1970)

Ahr & Youniss used paper cutouts of cats and dogs and red and yellow flowers, in an attempt to isolate factors that lead to class inclusion failures. They also varied the ratio between the subclasses (e.g., from four dogs and four cats to eight dogs and no cats) and the relational term used in the CI question (more A or more B, versus fewer A or fewer B). They found that only the subclass ratio had any strong effect (see Fig. 8.4). The greater the imbalance between subclasses, the more frequent the errors, but this tendency almost disappeared by age 10.

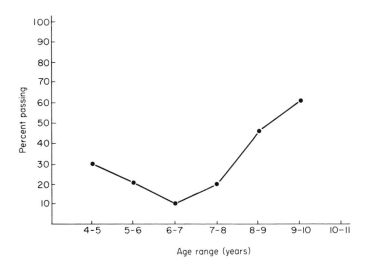

Fig. 8.3. Kofsky results on class inclusion.

Causes of Failure

The explanations offered for failure on the CI task can be broadly divided into two categories: processing failures and encoding failures. The former arise when the child is unable to make the appropriate subclass comparison; the latter result from a misinterpretation of the CI instructions.

As indicated earlier, Inhelder and Piaget suggest a processing failure.

> When answering "Are there more of the As or of the Bs?" he cannot compare the As with the Bs, and he compares them with the A's, precisely because he cannot handle class-inclusion. . . . He cannot think simultaneously of the part and the whole. . . [1964, p. 101].

The explanation offered by both Wohlwill (1968) and Ahr and Youniss (1970) is based upon a misinterpretation hypothesis. Wohlwill (1968) summarizes his findings thus:

> . . . the perception of two contrasting subclasses, unbalanced as to number, creates a strong tendency to translate a class inclusion question into a subclass comparison question. This tendency can be counteracted to some extent by procedures designed to weaken the set (counting the subclass and the superordinate class. . . , including extraneous objects. . .). It is presumably at its weakest when the items are presented in purely verbal form. . .[p. 462].

As already indicated, the experiments by Ahr and Youniss demonstrate that the greater the numerical imbalance between subclasses, the greater was the tendency to make the erroneous subclass comparison.

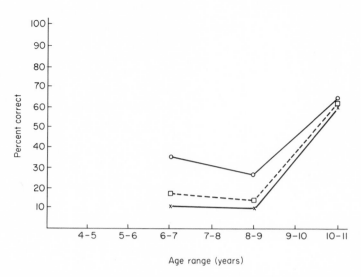

Fig. 8.4. Ahr and Youniss results on class inclusion. Circles indicate subclass ratio (A/A′) = 4:1; squares indicate average for all conditions: crosses indicate subclass ratio (A/A′) = 7:1.

It is not clear what the connection is between any of these reasons for failure and the effects of procedural variations. Procedural variations can be classified as changes in either the verbal instructions or in the physical stimuli. The verbal instructions can be varied in many ways to facilitate the appropriate comparison. Wohlwill notes that "even to an adult there appears something slightly tricky about such questions as 'Are there more pears or more fruit?' " Indeed we have discovered that normal adult subjects often give the wrong answer when the question is posed suddenly. The difficulty seems to follow from two interpretive steps: (a) The *or* is applied not to the two relational statements implied, "[more pears (than fruit)] or [more fruit (than pears)]?", but instead to the two classes: "[pears] or [fruit]?". (b) The *or* is interpreted exclusively rather than inclusively because that is its overwhelmingly more common usage.

It is easy for one familiar with the CI task to forget the initial confusing impact of the conjunction of these two interpretations. In a different form, the power of the exclusive interpretation of *or* becomes apparent (e.g., "Are there pears or fruit on the table?"), and the tricky nature of the CI question can easily take on a subtle pejorative tone (e.g., "In the APA are there more psychologists or more clinicians?"; "In the department are there more people or more students?").

Several variations in the wording of the question are apparent: "More A or more B?; more A than B or more B than A?; which is more, A or B?;" substituting *less* for *more*; etc. Similarly, one can imagine many stimulus

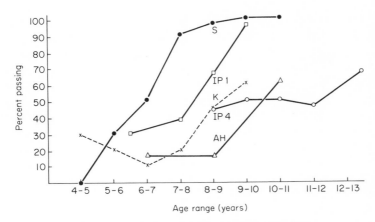

Fig. 8.5. Results of four studies of class inclusion.

variations, some of which have already been found to be influential: familiarity of objects or class name, subclass ratios, number of objects, similarity of objects, objects present, objects present but out of view, objects absent but enumerated, objects absent and *in extenso,* etc. The problem that one faces in generating these variations is that their effects must ultimately be interpreted, but the interpretation cannot be made upon the basis of any existing theory. Current theories are stated at a level of generality that makes it almost impossible to make specific predictions about the effects of the procedural variations listed previously.

The significant effect of different combinations of these variations is clear. Fig. 8.5, a composite of Figs. 8.1 to 8.4, shows the extremely wide range of performance on the CI task that is generated by the studies reviewed earlier. Consider, for example, Smedslund's study. His results indicate children reach the 50% mark on CI almost three years before the age reported by Kofsky and almost four years before Ahr and Youniss, and yet *a priori* his procedure would seem to be harder than the others because he used geometrical forms rather than objects having a natural semantic hierarchy (e.g., people and men), and his objects were not visible at the time the CI question was posed. We say "seem to be harder" because until we have a detailed model of the class inclusion process, we must rely upon our intuition for predictions about the effect of procedural variation.

AN INFORMATION PROCESSING APPROACH

Before proceeding to our methodological proposals, it seems appropriate to present a summary statement of the current state of research on class inclusion as we see it. On the one hand, we have Inhelder and Piaget's theoretical account and, on the other, the complex set of results obtained from the experimental studies. A gap exists between the hypothetical structures and processes which form the basis of the theory and the level of performance as represented by the experimental data. This arises from the fact that the theoretical account is presented at a level of generality which makes it uncertain as to whether it is sufficient to account for the complex and varied behavior which it purports to explain. Indeed, there is no way at all of determining what would be its consequences on the level of performance. A much more detailed account of the functioning of specific processes is necessary before these uncertainties can be dispelled.

The existence of a gap between the levels of theory and performance is not confined to the work of Piaget and his collaborators. The confines of the present paper will not permit an extended discussion of this point, but the same uncertainty regarding consequences in performance terms and sufficiency to account for behavior surrounds theories emanating from neobehaviorist sources such as Berlyne's (1965) account of directed thinking.

It is our contention that the information processing approach which follows provides a methodology which bridges the gap between theory and performance. During the last decade, information processing analysis has gained wide currency as a method of approach to the study of cognition. This approach assumes that for a broad range of cognitive activity, humans are representable as information processing systems. There are a few gross characteristics of the system (e.g., information transfer rates, size of immediate memory, seriality) that are sufficient to cause problem solving to take place in what Newell and Simon (1971) call a *problem space*. The problem space is a collection of symbolic representations and operations that are determined by the task environment and the problem space in turn determines the programs that can actually be used.

The most specific theory of human problem solving (Newell & Simon, 1972) deals entirely with adult subjects. Although the relevance of information processing models to theory construction in the developmental area has begun to be recognized (Lunzer, 1969; Biggs, 1969; Flavell & Wohlwill, 1969), most of these uses of the information processing approach in cognitive development have been at the metaphorical level. For example, Flavell & Wohlwill (1969) make the general statement that "intellectual development is essentially a matter of ontogenetic change in the content and organization of highly intricate 'programs' ... " When employed in this fashion, information processing analysis constitutes simply a different, rather than an improved, approach to the study of cognitive development. Theoretical statements employing only the metaphorical level of information processing analysis suffer from the same deficiencies as those already imputed to the theories of Piaget and Berlyne. It has been clearly demonstrated by Newell and Simon (1972), however, that the information processing approach can go far beyond the metaphorical level. When information processing analysis is combined with computer simulation, the result is a theorizing medium which provides both ease of detection of mutual contradictions and ambiguity, and an explicit method for examining the exact behavioral consequences of theoretical statements. These are precisely the attributes which the major theories of cognitive development lack.

Application of the information processing approach to the problems posed by cognitive development was advocated by Simon (1962), but up to the present, only a few studies of this type have been carried out (Gascon, 1969; Klahr & Wallace, 1970 a, b; Young, 1971). In an earlier paper, (Klahr & Wallace, 1970 b) we attempted to demonstrate that a set of tasks typically used to assess the stage of concrete operations calls upon a collection of fundamental processes that, when appropriately organized for each task, are sufficient to solve the problem posed. Our initial view of the information processing model of the child's performance on a typical Piagetian task was as follows:

> We believe that the major task facing the child who has just been presented with an experimental task is to assemble, from his repertoire of fundamental information handling processes, a routine that is sufficient to pass the task at hand. We view the information processing demands of the tasks as being analogous to the compilation and execution of a computer program. [See Figure 8.6]. Incoming visual and verbal stimuli are first encoded into internal representations. Then the assembly system attempts to construct, from its repertoire of fundamental processes, a task-specific routine that is sufficient to meet the demands of the verbal instructions. Having assembled such a routine, the system then executes it.

Detailed descriptions of three parts of the model were presented: the internal representation of objects, a collection of fundamental processes and a set of task-specific routines. We will briefly describe these elements below.

Representation

We propose an extremely simple representation, one that has long been used in a wide variety of information processing models of cognitive activity. The objects in the set of stimuli are represented as simple lists of values; the set itself is a list of objects; and the set also has attached to it a list that contains values appearing in the set, plus additional information about the set *qua* set, i.e., the *extensive* properties of the set; for example, quantitative symbols representing the relative amounts of different values. A representation for Smedslund's initial CI configuration is illustrated in Figure 8.7. In this example, the objects are represented by an arbitrarily ordered list of symbols, OB1, OB2, etc. Each object is described by a list of two values (color and shape) and the extensive list contains the values that appear in the collection, plus two quantitative symbols.

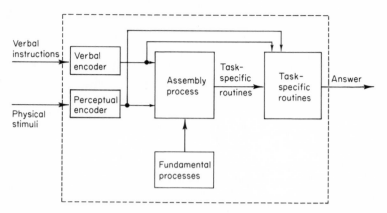

Fig. 8.6. Information processing model of task performance.

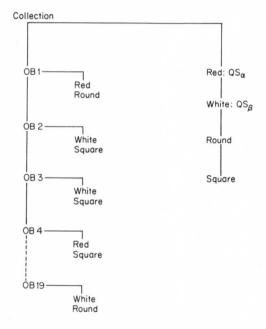

Fig. 8.7. A representation for Smedslund's initial CI configuration.

These symbols (QS_{RED} and QS_{WHITE})can be compared in magnitude by appropriate operations; this particular example illustrates a situation where both the value and amount of each color is available at the extensive level, while the extensive information about shapes concerns only the values.

As it exists, this specific example contains no spatial information. This rests on the explicit assumption that spatial arrangement is not important in the CI task, counter to the assumption implicit in the care with which the subject is usually presented with a mixed collection of objects. For modeling those studies where spatial arrangement is controlled, (e.g., Wohlwill, 1968) the representation presented here could be easily extended to include spatial information. (In fact, Wohlwill's results indicated that spatial arrangement had no significant effect on CI performance.)

Fundamental Processes

We postulate the existence of a collection of fundamental information processes that constitute the building blocks for the assembler in Figure 8.6 when it attempts to construct a task-specific routine. Several features of these processes, such as their error prone nature and their use of a simple motivational mechanism, are described fully in our original presentation (Klahr & Wallace, 1970 b). In this paper, we shall describe only a few features of a subset of the processes in order to give an example of what we call the *subroutine approach* to information processing models. This approach will be discussed subsequently and an alternate representation for information processing will be introduced.

The fundamental processes are described below in terms of a general form, a specific example, and a brief explanation.

1. $IS(\alpha, \beta) \rightarrow$ truth value. Ex. $IS(OB1, RED) \rightarrow$ TRUE. This process provides an answer to the question "Does object α have value β? It takes as input an object name and a value; it produces as output a truth value (i.e., "true" or "false") contingent upon the existence of the value on the list of values of the named object.

2. $NOTICE(\alpha) \rightarrow$ value. Ex. $NOTICE(OB1) \rightarrow$ TRIANGLE. This process provides a response to the command, "Name a value that object α possesses." It takes as input an object name and outputs some value possessed by that object. This usually involves selecting one of several potential outputs. The procedure for deciding which value is to be chosen is, at present, based on a simple, nonrandom rule for dealing with such choices among alternatives. This is based on an ordered list representing the relative saliency of values as a result of the child's experience to date. The item currently occupying top place in the list is selected.

In addition to selelcting values possessed by single objects, NOTICE can also operate on an array, collection, or set of objects (i.e., a list of objects). The output consists of a single object selected from the set.

3. $VALOF(\alpha \ \beta) \rightarrow$ value/nil. Ex. $VALOF(OB1, COLOR) \rightarrow$ RED. This process answers the question, "What is the value of attribute β for object α?" It finds the value of the input attribute on the input object. If a value of the attribute does not exist for that object, the output is nil.

The primary processes IS, NOTICE, and VALOF deal directly with the internal representations of the task situations, and, consequently, any change in the form of the representations would necessitate a change in these processes. None of the other processes deal directly with the task representations since they can obtain the necessary information through IS, NOTICE, and VALOF. These processes can be nested to represent a complex question. For example, the question, "Is Object 2 the same color as Object 3?" can be represented as IS[OBJECT 2, VALOF (OBJECT 3, COLOR)].

4. ATTOF(α)→ attribute. Ex. ATTOF(BLUE)→ COLOR. Given a value as input, ATTOF outputs the attribute which can assume that value. It answers the question, "What is the attribute for which α is a value?" This process makes use of lists each of which corresponds to an attribute and carries its values. These lists are regarded as being part of the child's structured experience.

5. FINDONE(set,α) → object/nil. "Find an object in the set with value α." Example: FINDONE(set,RED) → OB1. This process uses some of the other fundamental processes as its own components. First, it NOTICEs an object in the set, then it tests IS(OBx,RED). If it is, then FINDONE outputs the object name; if it is not, FINDONE either does another NOTICE or, depending upon the value of some motivational parameters not described here, it gives up.

6. FINDALL(set,α) → list of objects. "Find all the objects in the set with value α." This process operates by repeatedly executing FINDONE until either FINDONE returns a *nil* result, or FINDALL gives up.

Task Specific Routines

Such fundamental processes can be used as the components of a wide range of task specific classification routines. Consider for example, Kofsky's Exhaustive Sort task:

> A collection of blocks. . . . was shown to S. He was to choose a block and put it in a box along with all the others that were 'like it.' After the first box was filled, the procedure was repeated with the remaining blocks until all the blocks had been chosen.
>
> In an exhaustive sort, Ss consistently used an attribute to select the contents of each box and filled the box with all the blocks that possessed the criterial attribute (Kofsky, 1966, p. 195).

A task specific routine sufficient for success on exhaustive sorting can be assembled from the fundamental processes described above. The routine, written as a subroutine, works as follows:

1. Select a block from the collection and place it in the box (NOTICE).
   1.1 Select a value of the block (NOTICE).
2. Find all the blocks remaining in the collection that have the value selected in step 1.1. Place them in the box (FINDALL).

3. Determine the attribute of the value selected in step 1.1 (ATTOF).
4. Select a block from the remaining collection and place it in an empty box (NOTICE).
   4.1 If none are left, exit; output is content of boxes.
   4.2 If a block is found, go to step 5.
5. Find the value of the block just selected on the attribute determined in step 3 (VALOF).
6. Find all the blocks remaining in the collection that have the value determined in step 5 (FINDALL).
7. Go to step 4.

The actual routine for exhaustive sorting is shown in Figure 8.8 as a series of instructions in a computer programming language (POP-2, Burstall, Collins & Popplestone, 1968). The subroutine, EC calls upon several other subroutines that are programmed implementations of the fundamental processes described earlier.

Although the use of fundamental processes provides a convenient and explicit language for describing some of the detailed processing requirements of the tasks, in their current form they present certain technical and methodological difficulties. The closed subroutine representation has some severe shortcomings as a means for modeling cognitive development. First, there is an overly restrictive distinction between control and computation, a distinction that seems to have no psychological basis. Secondly, there is no straightforward manner in which relatively local and minor changes in the system can produce apparently qualitative improvements in performance. A third problem with the subroutine approach as we have used it is that the task specific routines must be assembled from the fundamental processes by an assembler of considerable power and scope. We have not yet found a reasonable model for such an assembler, and have instead sought a process representation that obviated the need for one.

PRODUCTION SYSTEMS
FOR DEVELOPMENTAL STAGES

In the past few years, a new form for describing information processing models of cognition has been proposed and successfully applied to a modest range of problem-solving activities (Newell, 1966; Newell & Simon, 1971). The models are posed in the form of a collection of independent rules, called productions, that together form a *production system* (PS). The rules are stated in the form of a condition and an action: $C \rightarrow A$. The condition refers to a combination of goals and knowledge elements that exist in the *knowledge state* of the PS, and the action consists of transformations on the knowledge state, including the generation, interruption and satisfaction of goals.

```
function EC set ⇒ olst; vars obx valx attl;
NOTICE (set) → obx; PLACE (obx, olst);
NOTICE (obx) → valx;
FINDALL (valx, set) → olst
ATTOF (valx) → attl;
loop: NOTICE (set) → obx; PLACE (obx, olst);
if obx = nil then exit;
VALOF (obx, attl) → valx;
FINDALL (valx, set) → olst;
goto loop end;
```

Fig. 8.8. Task specific routine for exhaustive sorting.

The PS operates under extremely simple rules. Interpretation always begins at the top of the PS (the first production), and the condition of each production is tested until one is satisfied. When a condition is satisfied, the associated action is taken, thus altering the knowledge state. Then the PS is re-entered at the beginning.

Thus far, PSs have proven most suitable for formulating models of sequentially linked behavior with many observable intermediate stages, e.g., verbal protocols of subjects analyzing chess positions (Newell & Simon, 1972). In this section, we shall attempt to extend the PS formulation into a domain in which there is little directly observable behavior between input and output, because we believe that this mode of model representation overcomes the shortcomings of the closed subroutine approach cited earlier.

There are two general variants of the CI task: those that deal only with *formal* class inclusion and those that mix formal inclusion with *semantic* inclusion. For example, in the Smedslund and Kofsky tasks, the inclusion relation derives not from any semantic properties of colors or shapes, but rather from the formal properties of the specific collection of objects. In those experiments using birds and animals, or daddies and men, the inclusion relation derives from both the formal properties of the collection and the semantic structure. Of course, whenever real objects are used (e.g., birds, dogs, daddies, etc.) it is impossible to isolate the effect of the semantic structure from the formal structure of the stimuli. For this reason, we believe that those CI tasks that use meaningless (in sense of having no semantic hierarchy) objects, such as Smedslund's (1964) and Kofsky's (1966) investigations, best test the formal ability to deal with class inclusion, independently of ability to deal with semantic hierarchies. Process models for performance on questions about semantic hierarchies have been proposed by Collins and Quillian (1972) and Meyer (1970), whereas the model we propose below deals only with formal class inclusion.

A Production System for "More"

The CI task is always posed in terms of a relation such as *more,* and thus our model for CI performance is imbedded in the context of the information processing generated by questions containing *more.* Our position is that the semantic basis of the term *more* is a production system. This production system, PS:MORE is illustrated in Figure 8.9 as a series of ordered production rules. We shall describe: the notation used in Figure 8.9; the general operation of the production system; a detailed explanation of each production rule; a trace of the system working on a specific problem; and finally, a summary of the logical basis of PS: MORE.

The production system is an ordered series of production rules, each rule consisting of a condition and an action, i.e., $C \rightarrow A$. The conditions and the actions refer to a knowledge state which can contain goals, values, quantitative symbols, operators, and verbal response symbols. Goals can be active, interrupted, or satisfied. The system obeys simple operating rules.

1. Initially, and after every action, the productions are considered in sequence, starting with the first (PA).
2. Each condition is compared with the contents of the knowledge state. If and only if *all* of the elements in a condition can be matched with elements (in any order) in the knowledge state, and tests on those elements are satisfied, then the condition is satisfied.
3. If a condition is not satisfied, the next production rule in the ordered list of production rules is considered.
4. If a condition is satsified, the actions to the right of the arrow are taken.
5. Actions can change the state of goals, replace elements, apply operators, or add elements to the knowledge state.
6. The knowledge state is a stack in which a new element appears at the top (at the left in Figure 8.10) pushing all else in the stack down one position.

The 11 numbered production rules in Figure 8.9 are specific to PS: MORE; in addition, we have three "housekeeping" productions (PA,PY,PZ). These three control the interruption, deletion, and reactivation of goals, and are thus of great generality beyond the scope of PS: MORE. They could have been eliminated from the system and included instead in the rules listed up to now. (E.g., "Rule 7: when two goals are simultaneously active, make the older one interrupted" could replace PA). We have included them here to demonstrate the facility with which one can specify many of the housekeeping functions of a PS in terms of production rules within that same system. The descriptions of the 14 production rules are:

PS: MORE

PA: $[\alpha]^+, [\beta]^+ \Rightarrow [\beta]^+ \leftarrow [\beta]$ %
P1: $[more] \uparrow, <X> \Rightarrow <X> \leftarrow$ "X"
P2: $[more] \uparrow, <=> \Rightarrow <=> \leftarrow$ "same"
P3:   more $\Rightarrow$ more $\leftarrow [more]^+$
P4: $[more]^+$ $\Rightarrow [compare]^+$
P5: $[compare] \uparrow, [more]$ % $\Rightarrow [more]$ % $\leftarrow [more] \uparrow$
P6: $[compare]^+, QS_x > QS_y \Rightarrow <X>, [compare]^+ \leftarrow [compare] \uparrow$
P7: $[compare]^+, QS_x < QS_y \Rightarrow <Y>, [compare]^+ \leftarrow [compare] \uparrow$
P8: $[compare]^+, QS_x, QS_y \Rightarrow <=>, [compare]^+ \leftarrow [compare] \uparrow$
P9: $[compare]^+, <X> \Rightarrow <X> \leftarrow [Quantify (<X>)]^+$
P10: $[Quantify (<X>)]^+, QS_x \Rightarrow [Quantify (<X>)]^+ \leftarrow [Quantify (<X>)] \uparrow$
P11: $[Quantify (<X>)]^+ \Rightarrow QS_x \leftarrow \leftarrow Q_n$
PY: $[\alpha] \uparrow \Rightarrow [\alpha] \uparrow \leftarrow$
PZ: $[\alpha]$ % $\Rightarrow [\alpha]$ % $\leftarrow [\alpha]^+$

NOTATION

$[\square]^+$	Active goal
$[\square]$ %	Interrupted goal
$[\square] \uparrow$	Satisfied goal
$<\square>$	Value
QS	Quantitative symbol
$a \leftarrow b$	Replace element *a* with element *b* in knowledge state
$a \leftarrow \leftarrow 0$	Apply operator 0 and add result *a* to knowledge state
"____"	Verbal response symbol

Fig. 8.9. Production system: MORE

PA: *If* there are two active goals in the knowledge state, *then* change the state of the older of the two from active to interrupted.

P1: *If* the goal [more] is satisfied *and* a value exists, *then* replace the value with a symbol for the verbal response of the value. (We assume that when such verbal response symbols exist they trigger an overt response, although we do not include any explicit mechanism for this.)

P2: *If* the goal [more] is satisfied *and* a symbol for equality exists, *then* replace the symbol with a symbol for a verbal response of "same."

P3: *If* the internal symbol for more exists, *then* replace it with the active goal [more].

P4: *If* the goal [more] is active, *then* add the active goal [compare] to the knowledge state.

P5: *If* the goal [compare] is satisfied *and* the goal [more] is interrupted, *then* change the goal [more] to satisfied.

P6: *If* the goal [compare] is active *and* two quantitative symbols exist *and* the first is greater than the second, *then* add the value name of the first to the knowledge state, *and* change the goal [compare] to satisfied.

P7: *If* the goal [compare] is active *and* two quantitative symbols exist *and* the first is less than the second, *then* add the value name of the second to the knowledge state, *and* change the goal [compare] to satisfied.

P8: *If* the goal [compare] is active *and* two quantitative symbols exist, *then* add a symbol for equality to the knowledge state *and* change the goal [compare] to satisfied.

P9: *If* the goal [compare] is active *and* a value name x exists, *then* add the active goal [quantify (x)] to the knowledge state.

P10: *If* the goal [quantify (x)] is active *and* a quantitative symbol for x exists, *then* change the goal [quantify (x)] from active to satisfied.

P11: *If* the goal [quantify (x)] is active, *then* apply a quantification operator to the internal representation for the set and add its result, quantitative symbol x, to the knowledge state. (*Which* quantification operator to apply is not specified in PS: MORE. We shall discuss this in the next section.)

PY: *If* there is a satisfied goal, *then* replace it with nothing; i.e., remove it from the knowledge state.

PZ: *If* there is an interrupted goal, *then* make it active.

Now let us trace out the sequence of actions for a specific input to the system. Assume that the question is not CI, but instead a subclass comparison question: "More red or more blue?" Assume also that there are, in fact, more blue things than red things in the display. The input to PS: MORE would be the output of a verbal encoder that produced symbols in the knowledge state for *more, red* and *blue.* This initial input is shown in line 1 of Figure 8.10. PS: MORE is entered with this initial knowledge state, and the conditions for PA, P1 and P2 are not satisfied. The condition of P3 is satisfied, and the symbol for *more* is replaced by the active goal [more]. The knowledge state at this point contains the active goal [more], *red* and *blue* (line 2). The PS is now re-entered at the top, and this time P4 is the first production rule to have its condition satisfied, thus generating the active goal [compare]. Note that (line 3) this new goal is placed before the active goal [more].

The PS is re-entered, and PA changes [more] from active to interrupted (line 4). The knowledge state now contains an active [compare], an interrupted [more] and two values. The first condition that finds a match in this knowledge state is P9, which matches the active [compare] and the value *red.* The action

Line	Production	Knowledge state after production is evoked				
1		more	red	blue		
2	P3	[M]$^+$	red	blue		
3	P4	[C]$^+$	[M]$^+$	red	blue	
4	PA	[C]$^+$	[M]%	red	blue	
5	P9	[Q(red)]$^+$	[C]$^+$	[M]%	blue	
6	PA	[Q(red)]$^+$	[C]%	[M]%	blue	
7	P11	QS_{red}	[Q(red)]$^+$	[C]%	[M]%	blue
8	P10	QS_{red}	[Q(red)]↑	[C]%	[M]%	blue
9	PY	QS_{red}	[C]%	[M]%	blue	
10	PZ	QS_{red}	[C]$^+$	[M]%	blue	
11	P9	[Q(blue)]$^+$	QS_{red}	[C]$^+$	[M]%	
12	PA	[Q(blue)]$^+$	QS_{red}	[C]%	[M]%	
13	P11	QS_{blue}	[Q(blue)]$^+$	QS_{red}	[C]%	[M]%
14	P10	QS_{blue}	[Q(blue)]↑	QS_{red}	[C]%	[M]%
15	PY	QS_{blue}	QS_{red}	[C]%	[M]%	
16	PZ	QS_{blue}	QS_{red}	[C]$^+$	[M]%	
17	P6	blue	QS_{blue}	QS_{red}	[C]↑	[M]%
18	P5	blue	QS_{blue}	QS_{red}	[C]↑	[M]↑
19	P1	"blue"	QS_{blue}	QS_{red}	[C]↑	[M]↑
20	PY	"blue"	QS_{blue}	QS_{red}	[M]↑	
21	PY	"blue"	QS_{blue}	QS_{red}		

Fig. 8.10. Trace of PS: MORE after the question: "More red or more blue?"

part of P9 replaces the value *red* with a new active goal of [Quantify *(red)*]. Like all new goals, it is placed at the beginning of the list of elements in the knowledge state (line 5). Next, PA detects two active goals and interrupts one of them. Then P11, detecting an active quantification goal, executes a quantify operator and adds a quantitative symbol for red to the knowledge state (line 7). P10's conditions for an active goal [quantify *(red)*] *and* a quantitative symbol for red are met and the goal [quantify *(red)*] is satisfied (line 8), and removed by PY (line 9).

At this point, the fact that all the goals in the knowledge state are interrupted is detected by PZ, which reactivates [compare]. A sequence of operations similar to lines 5 thru 9 is initiated: P9, PA, P11, P10, PY (lines 11 thru 15), leaving two quantitative symbols and two interrupted goals in the knowledge state. PZ then reactivates the goal [compare]. Now the knowledge state contains the requisite information to match the symbols in the conditions of P6, P7, and P8, but the conditions have the additional constraint that a given relation between the quantitative symbols must exist. Thus only one of the three productions can have its condition completely satisfied. In our example, it is P6, and the value *blue* is added to the knowledge state and [compare] is satisfied (line 17).

The combination of satisfied [compare] and interrupted [more] causes P5 to satisfy [more] (line 18) and this in turn causes P1 to produce the symbol for a verbal response of "blue" (line 19). The system then ticks over two more times, removing the satisfied goals and ending with a knowledge state as shown in line 21. At this point, there are no conditions in PS: MORE which are satisfied, and the system stops.

PS: MORE is a formal representation for the following casual analysis of the processing necessary to answer questions of the form: "more *x* or more *y*?" If the system wants to determine whether *x* is more than *y*, it must compare them quantitatively. In order to make a quantitative comparison, two quantitative symbols—one for each value—must be used. If a quantitative symbol is required, then some quantification must take place. Lines 1 to 15 in Figure 8.10 correspond to the execution of this sequence of events. Then with two quantitative symbols available, the system can make a comparison; having made the comparison it knows which of the two values is more, and it reports its result (Figure 8.10, Lines 16-21).

Quantification Operators

PS: MORE provides a context in which the quantification operator is applied. Recall that P11 says that if the goal is quantification of value *x*, then apply some (unspecified) quantification operator and produce a quantitative symbol for value *x*. We postulate two general modes of quantification with two variants of each mode (see Figure 8.11). One mode (Q1,Q2) consists of a sequential progression of noticing the objects on a list, incrementing a quantitative symbol, and marking the objects as they are processed to avoid double processing. The other mode (Q3,Q4) consists of the decomposition of a list into sublists by sequentially noticing objects and moving them from one list to a new list. Within modes, the differences are essentially between destructive and nondestructive processing. Q2 differs from Q1 in that it removes marks from objects (wipe), thus making them available for later recounting. Q4 differs from Q3 in that it makes a copy of the list before decomposing it into two sublists.

Both Q1 and Q3 are adequate for use in a MORE task involving disjoint subsets (e.g., "More red or more blue") but they are inadequate for the CI task, because they make it impossible for the second application of the quantification operator to deal with an intact list. That is, the requisite double processing of objects that are, for example, both pears and fruit, will fail if Q1 or Q3 is used.

Notice that Q4 first creates a copy of the set, then decomposes that copy into the required subsets. Thus at one point in the execution of PS: MORE using Q4, there exists simultaneously the superset *B* and the subsets *A* and *A'*. This is an explicit representation of the Genevan specification for success on CI. If we view

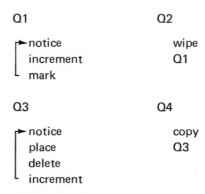

Fig. 8.11. Four modes of quantification.

the copy operation as the null transformation on a set, we can see its relevance to a wider range of concrete operational tasks. For example, in the development of reversible operations, the child must presumably be able to create copies of symbol structures about to be manipulated, or else he could never recognize when he had returned to the initial state.

Counting

We can relate the quantification operators to counting instructions by postulating a simple PS for counting (PS: COUNT). This PS, illustrated in Figure 8.12 consists of only two production rules. P12 transforms the internal symbol for "count" created by the verbal encoder into an active goal of counting. P13 tests for an active count goal and a value; if it finds both, it executes a chain of actions: wipe, application of Q1, elimination of the count goal and replacement of the value with a quantitative symbol for that value.

Children in the age range we are considering find no difficulty in repeatedly counting differently defined subsets from the same set of objects if they are given an explicit count instruction and a value before each count (e.g., "count the reds"; "count the squares"; "count the large ones"; etc.). The chain of actions in P13 represents the execution of a sequence that is not conditional upon anything in the knowledge state other than the initial condition.

Interpretation of CI Procedural Variations

The PS presented here (PS: MORE) works upon internal representations of the features of its environment; thus its performance depends critically upon the features of the external environment which become internalized, i.e., the problem space. Although we do not offer a model of either verbal or perceptual encoders, we have already suggested a possible internal representation for the physical stimuli, and in this section we shall attempt to interpret procedural

PS: COUNT

P12: count $\Rightarrow$ count $\leftarrow$ [count]$^+$
P13: [count]$^+$, $<X> \Rightarrow$ wipe, $<X> \leftarrow QS_x \leftarrow \leftarrow Q_1$, [count]$^+$ $\leftarrow$

Fig. 8.12. A production system for counting.

variations in CI in terms of different problem spaces that are available to PS: MORE.

First, let us consider two kinds of quantification of a collection of objects. The intensive properties of the set are carried in the complete description of individual objects, while the extensive properties are carried in the auxiliary list that describes aggregate set properties (see Figure 8.7). Quantification can be carried out at the intensive level by processing the individual elements of the set. Extensive quantification can be carried out by simply accessing, at the set level, the results of either prior intensive quantification, or prior direct input of extensive information about the set. When such information exists, there is no need for any of the Q's to be applied. This is represented in PS: MORE by P10 which says that if the goal is quantification of a value and a quantitative symbol for that value exists, then the quantification goal is satisfied.

For example, although Wohlwill interprets his verbal facilitation effect entirely in terms of a weakening of the perceptual set which fosters a misinterpretation of the CI question, his results are open to an alternative processing explanation. Presentation of a question such as "If I have six hats and four jackets, etc.", provides a direct input of the extensive quantative properties of the set, and precludes the necessity for any error-prone intensive quantification, using the Q's. Although it is still necessary to rely on the semantic hierarchy of hats and things to wear, and to combine the quantitative symbols, it is not necessary to doubly process single items.

The early age at which Smedslund found successful performance on CI can also be explained in terms of the creation of the requisite quantitative symbols prior to the posing of the CI question. His procedure (c.f., his questions 7 and 9) creates quantitative symbols for *both* of the subsets and thus necessitates only a single activation of P11, and the associated quantification operator. Furthermore, by removing the objects from view, he further inhibited any tendency to indulge in error-prone intensive quantification.

It appears that no such extensive assistance is provided in the Ahr and Youniss experiments and that the subject must work with the Q's at the intensive level. Like Wohlwill, Ahr and Youniss interpret the effect of subclass ratios (A/A') entirely in terms of the propensity to encode the CI question as a subclass comparison question. Here, too, we would suggest that, in addition to a misinterpretation, processing errors may constitute a partial explanation. In particular, the comparison of quantitative symbols, which in PS: MORE appears simply as a direct test in P6 and P7, has been found to be faster (and presumably easier) the greater the magnitude of the difference between the quantitative symbols being compared (Moyer & Landauer, 1967). This is consistent with Ahr and Youniss' finding that as the ratio of subclass to superclass (A/B) increases, so too does the difficulty of the problem. Further explication of PS: MORE would elaborate the comparison process to account for this effect.

Kofsky encouraged her subjects to work at the intensive level by instructing them to "point out objects being counted as they compared class and subclass" (1963, p. 103). Whether counting facilitates CI performance depends critically upon the order of counting prompts and CI questions. As we shall demonstrate below, in Kofsky's case, the counting did not occur at the most advantageous time. Furthermore, Kofsky's subjects had to apply PS: MORE to the same collection three different times, thus imposing considerable demands upon the marking and unmarking processes.

Effects of Training Procedures

The PS suggested here offers two main accounts of successful performance on CI, corresponding to the use of either a sequential marking quantification operation (Q2) or the creation of a copy of the set representation (Q4). One can distinguish in the literature two training techniques to move subjects from unsuccessful to successful CI performance which correspond roughly to these two quantification operators, i.e., from Q1 to Q2 or from Q3 to Q4.

Inhelder and Sinclair (1969) use a sensory motor training procedure in which at one point during an acting out of a series of experimenter-provided verbal instructions for constructing classes, "the total class . . . remains visible as an object of comparison while the child constructs his sublcasses. . . " The internalization of these sensory motor actions seems likely to encourage the ability to produce copies of internal representations of sets, which is the crucial distinction between Q3 and Q4.

However, most of the training literature appears to us to be interpretable in terms of the Q1 to Q2 transition. The best example of such training is Kohnstamm's (1963) procedure.* Children who failed CI were instructed to count the superset, to count the subset, to compare the resultant quantitative symbols ("what is more, three or two?"), to compare the quantitative symbols attached to values ("what is the most, three red blocks or two small blocks?"). At the aggregate level, Kohnstamm seems to be taking his children step by step through PS: MORE.

At a more detailed level, we can represent the effect of his procedure by replacing P11 with P11$'$ in PS: MORE, as illustrated in Figure 8.13. The original

---

*For an extended discussion of theoretical and procedural issues raised by training on CI see Kohnstamm (1967).

PS: MORE

$-$

$-$ {Before Training}

$-$

P11: $[\text{Quantify } (<X>)]^+ \Rightarrow \text{QS}_x \leftarrow \leftarrow \text{Q}_n$

PS: MORE′

$-$

$-$ {After Training}

$-$

P11′: $[\text{Quantify } (<X>)]^+ \Rightarrow [\text{Quantify } (<X>)]^+ \leftarrow [\text{count}]^+, <X>$

Fig. 8.13. Effect of counting training upon PS: MORE.

form of P11 is adequate for a "more" operation on any disjoint sets, but as we have seen, its adequacy for CI depends upon which Q is used. The result of counting training is to encourage the child to treat any quantification goal as a condition for activating a count goal, which ensures that the action chain for P13, including the crucial WIPE, is triggered. Thus, prior to training, the child, upon detecting a quantification goal, applies some quantification operator; after training a quantification goal generates a count goal.

Several sources of empirical support for this explanation exist. Wohlwill found that training in counting similar to Kohnstamm's led to a significant performance improvement. It appears that the relationship between the count instructions and the posing of the CI question is critical. For example, Kofsky's instructions to count occurred *after* the occurrence of the CI question, and thus could not serve to facilitate performance on an already complex version of CI, requiring three passes through PS: MORE.

Our own ongoing experiments with two forms of the CI task further support sensitivity of the process to the precise sequence of questions and hence to the order in which goals are generated. We presented groups of children found to fail Kofksy's version of CI with two variants of the task. The first of these corresponds directly to the Kohnstamm and Wohlwill training procedure. The following three questions were asked, with pauses for replies: "Count the squares. Count the reds. Are there more squares or reds?" The second condition consisted of single questions of the form: "Count the squares and count the reds and then tell me, are there more squares or more reds?" Although both conditions resulted in improved CI performance, there was a highly significant advantage to the first form over the second. As described previously, this seems to indicate that even when counting is mentioned prior to the generation of the goal [more] by the CI question, many subjects fail to use COUNT for quantification.

Transition

In this section we offer some general speculations on mechanisms underlying cognitive development. Our approach is to describe different stages in terms of different PSs, and then to postulate certain features of a transition mechanism that could produce changes from one system to the other. The most important feature of our model is the notion of an action chain, first used in PS: COUNT. An action (A_x) can be evoked either because its associated condition is satisfied $(C_x \rightarrow A_x)$ or because it has been linked to an action chain which has had the condition of its initial action satisfied $(C_i \rightarrow A_i A_j \dots A_x A_y)$.

A major alteration in the operation of a PS can be effected by a change in a single production rule such as the P11 to P11$'$ change described earlier. The result of such an alteration is to bring together two previously unconnected parts of a system that already had the requisite components, but did not evoke them in the appropriate sequence. The newly evoked production can have, as its action part, a previously formed chain of actions. This process might explain the success of brief training procedures in producing qualitative changes in performance.

Before extrapolating further on the general importance of such action chains in cognitive development, we will offer a brief neurophysiological aside. Recent work by Willows (1971) on the functioning of the brain of the mollusk *Tritonia* has revealed properties which bear a strong resemblance to the production situation outlined. Electrical stimulation of individual brain cells elicited responses from well-defined, limited parts of the animal's musculature, e.g., excitation of individual pedal-ganglion cells resulted in slight curling or turning movements by one side of its body. Excitation of single cells in a group near the central commissure joining the two halves of the brain, however, elicited a complete playing out of the animal's normal swimming escape response in all of its details: withdrawal, extension of its paddle-like organs and a series of body bending movements. This behavior did not require continued electrical stimulation during its duration: A brief stimulation of the cell (for less than a quarter of a second) was enough to set off the entire sequence of escape movements lasting for more than 30 sec. A microelectrode recording of the activity of the initial cell indicated that it did not continue exciting itself during this period. It frequently ceased firing altogether within 3 sec after the stimulation. The most likely explanation of these findings, in Willows' view, is that the cell triggered a series of firings by other neurons that drive the sequence of escape movements. Furthermore, Willows argues that this is not simply a chain of reflexes, in which one movement excites propriceptors in the muscles which then send impulses to the brain that stimulate the cells for the next movement. Studies of the isolated brain, in which no such feedback is possible, have shown that a central stimulation produces a playing back of the complete escape-swimming sequence, indicating that "the coordinated firing of its cells in the swimming pattern was obviously generated by the circuitry within the brain itself" (Willows, 1971, p. 74). There is a suggestive similarity between the neural events described and the hypothesized operation of actions on some occasions as single units evoked by appropriate conditions and on others as integrated elements in a chain of actions. However, since generalization across both phylogenetic divisions and cognitive levels is a hazardous tactic, we will not press the point further.

Our characterization of the sequence of cognitive development focuses upon the formation and decomposition of action chains. In any given task environment, successful functioning depends upon the existence of the appropriate ordered collection of productions. Continued experience in a stable task environment leads to a repeated evocation of the same sequence of actions. These actions then become effectively associated with one another, perhaps through generation of a set of productions in which the condition for one action is simply the immediately prior evocation of its predecessor (e.g., *if* A_i was just done, *then* do A_j). Such an action chain would not be sensitive to any aspects of the problem space other than its own immediate operation, although the processing required by the original conditions for each action would now be unnecessary.

With certain changes in the environment, a previously formed action chain may become inappropriate. For example, execution of A_i in the changed environment may no longer produce suitable inputs for A_j. Such a failure would result in the breaking of the action chain and the creation of an appropriate test. For example, the system with $C_a \rightarrow A_a A_b \ldots A_i A_j A_k$ might, upon an input failure to A_j, be modified to a system with $C_a \rightarrow A_a A_b \ldots A_i$, $C_i \rightarrow A_j A_k$, $C'_i \rightarrow A_m$.

It appears appropriate to conclude our paper by attempting to relate these theoretical suggestions to the corpus of cognitive developmental theory. The closest parallel to the two developmental processes outlined is to be found in the work of Werner (1967). The regulative principle of development, in his view, is the orthogenetic principle which states that wherever development occurs, it proceeds from a state of relative globality and lack of differentiation to a state of increasing differentiation and integration. The account of the course of developmental events within a PS which we have proposed appears to be consistent with this general principle. The function of a single production becomes increasingly specialized or differentiated and increasingly part of an integrated system as it first becomes a member of the ordered list of productions comprising a PS and then a component of a production chain.

A second fundamental feature of Werner's viewpoint is the importance accorded to mobility of developmental level of operation. As most generally conceived, mobility implies that once an organism attains highly stabilized structures and operations, it may or may not progress further. If it does, this will be accomplished through partial return to a genetically earlier, less stable level. Development follows a spiral course in which one has to regress in order to progress. An impressive illustration of the relationship between renewed development and regression on the biological plane is found in the processes of regeneration. At the amphibian level, regeneration consists of regressive as well as progressive phases. The regressive phase is prior to progression and involves de-differentiation of already specialized cells.

In speculating by analogy from these biological events to human behavior, Werner maintains that in creative reorganization, psychological regression involves two types of operations. The first is the de-differentiation or dissolution of existing schematized or automatized behavior patterns; the second consists in the activation of developmentally prior levels of behavior from which undifferentiated phenomena emerge. Repeated decomposition of action chains in unfamiliar situations would ultimately lead to a series of unitary productions. Our proposals for the development within a production system constitute obvious parallels to the two types of operations suggested by Werner.

The tenability of such a theoretical position rests partly upon the degree to which we can specify the mechanism that effects the proposed changes in the organism. A first step in the formulation of such a mechanism is the specification of what it is that is being changed. In this paper, we have argued that the system of interest is a production system and that changes in such systems can account for some important features of both training effects and the natural course of cognitive development.

PART V

FINAL COMMENT

John Richard Hayes received his undergraduate degree from Harvard University, and his doctorate from MIT. He joined the psychology faculty of Carnegie-Mellon in 1966, and a few years thereafter was drafted into service as Dean of our new College of Humanities and Social Sciences. Happily, he has now returned to full-time psychological research and teaching.

Dr. Hayes' early research (Hayes, 1958) had an alarmingly Skinnerian tone, but he was soon rescued for cognitive psychology, and served as chairman and editor of our 1969 Annual Symposium (Hayes, 1970).

CHAPTER 9

THE CHILD'S CONCEPTION OF THE EXPERIMENTER*

John R. Hayes

Carnegie-Mellon University

In my discussion of the papers in this volume, I will not attempt a summary or an overview. Simon has already done that in a very satisfactory way (Part I). Rather, I will focus on just three matters. First, I will discuss an issue raised by the papers of Cellérier (Part II) and of Klahr and Wallace (Part IV) concerning the role of simulation in developmental research. Second, I will discuss the Klahr and Wallace paper in part as an aid to the reader who may have become lost in the discussion of production systems and in part because I want to raise some substantive issues. Finally, inspired by the papers of Goodnow (Part III) and Klahr and Wallace, I will discuss language and social convention in the child's understanding of the task.

*The author wishes to express his thanks to Dr. Guy Groen for many helpful conversations.

To Simulate or Not to Simulate?

Cellérier makes it quite clear that for the present at least he sees considerable difficulties facing any attempt to program Piagetian developmental theory. He says, "It is quite clear that 'Programming Piaget' in the sense of simulating all Piaget-type situations would not be programming the essential Piaget, i.e., the *development* of intelligence. These experimental situations do not cover the whole scope of intelligent behavior in children, and even if they did, we would be left with a juxtaposition of independently evolving programs with no central unity and the job of writing the central coordinator program." He goes further,, "My impression is that Piaget's central concepts are not sufficiently specified in their present form to be programmable, . . ."

Cellérier's way of describing the situation is not likely to prompt investigators to rush to their computers. Klahr and Wallace, approaching the same scientific problem, take a very different view of the role of simulation in its solution. As they indicate in an earlier paper (Klahr & Wallace, 1970b), it is *because* Piaget's concepts (and those of other theorists) are not well specified that they feel it is important to simulate. Furthermore, their approach is doggedly and by principle, narrowly restricted to specific tasks. They say, "The decision to concentrate initially on a state description of one point in intellectual development before tackling the problem of the transition rule determining the passage from state to state in development is consistent with the line of approach advocated by Simon (1962) and Flavell and Wohlwill (1969)."

In this issue, my sympathies are strongly with Klahr and Wallace, perhaps because I share with them the information processing point of view. However, I justify my bias on empirical grounds. By attempting the simulation of a very specific task, they have indeed been able to come up with a new, very detailed, and testable hypothesis as to the nature of the developmental process reflected in the solution of class inclusion problems. Their approach, I feel, has been justified by its productivity. The testability of their model can be illustrated by reference to their counting program.

Counting and Ordering

As I understand Klahr and Wallace's hypothesis, it is this: Faced with a class inclusion problem such as "are there more roses here or more flowers?" all children start by searching for estimates of the quantity of roses and the quantity of flowers. If they already have such estimates stored in memory, the problem is solved. Otherwise, they must generate new quantity estimates. It is here in the generation of quantity estimates that younger and older children differ crucially. In fact, Klahr and Wallace describe two modes for estimating quantity, each of which has a younger and an older version. First I will describe the Q1, Q2 mode—Q1 for the younger child's version and Q2 for the older.

In Q1, the child notices each rose in succession, and as he notices it he increases his estimate of quantity and at the same time, marks the rose as one he has seen before so that he will not count it again. This procedure gives him a reasonable estimate of the quantity of roses. Now the child goes on to estimate the quantity of flowers in the same way. However, since the roses have already been marked as having been seen before, he does not include them in his flower count. Therefore, his estimate of the quantity of flowers is too low. When the roses constitute more than half of the flowers, the child answers that there are more roses than flowers.

Incidentally, there is nothing in the Klahr-Wallace model which requires that the child estimate roses first and then flowers. Perhaps there should be, for consider what happens if the child first estimates flowers and then roses. He will get a good estimate of the quantity of flowers, but then having marked all the flowers as ones which have been seen before, he will find no roses at all! It seems doubtful that such a prediction could be supported empirically.

The older child's version, Q2, differs from Q1 in just one way. After completing the first count (either roses or flowers), the child wipes out the marks he has made to prevent double counting. This allows him to obtain good quantity estimates for both roses and flowers.

In the second mode of quantity estimation, Q3 is the younger child's version and Q4 the older. Let us assume that the child using Q3 starts by estimating the quantity of roses. He notices each flower in turn and if it is a rose, he adds it to the rose list, deletes it from the flower list, and increases his quantity estimate for roses. This gives him a reasonable estimate of the quantity of roses. Next he tries to estimate the quantity of flowers. He does this using the list from which the roses have been deleted and therefore gets a quantity estimate for the flowers which is too low.

The same order problem exists for Q3 and for Q1. If the child using Q3 starts with flowers, he will get a good quantity estimate for flowers and find no roses at all. I strongly suspect that the model needs modification on this point.

In using Q4, the child does just what the child using Q3 does with the exception that he makes and saves a *copy* of the original list of flowers. Thus, in making his second quantity estimate, the child does not have to rely on a list from which deletions have been made. Klahr and Wallace point out that the concept of a copy may be very useful in discussing reversibility, since the copy could be used to verify the return to the initial state.

While I plainly have some doubts about the completeness of the Klahr and Wallace model, I feel that the power of their approach is enormous. If they are wrong, it will soon become apparent and new models can be constructed to replace the rejected ones.

Language and Social Convention

Goodnow convinced me that the child's understanding of rather subtle linguistic and social conventions may well influence his performance on tasks which are intended to measure his cognitive functioning (e.g., IQ tests). Klahr and Wallace convinced me that the understanding of linguistic conventions may well influence performance in the class inclusion problem. I agree that there *is* something tricky about class inclusion questions like, "Are there more roses or more flowers in the garden?". They bear a kinship to other anomalous questions such as "Is it warmer in the afternoon than it is in the summer time?" and "Do you prefer lettuce to other people?".

Thus convinced, I went home and questioned my daughters, all of whom, incidentally, are beyond the age at which they could be expected to fail the class inclusion problem. Specifically, I asked them, "What would you think if someone asked you, 'Are there more roses in the garden or more flowers?'". My 8-year-old answered in a very straightforward way, "I would think there were more flowers." My 13-year-old, on the other hand, answered, "I'd think he was putting me on." In much the same vein, when I asked, "Is it warmer in the afternoon than it is in the summertime?" the older two girls, 11 and 13, simply laughed, but the youngest considered the question carefully and decided that on balance it was warmer in the summertime.

What these observations suggest to me is, that in different children, such questions lead to very different interpretations of the task to be performed. Indeed, older children may not feel there is a task to be performed at all. Second, my observations suggest that the child's manner of interpreting such anomalous questions may be a developmental variable. Let me expand on this point. In listening to speech, we very often have to "fix it up" in the sense that we have to interpret what the speaker meant from what he said rather than simply taking his words at face value. The speaker may mispronounce a word, he may select the wrong word, or he may mangle a construction. In all of these cases, a skillful listener will recognize the resulting anomaly and attempt to reconstruct what the speaker should have said. To do this requires the listener to have a good model of the speaker. Some situations of fairly common occurrence can make considerable demands on the listener's ability to construct a good model of the speaker. Detecting dishonesty, irony, and misunderstanding, e.g., cases in which speaker and listener use the same word for different concepts, all put severe demands on the listener's ability to model the speaker. Another peculiar situation which may give the young child some difficulty is the one in which the speaker enters in the role of teacher or experimenter. In this role, the speaker may ask questions not because he wants the indicated information, but rather because he wants to determine if the listener has that information. A child who was not aware of the possibility of this testing role might be especially likely to find the class inclusion questions anomalous.

On the basis of these considerations and without any real empirical support, I would like to propose that the child's ability to build a correct model of the speaker progresses through a developmental sequence, and that this sequence is represented roughly by the list of situations in Table 9.1, ordered from easiest for the child to handle to those which are most difficult. The real ordering in the list is given by the class shown in the right hand column. I feel that the lexical, sentential, and interpersonal class probably are ordered developmentally, but make no argument for ordering of the items within the classes.

We might apply this developmental ordering to the class inclusion problem as follows. For the young child, there is only one available way of dealing with anomalous question. He must assume that the speaker has chosen the wrong word, e.g., "flowers," to express his real intent. The older child, on the other hand, can deal with the anomaly by assuming that the speaker is a teacher-experimenter and may therefore be expected to ask questions of this "obvious" sort.

Many investigators have been concerned with the problem of differentiating the child's understanding of what the task is from his ability to perform it. For example, Braine and Shanks (1965, 1966) studying conservation of size and shape, found that at roughly 5-years old, the child is able to make a distinction between "real" and apparent properties of objects. They find that for the child between five and seven, getting the correct response to size conservation questions depends critically on making it clear to the child that he should judge "real" rather than apparent size. They suggest that the child simply assumes that the experimenter is referring to apparent size unless he makes it very clear that he has "real" properties in mind. We have suggested already that this sort of misunderstanding might be very difficult for the child to handle without the experimenter's help.

Piaget himself has often been concerned with the possibility that the child has misunderstood the task instructions. For example, in describing his classic studies of class inclusion he says, "It might be argued that the child's difficulty in mentally constructing two simultaneous sets is not due to the irreversibility of his thought, as we have just suggested, but merely to lack of understanding of his instructions. Might he not think that two necklaces were actually to be made with the same material? It was precisely with this possibility in mind that we finally used two sets of beads in two separate boxes, and as we have seen, this technique made little difference in the results. The difficulty is therefore not due to verbal misunderstanding." (Piaget, 1952, p. 179) I will qoute from the same source an example of the evidence to which Piaget referred.

TABLE 9.1
Some Factors Involved in a Developmental Sequence of the Child's Model of the Speaker

Situation	Example	Class
Mispronunciation	Will you have some Pasgetti?	Lexical
Incorrect choice of word	Mommy, can I eat [feed] the cat?	Lexical
Subject-object interchange	Stop it, I'm hurting you.	Sentential
Incorrect voice	The girl was watered by the plants.	Sentential
Incorrect negation, etc.	Nobody don't likes me.	Sentential
Dishonesty	The cat cut those triangles in the potted plant.	Interpersonal
Irony	Sure I like your article.	Interpersonal
Misunderstanding	Yes, I think missionaries have good taste too.	Interpersonal
Testing	How many fingers do you have?	Interpersonal

Tap $(5; 6)$ $\cdots$ Tap was then given two sets of beads in two sets of boxes, each one contained 20 brown and 18 green all made of wood. "The little girl who has this box makes her necklace with the brown beads, and the girl who has the other box makes her necklace with the wooden beads in it. Which necklace will be longer?"–"*The brown ones because they are more.*"–"And what color will the necklace of wooden beads be?–*Only green.*"

With these results, Piaget certainly casts doubt on the particular hypothesis of verbal misunderstanding which he had in mind. However, it strikes me that these very same results also cast doubt on Piaget's own interpretation of the class inclusion data—namely that the child cannot simultaneously conceive of a class and a subclass of that class. In this new version of the problem, the child is not required to conceive class and subclass simultaneously—yet he still fails. These results, however, are consistent with the interpretation that the child treats the experimenter's question as anomalous and fixes it up.

Wohlwill (1968) found that children perform better on class inclusion problems when they are presented verbally than when they are presented pictorially. He attributes this difference to a perceptual set induced by the pictorial presentation which leads the child to compare subclasses rather than to compare subclass with superclass. I find it easy to assimilate this aspect of Wohlwill's position to my own by assuming that Wohlwill's perceptual set is really a tendency of the child to use the presented visual displays in addition to the experimenter's words to decide what the experimenter has in mind. Wohlwill also says, however, ". . . there are certain indications that the effect of a perceptual set are only superimposed on factors of a more intrinsic nature, relating to the child's level of cognitive development." The evidence which Wohlwill presents to support this position is that, with respect to the class inclusion problem, the difference between verbal and pictorial conditions is largest for children at a relatively advanced state of development. To put it simply, it seems as though verbal presentation helps the child in a class inclusion problem only if he almost has it anyway.

This position of Wohlwill's accords well with that of the Geneva school in that it assigns to the problem of understanding the task, a strictly secondary role which may be superimposed on the more primary processes concerning the development of logical structures in the child. In discussing verbal misunderstanding in the class inclusion problem, Inhelder and Piaget (1964) say, "We cannot accept the answer that they did not understand the language we used. In every single case, we took good care that they did. On the other hand, if there was a systematic, verbal misunderstanding, this would itself require an explanation in terms of logical structure [p. 104]."

Wohlwill and Inhelder and Piaget may well be right in their position, but I do not think, by any means, that they have proved their point nor do I believe that they have even stated the question fairly. In discussing the problem of task misinterpretation, we should consider two parallel lines of development. One of these is the familiar line concerned with the development of logical structures such as groups and lattices. The other is the line concerned with the developing ability of the child to construct a model of the speaker as an intelligence similar to, but progressively more divergent from, the self. This line of development is clearly a close relation to and must include the concept of egocentrism.

If we are willing from the outset to consider the possibility of two such parallel lines, then the arguments of Wohlwill and of Inhelder and Piaget lose their force. A systematic, verbal misunderstanding would indeed require an explanation, but it need not be in terms of logical structure. It might instead be in terms of the child's ability to construct a model of the speaker.

I consider the question interesting enough to deserve a fair hearing and feel that by studying the child's conception of the experimenter, and how he builds a model of him as a speaker, that the topic of development can be enriched.

CHAPTER 10

REPLY TO HAYES:
ON THE VALUE OF THEORETICAL PRECISION

David Klahr

and

J. G. Wallace

Carnegie-Mellon University

University of Warwick

First of all, we take issue with the use of the term "estimation" as a description of the quantification process used by the child. P11 says that if the quantification goal is active, then some quantification operator should be applied and its result, a quantitative symbol, should be added to the knowledge state. The type of quantification operator that is applied at this point will determine the value and form of the quantitative symbol. Although it might be an estimate, particularly if the environmental conditions make other forms of quantification impossible (e.g., $n > 1000$, or T-scope presentation), the quantification operators that we have described thus far are in no sense estimators. Similarly, in the condition where direct verbal input places the requisite quantitative symbols in the knowledge space, it is misleading to consider such quantitative symbols as estimates. (On the other hand, if the questions in the

183

verbal condition had been stated: "If I had a whole bunch of dogs and a few cats would I... etc.," the directly inputed quantitative symbols could correctly be described as estimates.) It is important to differentiate between various approaches to quantification (counting, subitizing, estimation) if one is to attempt, ultimately, to describe a PS: MORE that works for both large and small collections of objects. The only quantification operators described in our paper are based upon various forms of enumeration of small collections.

As a second major point, Hayes' description of the sensitivity of PS: MORE to the order of the quantification attempts raises several important points about process models in general and PS: MORE in particular. One of the benefits of specifying a process model in an unambiguous form is that the model becomes extremely falsifiable, both logically and empirically, and thus amenable to specific extensions, modifications and revisions. Hayes correctly notes that when PS: MORE is using Q1 or Q3, if it quantifies the superset before the subset, then by the time that the subset quantification is attempted, all the objects will have been marked. However, Hayes does not carry the analysis through in terms of the production system, and thus fails to take advantage of the precision with which the model is stated. He says that in this circumstance the child "... will find no roses at all!" "It seems doubtful," he goes on, "that such a prediction could be supported empirically."

The prediction that the child will find no roses is not a prediction that follows from an analysis of PS: MORE, nor is it a prediction that is, as stated, empirically testable. However, Hayes *has* detected an ambiguity in PS: MORE, and we shall indicate its specific sources and potential solutions, as well as the testable empirical predictions that derive from it.

Consider what happens if the superset has been quantified first, using Q1 or Q3, and all the elements in the set have been marked when the second quantification attempt takes place. The quantification operator could simply return a nil value, and the quantitative symbol placed in the knowledge state would correspond to zero. The comparison in P6 would then select the quantitative symbol for the superset as being greater than that for the subset, i.e., PS: MORE would produce the correct answer. The empirical prediction depends upon the assumptions we make about the order in which the sets are quantified. PS: MORE and the interpretation rules for production systems dictate that the order of quantification is determined entirely by the order in which the set names initially appear in the knowledge state. This order is in turn determined by the verbal encoder, about which we currently have little to say. However, since the order in which superset and subset names are presented is usually balanced in CI experiments, let us assume that the net result is that on the average the superset is quantified before the subset half of the time. This would lead to a testable empirical proposition based upon the return of a zero symbol for the subset. The prediction is that the youngest children, those who use Q1 or Q3, will be correct on CI about half the time. This prediction is not supported by the existing empirical data. All of the studies reported show that the youngest children's performance is well below the chance level. Thus, simply specifying that the Q's can return a nil symbol that can then be compared to the other quantitative symbol produces a prediction based upon PS: MORE that is refuted by the data.

The additions that PS: MORE needs in order to avoid this problem involve several complex issues that we have attempted to circumvent in our initial PS. However, since Hayes has found a crack in the foundation, we will at least discuss the form of the mortar, although the space limitations prohibit us from actually making the repairs.

The simplest solution would be to define quantification operators that produce a failure signal upon finding that there are no elements of the value currently being quantified. This would require additional productions to detect this special result and to create and process failed goals. As it now stands, PS: MORE has no productions, general or specific, to deal with failed goals, or with operators that fail, but as we shall indicate below, such productions are necessary in any system that is to function in an environment that often provides unsuitable inputs. In fact, as we argue in our paper, a fundamental part of the developmental process depends upon the ability to detect precisely these situations.

However, this proposed simple extension has difficulty dealing with a situation in which there are in fact no objects of the type indicated. In the case of a collection of flowers, we expect a correct response to the question "more flowers or more animals?", even though at an intermediate stage in processing the quantification operator returned a nil signal. Notice, however, that questions like "more flowers or more animals" when asked of a collection of flowers are a bit like Hayes' conundrums: "Warmer in the summertime or in the evening?" For both questions, the system should detect some conflict when attempting to quantify or to compare the results of the quantification.

We believe that the production of solution to any of these questions, whether anomalous or not, includes a process of *verification*, and this verification process is what is absent in PS: MORE. The function of a verification process is simply to check the results of operator application to ensure that the operator did in fact produce a result, and that the result is consistent with other results. A PS: MORE with verification productions would check for zero quantitative symbols. If it found any, it would try again, this time with a different order of quantification attempts. Such a strategy would circumvent the problem noted by Hayes, while still producing the correct reply to our question about flowers and animals.

This extension to PS: MORE—the addition of a verification procedure—is the general form of our solution to Hayes' problem. Verification procedures are essential in any model that purports to understand the growing ability of children to deal with misleading perceptual cues, or to coordinate results from several quantification processes.

The specific form of the productions that deal with verification and with failed goals depends upon the assumptions we make about how long the marked objects remain marked. The issue of the decay of marking information is related to the concept of an episode in a problem-solving situation. (Newell, 1968). Marks cannot be permanent, otherwise a collection could never be quantified more than once. It seems reasonable, for example, to assume that after each experimenter intervention (on the order of 5 sec) that marking information either is removed or has decayed. On the other hand, our analysis of the difficulty on CI rests upon the assumption that the marks remain at least as long as it takes to end one quantification and start the next. (By Simon's estimates, this is under 1 sec.) Thus we might view the marks as permanent with respect to an episode. One function of productions that handle failed goals is to enable the system to trace its steps backward to some appropriate point, carrying with it enough information to avoid going down the same path again. Thus we could add production rules whose effect would be to detect the failed goal and to back up far enough to reverse the order of the quantification attempts.,

However, this raises a problem. Upon the second attempt to quantify the subset, this time before the superset, are the elements of the set still marked, or can we assume that they are gone? Although the latter assumption eliminates the problem noted by Hayes, we feel a bit uncomfortable at this point in making any strong statement about the manner in which marked objects become unmarked. Alas, this technical problem, unlike the marks, will not decay over time.

REFERENCES

Ahr, P. R. & Youniss, J. Reasons for failure on the class inclusion problem. *Child Development,* 1970, **41**, 131-143.

Arnheim, R. *Art and visual perception.* Berkeley, Calif.: Univ. of California Press, 1954.

Arnheim, R. *Visual thinking.* Berkeley, Calif.: Univ. of California Press, 1969.

Atkinson, R. C., Hansen, D. N. & Bernbach, H. S. Short-term memory with young children. *Psychonomic Science,* 1964, **1**, 255-256.

Baker, S. J. A developmental study of variables affecting the processing of task-relevant and task-irrelevant information. Unpublished doctoral dissertation. Ann Arbor, Mich.: Univ. of Michigan, 1970.

Bartlett, F. C. *Thinking.* London: Allen & Unwin, 1958.

Belmont, J. M. & Butterfield, E. C. The relations of short-term memory to development and intelligence. *In* L. Lipsitt & H. Reese (eds.), Vol. 4, *Advances in child development and behavior.* New York: Academic Press, 1969. Pp. 29-82.

Bereiter, C. & Engelmann, S. *Teaching disadvantaged children in the preschool.* New Jersey: Prentice-Hall, 1966.

Berlyne, D. E. *Structure and direction in thinking.* New York: Wiley, 1965.

Bever, T., Fodor, J. & Weksel, W. On the acquisition of syntax: A critique of "contextual generalization." *Psychological Review,* 1965, **72**, 467-482.

Biggs, J. B. Coding and cognitive behaviour. *British Journal of Psychology,* 1969, **60**, 287-305.

Birch, H. G. & Belmont, L. Auditory-visual integration in normal and retarded readers. *American Journal of Orthopsychiatry,* 1964, **34**, 852-861.

Birch, H. G. & Belmont, L. Auditory-visual integration, intelligence and reading ability in school children. *Perceptual & Motor Skills,* 1965, **20**, 295-305.

Blair-Hood, H. An experimental study of Piaget's theory of the development of the number in children. *British Journal of Psychology,* 1962, **53**, 273-286.

Blank, M., Weider, S. & Bridger, W. Verbal deficiencies in abstract thinking in early reading retardation. *American Journal of Orthopsychiatry,* 1968, **38**, 823-834.

Braine, M. D. S. On learning the grammatical order of words. *Psychological Review,* 1963, **70**, 323-348.

Braine, M. D. S. & Shanks, B. L. The development of conservation of size. *Journal of Verbal Learning and Verbal Behavior,* 1965, **4**, 227-242.

Braine, M. D. S. & Shanks, B. L. The conservation of a shape property and proposal about the origin of the conservation. *Canadian Journal of Psychology,* 1966, **19**, 197-207.

Brett, G. *Kinetic Art.* London: Studio Vista, 1969.

Broadbent, D. E. *Perception and communication.* New York: Macmillan (Pergamon), 1958.

Brofsky, H. & Bamberger, J. *The art of listening.* New York: Harper, 1969.

187

Burstall, R. M., Collins, J. S. & Popplestone, R. S. *POP-2 Papers,* Edinburgh: Oliver & Boyd, 1968.

Caldwell, E. C. & Hall, V. C. The influence of concept training on letter discrimination. *Child Development,* 1969, **40**, 63-71.

Carmichael, L. (ed.) *Manual of child psychology,* New York: Wiley, 1954.

Carter, Dorothy J. Response to the successively-presented Mueller-Lyer Illusion as a function of interstimulus interval. *Proceedings of the American Psychological Association,* 1970, 293-294.

Chomsky, N. *Aspects of the theory of syntax.* Cambridge, Mass.: MIT Press, 1965.

Chomsky, N. *Cartesian linguistics.* New York: Harper, 1966.

Cole, M., Gay, J., Glick, J. A., & Sharp, D. W. *The Cultural context of learning and thinking.* New York: Basic Books, 1971.

Collins, A. M. & Quillian, M. R. Experiments on semantic memory and language comprehension. *In* L. W. Gregg (ed.), *Cognition in learning and memory.* New York: Wiley, 1972.

Comalli, P. F. Perceptual changes to visual illusions in childhood, adulthood, and old age. Paper presented at the Biennial Meeting of the Society for Research in Child Development, Santa Monica, 1969.

Crowder, R. G. The role of one's own voice in immediate memory. *Cognitive Psychology,* 1970, **1**, 157-178.

De Valois, R. L. Analysis of brightness and color by primate visual systems. Invited Address, American Psychological Association, 1970.

Denner, B. Representational and syntactic competence of problem readers. *Child Development,* 1970, **41**, 881-887.

Druker, J. F. & Hagen, J. W. Developmental trends in the processing of task-relevant and task-irrelevant information. *Child Development,* 1969, **40**, 371-382.

Ebert, P. & Pollack, R. H. Magnitude of the Mueller-Lyer Illusion as a function of hue, saturation, and fundus pigmentation. Paper presented at the Annual meeting of the Eastern Psychological Association, 1971.

Ervin, S. M. & Miller, W. R. Language development. In *Child Psychology* (Sixty-second Yearbook, National Society for Study of Education), Part 1. Chicago, Ill.: Univ. of Chicago Press, 1963. Pp. 108-143.

Farnham-Diggory, S. Self, future and time: A developmental study of the concepts of psychotic, brain-damaged and normal children. *Monographs of the Society for Research in Child Development,* Serial No. 103, 1966.

Farnham-Diggory, S. Symbol and synthesis in experimental 'reading'. *Child Development,* 1967, **38**, 221-231.

Farnham-Diggory, S. Cognitive synthesis in Negro and white children. *Monographs of the Society for Research in Child Development,* 1970, **35** (2, Whole No. 135).

Farnham-Diggory, S. *Cognitive processes in education.* New York: Harper, 1972.

Farnham-Diggory, S. & Bermon, M. Verbal compensation, cognitive synthesis, and conservation. *Merrill-Palmer Quarterly,* 1968, **14**, 215-228.

Feigenbaum, E. A. The simulation of verbal learning behavior. *In* E. A. Feigenbaum & L. Feldman (eds.), *Computers and Thought.* New York: McGraw-Hill, 1963. Pp. 297-309.

Fisher, G. H. *The frameworks for perceptual localization.* Newcastle Upon Tyne: Ministry of Defense, 1968.

Flavell, J. H. Developmental studies of mediated memory. *In* L. Lipsitt & H. Reese (eds.), Vol. 5, *Advances in Child Development and Behavior.* New York: Academic Press, 1970.

Flavell, J. H. Stage-related properties of cognitive development. *Cognitive Psychology,* 1971, **2**, 421-453.

Flavell, J. H., Beach, D. R., & Chinsky, J. M. Spontaneous verbal rehearsal in a memory task as a function of age. *Child Development*, 1966, 37, 283-299.

Flavell, J. H. & Wohlwill, J. F. Formal and functional aspects of cognitive development. *In* D. Elkind and J. H. Flavell (eds.) *Studies in cognitive development.* New York: Oxford University Press, 1969. Pp. 67-120.

Fodor, J. & Garrett, M. Some reflections on competence and performance. *In* J. Lyons and R. J. Wales (eds.), *Psycholinguistic papers.* Univ. of Edinburgh Press, 1966.

Gascon, Jean. *Modèle cybernétique d'une sériation de poids.* Masters thesis, Université de Montreal, 1969 (a).

Gascon, Jean. Modèle cybernétique d'une sériation de poids chez les enfants, *Modeles cybernétiques de la pensee,* 2. Université de Montreal, 1969 (b).

Gesell, A. & Ames, L. B. The development of directionality in drawing. *Journal of Genetic Psychology*, 1946, 68, 45-61.

Ghent, L. B. Form and its orientation: a child's eye view. *American Journal of Psychology*, 1961, 74, 177-190.

Goffman, E. *The presentation of self in everyday life.* Edinburgh: University of Edinburgh Social Sciences Research Centre, 1956.

Goffman, E. *Strategic interaction.* Philadelphia: Univ. Pennsylvania Press, 1969.

Gombrich, E. H. *Art and illusion.* Princeton: Princeton Univ. Press, 1960.

Goodnow, J. J. A test of milieu differences with some of Piaget's tasks. *Psychological Monographs*, 1962, 176, No. 36 (Whole No. 555).

Goodnow, J. J. Problems in research on culture and thought. *In* D. Elkind & J. H. Flavell (eds.), *Studies in cognitive development.* New York: Oxford University Press, 1969. Pp. 439-462 (a).

Goodnow, J. J. Cultural variations in cognitive skills. *In* D. R. Price-Williams (ed.), *Cross-cultural studies.* Middlesex: Penguin, 1969. Pp. 246-264. (b)

Goodnow, J. J. Matching auditory and visual series: Modality problem or translation problem? *Child Development*, 1971, 42, 1187-1201.

Goodnow, J. J. & Levine, R. The grammar of action: Sequences and syntax in children's copying. *Cognitive Psychology*, 1972, in press.

Goulet, L. R. Verbal learning in children: Implications for developmental research. *Psychological Bulletin*, 1968, 69, 359-376.

Greene, R. T. & Lawson, R. B. Ponzo wedge effects upon stereoscopic size and distance. Paper presented at the annual meeting of the Eastern Psychological Association, 1970.

Hagen, J. W. The effect of distraction on selective attention. *Child Development*, 1967, 38, 685-694.

Hagen, J. W. & Frisch, S. R. The effect of incidental cues on selective attention. Report No. 57, USPHS Grant HD 01368. Center for Human Growth and Development, Univ. of Michigan, 1968.

Hagen, J. W. & Huntsman, J. Selective attention in mental retardates. *Developmental Psychology*, 1971, 5, 151-160.

Hagen, J. W. & Kingsley, P. R. Labeling effects in short-term memory. *Child Development*, 1968, 39, 113-121.

Hagen, J. W. & Sabo, R. A. A developmental study of selective attention. *Merrill-Palmer Quarterly*, 1967, 13, 159-172.

Hagen, J. W. & West, R. F. The effects of a pay-off matrix on selective attention. *Human Development*, 1970, 13, 43-52.

Hagen, J. W., Meacham, J. A. & Mesibov, G. Verbal labeling, rehearsal, and short-term memory. *Cognitive Psychology*, 1970, 1, 47-58.

Hall, V. C., Salvi, R., Seggev, L., & Caldwell, E. Cognitive synthesis, conservation, and task analysis. *Developmental Psychology,* 1970, **2**, 423-428.

Hanfmann, E. A study of personal patterns in an intellectual performance. *Character and Personality,* 1941, **9**, 315-325.

Hayes, J. R. The maintenance of play in young children. *Journal of Comparative and Physiological Psychology,* 1958, **51**, 788-794.

Hayes, J. R. (ed.). *Cognition and the development of language.* New York: Wiley, 1970.

Hearnshaw, L. S. Temporal integration and behavior. *Bulletin of British Psychological Society,* 1956, **9**, 1-20.

Hilgard, E. R. & Bower, G. W. *Theories of learning,* (3rd ed.) New York: Appleton, 1966.

Hilgard, E. R., Marquis, D. G. & Kimble, D. G. *Conditioning and learning.* New York: Appleton, 1961.

Holt, J. Sesame Street as a detour. *Washington Post,* 1971 (May 2nd).

Hopcroft, J. & Ullman, J. *Formal languages and their relation to automata.* Reading, Mass.: Addison-Wesley, 1969.

Ilg, F. L. & Ames, L. B. *School readiness.* New York: Harper, 1964.

Inhelder, B. & Piaget, J. *The early growth of logic in the child.* New York: Harper, 1964.

Inhelder, B. & Sinclair, H. Learning cognitive structures. *In* Mussen, *et al.* (eds.), *Trends and issues in developmental psychology.* New York: Holt, 1969. Pp. 2-21.

Inhelder, B., Bovet, M. & Sinclair, H. Développement et apprentissage. *Revue suisse de psychologie,* 1967, **26**, No. 1, 1-23.

Jarrard, L. (ed.). *Cognitive processes of nonhuman primates.* New York: Academic Press, 1971.

Jennings, J. R. *Cardiac reactions associated with different developmental levels of cognitive functions.* Unpublished PhD dissertation, Univ. of California at Berkeley, 1969.

Jensen, A. R. How far can we boost IQ and scholastic achievement? *Harvard Educational Review,* 1969, **39**, 1-123.

Keeney, T. J., Cannizzo, S. R. & Flavell, J. H. Spontaneous and induced verbal rehearsal in a recall task. *Child Development,* 1967, **38**, 953-966.

Kendler, H. H. & Kendler, T. S. Vertical and horizontal processes in problem solving. *Psychological Review,* 1962, **69**, 1-16.

Kendler, T. S. Development of mediating responses in children. *In* J. C. Wright and J. Kagan (eds.). Basic cognitive processes in children. *Monographs of the Society for Research in Child Development,* 1963, **28**(2), 33-52.

Kingsley, P. R. & Hagen, J. W. Induced versus spontaneous rehearsal in short-term memory in nursery school children. *Developmental Psychology,* 1969, **1**, 40-46.

Klahr, D. & Wallace, J. G. The development of serial completion strategies: An information processing analysis. *British Journal of Psychology,* 1970, **61**, 243-257. (a).

Klahr, D. & Wallace, J. G. An information processing analysis of some Piagetian experimental tasks. *Cognitive Psychology,* 1970, **1**, 358-387. (b)

Kleinmuntz, B. (ed.) *Problem solving: Research, method and theory.* New York: Wiley, 1966.

Koenigsberg, R. An evaluation of procedures for improvement of orientation discrimination in pre-school children. Unpublished doctoral dissertation, the George Washington University, 1971.

Kofsky, Ellin. *Developmental scalogram analysis of classificatory behavior.* Unpublished PhD dissertation, Univ. of Rochester, 1963.

Kofsky, Ellin. A scalogram study of classificatory development. *Child Development,* 1966, **37**, 191-204.

Köhler, W. & Wallach, H. Figural aftereffects: An investigation of visual processes.

Proceedings of the American Philosophical Society, 1944. 88, 269-357.

Kohnstamm, G. A. An evaluation of part of Piaget's theory. *Acta Psychologica,* 1963, **21,** 313-356.

Kohnstamm, G. A. *Piaget's analysis of class inclusion: Right or wrong?* The Hague: Mouton, 1967.

Labov, W. *A study of non-standard English.* Washington, D.C.: Center for Applied Linguistics, 1969.

Lashley, K. S. The problem of serial order in behavior. *In* L. A. Jeffress (ed.), *Cerebral mechanisms in behavior: The Hixon symposium.* New York: Wiley, 1951.

Laurendeau, M. & Pinard, A. Réflexions sur l'apprentissage des structures logiques. *In* F. Bresson & M. de Montmollin (eds.). *Psychologie et épistémologie génétiques.* Paris: Dunod, 1966. Pp. 191-210.

Leibowitz, H. W. & Judisch, J. M. The relation between age and the magnitude of the Ponzo Illusion. *American Journal of Psychology,* 1967, **80,** 105-109.

Leibowitz, H. W., Brislin, R., Perlmutter, L. & Hennessy, R. The Ponzo perspective illusion as a manifestation of space perception. *Science,* 1969, **166,** 1174-1176.

Lunzer, E. A. *The regulation of behavior.* Staples Press, 1969.

Luria, A. R. The directive role of speech in development and dissociation. *Word,* 1959, **15.**

Luria, A. R. *The role of speech in the regulation of normal and abnormal behavior.* New York: Macmillan (Pergamon), 1961.

Maccoby, E. E. & Hagen, J. Effects of distraction upon central versus incidental recall: Developmental trends. *Journal of Experimental Child Psychology,* 1965, **2,** 280-289.

McGhee, Paul E. Cognitive development and children's comprehension of humor. *Child Development,* 1971, **42,** 123-138.

McLaughlin, G. H. Psychologic: A possible alternative to Piaget's formulation. *British Journal of Educational Psychology,* 1963, **33,** 61-67.

Meyer, D. E. On the representation and retrieval of stored semantic information. *Cognitive Psychology,* 1970, **1,** 242-300.

Miller, G. A. The magical number seven: Plus or minus two. *Psychological Review,* 1956, **63,** 81-97.

Miller, G. A. & Selfridge, J. A. Verbal context and the recall of meaningful material. *American Journal of Psychology,* 1950, **63,** 176-185.

Miller, G. A., Galanter, E. & Pribram, K. H. *Plans and the structure of behavior.* New York: Holt, 1960.

Milner, B. Hemispheric specialization and memory in man. Paper presented to Carnegie-Mellon Colloquium, November, 1970.

Minsky, M. & Papert, S. *Perceptrons: An introduction to computational geometry.* Cambridge, Mass.: M.I.T. Press, 1969.

Moyer, R. S. & Landauer, T. K. Time required for judgments of numerical inequality. *Nature,* 1967, **215,** 1519-1520.

Mussen, P. H. (ed.). *Carmichael's manual of child psychology.* New York: Wiley, 1970.

Neisser, U. *Cognitive Psychology.* New York: Appleton, 1967.

Newell, A. Studies in problem solving: Subject 3 on the Crypt-arithmetic task DONALD + GERALD = ROBERT. Carnegie Institute of Technology, July, 1967.

Newell, A. On the analysis of human problem solving protocols. *In* J. C. Gardin & B. Javlin (eds.), *Calcul et formalization dan les sciences de l'homme.* Center de la Recherche Scientifique, 1968. Pp. 146-185.

Newell, A. & Simon, H. A. *Human problem solving.* Englewood Cliffs, New Jersey: Prentice Hall, 1972.

Norman, D. A. *Memory and attention.* New York: Wiley, 1969.

Noton, D. & Stark, L. Scanpaths in eye movements during pattern reception. *Science,* 1971, **171**, 308-311.

Page, S. C. The transition from concrete to formal thinking. Unpublished doctoral dissertation, Australian National Univ., 1971.

Parrish, M., Lundy, R. M. & Leibowitz, H. W. Hypnotic age-regression and magnitudes of the Ponzo and Poggendorff illusions. *Science,* 1968, **159**, 1375-1376.

Pascual-Leone, J. A mathematical model for the transition rule in Piaget's developmental stages. *Acta Psychologica,* 1970, **32**, 301-345.

Piaget, J. *The child's conception of physical causality.* London: Kegan Paul, 1930.

Piaget, J. *The child's conception of number.* New York: Humanities, 1952.

Piaget, J. *The mechanisms of perception.* New York: Basic Books, 1969.

Piaget, J. *Structuralism.* New York: Basic Books, 1970. (a)

Piaget, J. *L'épistémologie génétique (Que sais-je?)*, Presses universitaires de France, Paris, 1970. (b)

Piaget, J. *Biology and knowledge.* Chicago, Ill.: Univ. of Chicago Press, 1971.

Piaget, J. & Inhelder, B. *The psychology of the child.* New York: Basic Books, 1969.

Piaget, J. & Szeminska, A. *The child's conception of number.* Routledge & Kegan Paul, London, 1952.

Pinard, A. & Laurendeau, M. Stage in Piaget's cognitive-developmental theory: Exegesis of a concept. *In* D. Elkind & J. H. Flavell (eds.), *Studies in cognitive development.* London and New York: Oxford Univ. Press, 1969. Pp. 138-145.

Pollack, R. H. Figural aftereffects as a function of age. *Acta Psychologica,* 1960, **17**, 417-423.

Pollack, R. H. Contour detectability threshold as a function of chronological age. *Perceptual and Motor Skills,* 1963, **17**, 411-417.

Pollack, R. H. Simultaneous and successive presentation of elements of the Mueller-Lyer figure and chronological age. *Perceptual and Motor Skills,* 1964, **19**, 303-310.

Pollack, R. H. Hue detectability thresholds as a function of chronological age. *Psychonomic Science,* 1965, **3**, 351-352. (a)

Pollack, R. H. Backward figural masking as a function of chronological age and intelligence. *Psychonomic Science,* 1965, **3**, 65-66. (b)

Pollack, R. H. Some implications of ontogenetic changes in perception. **In** D. Elkind & J. H. Flavell (eds.), *Essays in cognitive development: Studies in honor of Jean Piaget.* London and New York: Oxford Univ. Press, 1969. Pp. 365-407.

Pollack, R. H. Magnitude of the Mueller-Lyer illusion as a function of hue in the absence of lightness contrast. *Proceedings of the American Psychological Association,* 1970, 53-54. (a)

Pollack, R. H. Mueller-Lyer illusion: Effect of age, lightness contrast, and hue. *Science,* 1970, **170**, 93-95. (b)

Pollack, R. H. & Silvar, S. Magnitude of the Mueller-Lyer illusion as a function of the pigmentation of the *fundus oculi. Psychonomic Science,* 1967, **8**, 83-84.

Pollack, R. H., Ptashne, R. I. & Carter, D. J. The effects of hue and intelligence on the dark interval threshold. *Perception and Psychophysics,* 1969, **6**, 50-52.

Polya, G. *How to solve it.* New York: Doubleday, 1957.

Quina, M. The Ponzo figure: One or two illusions. *Proceedings of the American Psychological Association,* 1971, 175-176.

Quina, M. & Pollack, R. H. A parametric investigation of the Ponzo Illusion under conditions of tachistoscopic exposure. *Proceedings of the American Psychological Association,* 1971, 77-78. (a)

Quina, M. & Pollack, R. H. The Ponzo figure: One or two illusions. *Proceedings of the American Psychological Association,* 1971. (b)

Reese, H. W. Verbal mediation as a function of age level. *Psychological Bulletin,* 1962, 59, 502-509.

Sabo, R. A. & Hagen, J. W. A developmental study of perceptual and cognitive factors affecting selective attention. Paper presented at biennial meetings of the Society for Research in Child Development, Minneapolis, 1971.

Siegel, A. W. Variables affecting incidental learning in children. *Child Development,* 1968, 39, 957-968.

Siegel, A. W. & McBurney, D. H. Estimation of line length and number: A developmental study. *Journal of Experimental Child Psychology,* 1970, 10, 170-180.

Sigel, I. E. How intelligence tests limit understanding of intelligence. *Merrill-Palmer Quarterly,* 1963, 9, 39-56.

Siklóssy, L. & Simon, H. Natural language learning by computer. *In* H. Simon & L. Siklóssy (eds.) *Representation and Meaning.* Englewood Cliffs, New Jersey. Prentice-Hall, 1972.

Silvar, S. D. & Pollack, R. H. Racial differences in pigmentation of the fundus oculi. *Psychonomic Science,* 1967, 7, 159-160.

Simon, H. A. An information processing theory of intellectual development. *In* W. Kessen & C. Kuhlman (eds.), Thought in the young child. *Monographs of the Society for Research in Child Development,* 1962, 27, No. 2, pp. 150-155.

Simon, H. A. An information-processing explanation of some perceptual phenomena. *British Journal of Psychology,* 1967, 58, 1-12.

Simon, H. A. *The sciences of the artificial.* Cambridge, Mass.: M.I.T. Press, 1969.

Simon, H. A. & Barenfeld, M. Information processing analysis of perceptual processes in problem solving. *Psychological Review,* 1969, 76, 473-483.

Simon, H. A. & Kotovsky, K. Human acquisition of concepts for sequential patterns. *Psychological Review,* 1963, 70, 534-546.

Simon, H. A. & Newell, A. Computer simulation of human thinking and problem solving. **In** W. Kessen & C. Kuhlman (eds.), Thought in the young child. *Monographs of the Society for Research in Child Development,* (2, Whole No. 83), 137-150.

Sjöstrom, K. P. & Pollack, R. H. The effect of simulated receptor aging on two types of visual illusions. *Psychonomic Science,* 1971, 23, 147-148. (a)

Sjöstrom, K. P. & Pollack, R. H. Simulated receptor aging in the study of ontogenetic trends of visual illusions. *Proceedings of the American Psychological Association,* 1971. (b)

Skoff, E. & Pollack, R. H. Visual acuity in children as a function of hue. *Perception and Psychophysics,* 1969, 6, 244-246.

Smedslund, J. Concrete reasoning: A study of intellectual development. *Monographs of the Society for Research in Child Development,* 1964, Serial No. 93.

Smedslund, J. Microanalysis of concrete reasoning: I. The difficulty of some combinations of addition and subtraction of one unit. *Scandinavian Journal of Psychology,* 1966, 7, 145-145. (a)

Smedslund, J. Microanalysis of concrete reasoning: III. Theoretical overview. *Scandinavian Journal of Psychology,* 1966, 7, 164-167. (b)

Sperry, R. The great cerebral commissure. *Scientific American,* 1964.

Spiker, C. C. Verbal factors in the discrimination learning of children. *In* J. Wright and J. Kagan (eds.), Basic cognitive processes in children. *Monographs of the Society for Research in Child Development,* 1963, 28 (2), 53-69.

Stambak, M. Le problème des rythmes dans le développement de l'enfant et dans les dyslexies de l'évolution. *Enfance,* 1951, 4, 480-502.

Stambak, M. Trois épreuves de rythme. *In* R. Zazzo (ed.), *Psychologie de l'enfant et méthode génétique.* Neuchâtel: Delacraux & Niestlé, 1962. Pp. 81-94.

Starr, A. S. The diagnostic value of the audito-vocal digit memory span. *Psychological Clinic*, 1923, 15, 61-84.

Vurpillot, E. The development of scanning strategies and their relation to visual differentiation. *Journal of Experimental Child Psychology*, 1968, 6, 632-640.

Wallace, J. G. *Concept growth and the education of the child.* National Foundation for Educational Research in England and Wales, Slough, 1965.

Wallace, J. G. *Stage and transition in conceptual development.* National Foundation for Education Research in England and Wales, Slough (in press), 1971.

Wapner, S., Werner, H. & Comalli, P. F., Jr. Perception of part-whole relationships in middle and old age. *Journal of Gerontology*, 1960, 15, 412-416.

Werner, H. The concept of development from a comparative and organismic point of view. *In* D. Harris (ed.), 2nd ed., *The concept of development.* Minneapolis, Minn.: Univ. of Minnesota Press, 1967.

Wickelgren, G. G. Brightness contrast and length perception in the Mueller-Lyer illusion. *Vision Research,* 1965, 5, 141-150.

Williams, D. Computer program organization induced from problem examples. *In* H. A. Simon & L. Siklóssy (eds.), *Meaning and Representation.* Englewood Cliffs, New Jersey: Prentice-Hall, 1972.

Willows, A. O. D. Giant brain cells in mollusks. *Scientific American,* 1971, 224, 69-75.

Wohlwill, J. F. Responses to class-inclusion questions for verbally and pictorially presented items. *Child Development,* 1968, 39, 449-465.

Wohlwill, J. F. & Weiner, M. Discrimination of form orientation in young children. *Child Development,* 1964, 35, 1113-1125.

Young, R. Production systems for children's seriation behavior. C.I.P. Working Paper, No. 202, Psychology Department, Carnegie-Mellon Univ., 1971.

Author Index

Numbers in italics refer to the pages on which the complete references are listed.

Subject Index

A

Accommodation, 104
Artificial intelligence, 20
Assimilation, 104
  reciprocal, 113, 116, 121
Attention, 14-17, 22, 52-53
  selective, 66, 72

B

Block-and-dot task, 53-54
Block tapping span, 46-52
  reversals in, 47

C

Central memory, 66-72, 76
Chunks, in memory, *see* Short-term memory
Class inclusion, 12, 17-18, 61, 105, 126, 134-
    139, 143-172, 176-181
  decomposition scheme and, 122
  misinterpretation in, 151-153, 178-181
  role of language, 180-181
  subclass size variation, 111-113
Cognitive synthesis, 43-46
  of color and form, 54-59
Compensation, 44, 104, 110-114
  conflict and, 113
Computer simulation, *see also* Human pro-
    grams
  absence of Piaget's views on, 116

explanation and, 18-20
language learning, 21
of seriation, 119-120
of "the essential Piaget," 118, 176
problem-solving, 21
Conservation, 44-45, 105-111
  effects of class inclusion training, 113
  of length, 109
  of numerical quantity, 105-107, 109
  matchstick experiments, 106-111
  steps in attaining, 109-111
Contextual associations, 61

D

Digit span, 7-8, 46-52

E

EPAM (Elementary Perceiver and Memorizer),
  15-16
Epistemology, 20, 103-104, 113, 117
Equilibrium, 104, 120
  disturbances and, 114
Equivalence matching, 43, 45-46, 53-60,
  86-94
Explanation
  computer programs and, 18-20
  nature of, 18-22
  Piaget's views of, 116
  sensory-motor versus verbal, 10

DATE DUE

11/29			
JY 13 '80			